KATE AITKEN'S

CANADIAN COOK BOOK

by

KATE AITKEN

Food Editor

The Standard

First Edition

Introduction by Elizabeth Driver
Essays by the Aitken Family

whitecap

JUN 2 3 2004

Copyright © 2004 Estate of Kate Aitken
First published in 1945 by The Montreal Standard

Cover and interior photographs provided by the Estate of Kate Aitken
Printed in Canada

National Library of Canada Cataloguing in Publication Data

Aitken, Kate, 1891-1971
    Kate Aitken's Canadian cook book / Kate Aitken ; introduction, Elizabeth Driver.

(Classic Canadian cookbook series)
Includes index.
First published : Montreal : The Standard, 1945.
ISBN 1-55285-591-0

    1. Cookery. I. Title. II. Title: Canadian cook book. III. Series.

TX715.6.A483 2004   641.5   C2004-900172-8

The publisher acknowledges the support of the Canada Council for the Arts and the Cultural Services Branch of the Government of British Columbia for our publishing program. We acknowledge the financial support of the Government of Canada through the Book Publishing Industry Development Program for our publishing activities.

Please note that the ingredients, methods and cooking times listed in this book are consistent with the kitchen appliances and techniques that were in use in 1945. Current equipment and supplies may produce different results that are inconsistent with contemporary food safety theories.

Visit our website at www.whitecap.ca.

KATE AND HER COOKBOOK

by Elizabeth Driver

When the publishers of the *Montreal Standard* newspaper launched *Kate Aitken's Canadian Cook Book* in 1945, its author needed no introduction to Canadians. Kate Aitken, née Scott (1891–1971), was already a household name—"Mrs. A." to her fans—and one of Canada's culinary experts. Shortly after her marriage in 1914, she started a farm and canning operation in Beeton, Ontario, the small town northwest of Toronto where she was born, and over the course of several decades, her career involved all aspects of the food business, as an entrepreneur, educator, writer, broadcaster, and government-appointed advocate for food conservation during World War II.

Kate's energy was legendary and her output prodigious. Some of the ways in which she became familiar to Canadian cooks are noted in the brief essays by her family that are printed in this edition of *Kate Aitken's Canadian Cook Book*—her lectures to rural Ontario women in the 1920s, when she was on the

Women's Institute staff of the province's Department of Agriculture; her long-time association with the Canadian National Exhibition in Toronto, where she opened a "Country Kitchen" in 1923 to sell her preserves and baked goods, gave cooking demonstrations to thousands over the years, and became Director of Women's Activities in 1938; and her stint in the 1940s as Women's Editor at the *Montreal Standard.* Her radio broadcasts and cooking schools were usually sponsored by companies that manufactured national brand-name products, for which she wrote recipe pamphlets or small booklets. In 1934, for example, she authored five titles in a series for Ogilvie Flour Mills in Montreal, to promote its Royal Household Flour. For Canada Starch Ltd, maker of corn starch, corn syrup, and corn oil, she produced the "52" series in 1940 and *Cooking Gossip* bulletins. In the 1940s and 50s, listeners to her broadcasts on CFRB for Tamblyn drug stores collected the monthly *Good News* recipe brochures. During the war years, when the Canadian National Exhibition was temporarily suspended and the country faced rationing, she provided guidance to Canadian housewives in her position as Supervisor of Conservation in the Consumers Branch of the Wartime Prices and Trade Board.

Kate Aitken's Canadian Cook Book, which appeared when she was in her mid-fifties, was her first full-length, hard-cover cookbook and it represented nearly a lifetime of experience.

Canadians, who regularly welcomed Kate into their homes with each radio broadcast, could now consult their trusted friend, whenever needed, by turning to the pages of the cookbook. As the author herself explains in the Foreword, it was published "to give [Canadian women] a handy inexpensive guide to healthful living" because "the health of the people of Canada" lies in their hands. She devotes the first chapter to "menu building," giving special attention to the role of vitamins, minerals, and recommended amounts of different foods. The recipe selection is for families—You will not find fancy hors d'oeuvres or many elaborate dishes for entertaining. Instead, there are luncheon and supper dishes, such as Macaroni and Cheese; main courses featuring Canadian canned salmon; classic Chicken Pot Pie; and in the meat section, information about cuts, the best cooking methods, and basic dinner fare, such as Broiled Hamburgers, Rolled Meat Loaf, Lamb Stew, Sausages de Luxe, and four recipes for liver (since nutritionists "recommend liver in the diet at least once a week"). Kate offers a wide variety of desserts in favourite flavours—from rhubarb, apple, and summer berries, to maple, butterscotch, and chocolate, plus Taffy Apples and Divinity Fudge for the real sweet tooth. No one knew better than she how to preserve the bounty of Canada's harvest; her instructions for canning, preserving and pickling were definitive for the time, and her recipes set the standard for Nine-Day

Pickles, Chili Sauce, and Pickled Watermelon Rind. Kate had no formal home economics training and would have first learned about cooking from her mother in the 1890s. It's not surprising, therefore, that her repertoire also reflects 19th-century tastes for Raspberry Vinegar (a refreshing summer drink), Johnny Cake, using the pioneer staple of cornmeal, and Canadian Fruit Cake, incorporating diced salt pork. Conscious that some women in 1945 may still have had stoves without temperature gauges, she added an "Oven Guide" that relates the now obsolete descriptions for oven heat of "slow," "moderate," "fairly hot," and "hot," to the corresponding Fahrenheit degrees. Yet, at the same time, in the "Eat and Keep Slim" chapter, she set out a "diet...for the woman who really wants to reduce," addressing what would become an increasing desire of post-war Canadians to control their weight. And, in "Notes to Brides" below some recipes, she spoke directly to the new cook, just starting out on married life.

There were four distinct versions of *Kate Aitken's Canadian Cook Book* before the author died in 1971: the first edition (reproduced here) and editions in 1950, 1953, and 1964, plus annual reprints from 1965 to 1971, and in 1973, 1975, 1982, 1987, 1990, and 1992. Many people fondly remember sharing time in the kitchen with their mothers, following the new section at the back of the 1964 version called "Your Daughter's Second Trade—Homemaking," which gives recipes and advice for teaching girls to cook, for the ages of six, eight, ten, twelve, thirteen, "between fourteen and seventeen," and when "your daughter is launched." Another significant addition to the 1964 version was "Canadian Provincial Recipes," presenting typical regional foods.

What accounts for the enduring fame of Kate and her cookbook? Other cookery teachers and writers emerged in Canada in the 1920s and 1930s, sometimes benefitting, like Kate, from the new medium of radio, the public's fascination with cooking demonstrations, and the advertising dollars of the country's expanding food industries, but none had her staying power. One rising star in the 1930s was Toronto's Jessie Read, who broadcast for Consumers' Gas Co., became a columnist for the *Telegram* newspaper, attracted thousands of women to Canada's "first cooking school talking picture" in 1936, and had published *Three Meals a Day* in 1938, but her life was cut tragically short by illness in 1940. Another well-known figure was Mary Moore, whose daily cookery columns were syndicated in newspapers across Canada from 1928 to 1978, close to the same period as Kate's working life, and who, like Kate, also wrote commercial recipe pamphlets. However, Mary Moore did not enjoy the close familiarity that radio brought to Kate. Nellie Pattinson's *Canadian Cook Book,* first published in 1923 and reprinted many times through the century, garnered a national profile, but Pattinson herself never ventured beyond the classrooms of Central Technical School and died in 1953. Another of Kate's contemporaries was Katherine (Kay) Caldwell Bayley, who was influential as the Food Editor of the *Canadian Home Journal,* but hid her identity behind pseudonyms (Ann Adam, Anna Lee Scott) for advertising cookbooks and newspaper food columns. Kate's genius was that she parlayed her farming and kitchen skills, first into a successful freelance business (canned goods and cooking schools), then into a broadcasting career that evolved beyond the culinary to political and cultural affairs and which culminated in her appointment to the Board of Governors of the Canadian Broadcasting Corporation in 1959. Also to her advantage was that *Kate Aitken's Canadian Cook Book* appeared just as World War II ended, filling what would be a void in cookbook publishing until new authors rose to prominence from the late 1950s on (such as Helen Gougeon, Jehane Benoit, Margo Oliver, Edna Staebler).

Generations of Canadian women turned to Kate as an authority in the kitchen. This reprint of *Kate Aitken's Canadian Cook Book* stands as a testament to the traditions of Canadian home cooking in the 20th century.

From Her Family

Mrs. A with world-record hen from Sunnybank Farm, Beeton.

While her husband, Henry, operated the family feed mill in Beeton, Ontario, Kate tended to the family farm located across the road. Kate ambitiously planned a farm that had apple orchards, fruits, vegetables and poultry. Her dream became a reality.

From a modest beginning of twelve white Wyandotte chicks, she built a flock of chickens that gained world records and renown. Her fruit and vegetable gardens flourished as did the orchards. Soon she had more produce than she knew what to do with. Ever ambitious, Kate started a home-canning enterprise together with a garden stand. Her canned produce was sought after not only by the local townsfolk, but also by the residents and restaurants of Toronto.

Because she was a female pioneer in agriculture and because her experimental work had such spectacular results, the provincial and federal Departments of Agriculture asked for her assistance. They employed her to give lectures across Canada on such varied topics as high-production hens and dairy cows, canning and food preparation. After six years of criss-crossing Canada, Kate returned to her roots at the family farm. Then the Great Depression came. Kate had to leave the farm again. New horizons and new ventures challenged her. She answered the call.

"And now here's Mrs. A", the radio speaker announced. With that, one and a half million listeners' ears tuned in. Canada's most popular woman was about to speak to them in their homes once again. She could have been sitting at the kitchen table with them. They loved her. They appreciated her down-home advice, and thanked her for her no-nonsense, sensible recipes. She was the women's voice of Canada.

Mrs. A's broadcasting debut was not planned. While in the midst of a cooking seminar in the Maritimes, the distraught manager of the local radio station burst in. Could she please help him? His regular broadcaster had been involved in an accident. The preparation of the cake at the seminar was completed live on radio. It drew rave reviews.

Within a very short period, Mrs. A was being broadcast on the radio three times a day, five days a week, thirty-nine weeks of the year, to her adoring Canadian audience. The remaining weeks of the year, she travelled the world and brought back her observations to her listeners.

Mrs. A's broadcasts did not come just from the studio. She visited her lis-

teners from all corners of Canada and the world. With her portrayals, she expanded their horizons. They could visit where they would never go. Mrs. A's audience experienced Hitler's speech from the Chancellery; attended the wedding of Princess Elizabeth and her later coronation; were present when refugees tried to flee Hungary, and numerous other events.

In 1957, Mrs. A retired from broadcasting.

In her lifetime, Mrs. A travelled more than two million miles, visiting fifty-four countries, and all the provinces of Canada. She served her country and reported the latest in world and Canadian developments to her radio audience.

Mrs. A had the unique ability of being in the wrong place at the right moment and vice versa. She was present and reported on the border closings by China and Korea. She was in Kenya at the start of the uprisings. She saw children kill a border guard to escape from Hungary.

Mrs. A, on a trade mission for Canada, successfully negotiated with Mussolini for the sale of Canadian wheat to Italy. During World War II she brought solace to Canadian families who had loved ones serving overseas.

Her audience sat next to her while she took tea with King George VI and Queen Mary, and were enthralled by her interviews of Hitler, Mussolini, Franklin Roosevelt, McKenzie King, Louis St. Laurent, Lester Pearson and a multitude of others. She brought the world into the homes of Canadian families.

War correspondent in Europe in the summer of 1943.

Mrs. A conducted the Canadian National Exhibition's first cooking school in 1923. She also lectured in the Maritimes and at the Chicago World's Fair on the subject of homemaking and its joys. She continued to serve the provincial and federal governments with projects when they requested her assistance.

In 1938, the executive branch of the C.N.E. decided that they wished to expand the women's program to stimulate increased attendance. They asked Mrs. A to become the Director of Women's Activities and she accepted. It turned out to be a wise decision on the part of the C.N.E.

Mrs. A introduced programs that appealed to all walks of life. Her programs were creative and innovative. No longer was the program just a cooking show. It was a time of celebration and education – fashions, special displays, food, school art, home furnishing and decoration, cosmetics, and handicrafts. Daily luncheons were hosted by Mrs. A to acknowledge the contribution of women to their families and to their countries. Not only in attendance were women of fame – Eleanor Roosevelt, Princess Juliana, and Lady Mountbatten— but even more importantly, women of Canada who had distinguished themselves, their families and their country by their contributions.

Canadian National Exhibition in 1951: Eleanor Roosevelt (centre);
Mrs. R. C. Berkinshaw, wife of the president of the C.N.E. (left); Mrs. A.

Nestled in the woods on the Credit River, near Streetsville, Ontario, sat Sunnybank Acres—Mrs. A's pride and joy. Surrounded by beautiful wildflowers in the woods, flower gardens and wildlife, this was Mrs. A's headquarters. It was at Sunnybank Acres that she came up with the ideas for her radio and television shows.

Surrounded by natural beauty, Mrs. A wrote her newspaper columns and her many books. She received

Sunnybank Acres in the spring of 1955.

260,000 letters a year, each of which she insisted be answered. At one point she had twenty-one secretaries helping her. She personally signed each letter.

Mrs. A's home had two large kitchens that were constantly on the go. Every recipe that went into her cookbooks was personally tested.

Mrs. A retired from broadcasting in 1957. She did not, however, retire from public service. She continued to devote her energies to the United Nations, UNICEF, while serving as a board member of the Canadian Broadcasting Corporation.

Sunnybank Acres was heaven to Mrs. A's nine grandchildren. There were adventures in the woods, frogs to catch, swimming in the river and, of course, football using the rose gardens as decoys. At night, they would gather round the fireplace and let their imaginations roam as Mrs. A took them on a journey to far away places.

KATE AITKEN
Food Editor, THE STANDARD.

FOREWORD

We often laugh at ourselves for clipping and copying recipes, for saving those bits of paper long after they're torn and creased, for hoping that eventually we will get round to trying the recipes. But after all it's quite understandable, for food is our business. We buy it, prepare it, serve it. Three times a day and 365 days a year our first question is, "What shall we eat?"

That's the reason this book has been published, to give you a handy, inexpensive guide to healthful daily living. In the hands of Canadian women lies the health of the people of Canada. Food is our business. It's an intelligent business and its dividends are paid daily in the health and happiness of the members of our family.

CHAPTER INDEX

CHAPTER 1

Daily Menu Building

Vitamins have become a part of daily life, but not so many of us realize that, for health, vitamins and minerals should go hand in hand.

WHAT VITAMINS ARE NECESSARY?

Vitamin	*Use in Body*	*Best Sources*
A	For normal vision	Leafy greens Yellow vegetables and fruits Egg Liver Milk
B1 (Thiamin)	For good appetite, good digestion and steady nerves	"Enriched" and whole grain bread and cereal Dried peas and beans Peanuts Pork and Liver
C (Ascorbic Acid)	For healthy teeth, gums, bones and blood vessels	Citrus fruits Tomato juice Leafy greens Potato
D	For normal development of teeth and bones	Salmon, sardines, mackerel and fish liver oils. Vitamin D milk Egg yolk
G (Riboflavin)	For healthy skin and eyes	Liver and Kidney Lean beef Leafy greens Milk
Niacin (Nicotinic acid)	For healthy skin	"Enriched" and whole grain bread and cereal Liver, lean Meats

WHAT MINERALS ARE NECESSARY?

Mineral	Use	Best Sources
Iron	For healthy red blood cells	Dried fruits Liver, lean Meats Dried peas or beans Whole grain cereals Green vegetables Molasses Eggs
Calcium	For strong bones and teeth	Cheese Milk Leafy greens
Phosphorus	For development of healthy bones and teeth	Cereals Cheese Eggs Milk Meat Fish Dried peas or beans

WHAT SHOULD WE EAT DAILY?

Food	Average Adult (Moderately active)	Average Child (10-12 years)
Milk	1 pint	1 quart
Meat or Fish	1 or more servings of a wide variety Liver once a week	Same as adult
Eggs	1 egg Dried peas or beans may be substituted 3 times a week	Same as adult
Vegetables	1 leafy green or yellow and 1 other (serve one raw) 1 potato	Same as adult
Fruits	½ cup citrus or 1 cup tomato juice plus other fruits (raw, cooked or canned)	¾ cup citrus or 1½ cups tomato juice plus other fruits (raw, cooked or canned)
Bread and Cereals	3 servings whole grain or "enriched" bread or cereal	Same as adult
Butter	2 tablespoons	2-3 tablespoons

CHAPTER 2

Appetizers

CHEESE BITES

Temperature: 350°F.

Time: 15-20 minutes

8 thin slices bread
2 tablespoons melted butter
1 cup cheese, grated
2 eggs, slightly beaten

½ teaspoon salt
¼ teaspoon paprika
Dash of cayenne
1 cup milk

Slice the bread; cut off the crusts; brush with melted butter. Spread 4 slices with the grated cheese; add the remaining 4 slices to make sandwiches. Cut in fingers; place in an oiled baking dish. Slightly beat the eggs; add the seasonings and milk. Pour over the sandwich fingers; bake till golden brown. Serve hot with fruit cocktails. Serves 6.

CHEESE DREAMS

Temperature: 415°F.

Time: 6-8 minutes

1¼ cups cheese, grated
1 egg, lightly beaten
3 tablespoons cereal cream

⅛ teaspoon salt
Dash of pepper and paprika
10 slices bread

Use old cheese if you can get it. Combine the cheese, egg, cream and seasonings; blend well. Cut the crusts from the bread; cut the slices in half. Toast on one side; spread the untoasted side with the cheese mixture. Bake in the oven until the cheese is puffy and toasted. Yield: 40 squares.

CHEESE WAFERS

Temperature: 400°F.

Time: 3-5 minutes

Small crisp wafers
1 egg, slightly beaten
½ cup tomato juice
¼ teaspoon dry mustard

½ teaspoon salt
Dash of pepper and
cayenne
2 cups cheese, grated

Spread the wafers singly on a cookie sheet. Beat the egg lightly; add the tomato juice and seasonings; pour into the top of a double boiler; heat to scalding over boiling water. Add the grated cheese; cook, stirring occasionally, until the mixture is smooth and thick (about 15 minutes). Cool; spread a spoonful on each cracker. Broil in a fairly hot oven till the cheese bubbles. Serve hot. This will make a pint of cheese mixture. Store it in the refrigerator to use on crackers, toast, or spooned over meat balls.

CHEESE SQUARES

Temperature: 375°F.   Time: 7 minutes
12 fresh bread cubes, 3" square   1 cup cheese, grated
  1 egg   ¼ teaspoon salt
1 tablespoon milk   Dash of cayenne
  1½ tablespoons melted butter

Cut the bread in cubes. Beat the egg till light; add the milk and melted butter. Roll the bread cubes in this mixture, then in a mixture of the cheese and seasonings. Place the cubes on a rack on a cookie sheet; toast till the cheese melts. Serve hot from the oven. Yield: 12 squares.

CRANBERRY COCKTAIL

2 cups cranberries   ¼ cup sugar
  2 cups water   2 cloves or ½ stick cinnamon

Wash and pick over the cranberries. Add the water; simmer gently till tender; strain through a cheesecloth. To the juice add the sugar and the spice you like best. If you don't like a spiced cocktail, add orange or lemon rind. Simmer for 5 minutes; chill; serve in clear glasses with cheese crackers. Yield: 6 servings.

BROILED GRAPEFRUIT

Cut the grapefruit in half; remove the seeds and the skin between the sections. Sprinkle very lightly with salt; chill until just before serving. Sprinkle each grapefruit with a mixture of brown sugar and nutmeg (½ cup brown sugar mixed with ⅛ teaspoon nutmeg); broil in hot oven till sugar bubbles. Serve warm.

LIME MELON CUP

Scoop out balls of ripe melon, using 2 or 3 different kinds to get color contrast. Fill cocktail glasses ⅔ full with melon balls; add ⅓ cup fresh lime juice to each. Chill; garnish with slices of candied cherries.

SPICED TOMATO COCKTAIL

4 cups canned tomato juice   1 tablespoon mixed pickling
  2 tablespoons lemon juice   spice
1 teaspoon salt   1 stalk celery, chopped
  2 teaspoons white sugar   1 teaspoon parsley, chopped
1 medium onion, chopped   1 teaspoon chili sauce
  2 bay leaves

Combine all the ingredients; blend well. Chill until ready to serve. Strain; serve with tasty wafers. 8 servings.

POTATO CHIP TASTY BITS

Buy potato chips; crisp before using. Scrape some onion; 1 teaspoon is just right for a 4-ounce package of cream cheese. Soften the cheese with a fork; add the onion, some salt and pepper and a speck of cayenne. Pile by spoonfuls on top of the potato chips and serve. Serves 6.

RHUBARB COCKTAIL

3 cups cold water
¾ cup white sugar
¼ teaspoon cream of tartar
6 cups rhubarb, diced
1-3″ stick cinnamon

1 tablespoon orange rind, grated
1 teaspoon lemon rind, grated
2 tablespoons lemon juice
½ cup orange juice

Measure 1 cup water, the sugar and cream of tartar into a saucepan; boil together for 5 minutes; cool. Combine the remaining 2 cups of water and the rhubarb; add the cinnamon, grated orange and lemon rind. Simmer for 8 minutes; strain. Add the cooled syrup and the fruit juices. Pour into a sterile jar and store in the refrigerator. Before serving, add an equal quantity of ice water or ginger ale. Serves 8.

TOMATO JUICE COCKTAIL

5 cups tomato juice
1 teaspoon onion, grated
2 teaspoons celery, chopped
2 teaspoons horseradish

3 tablespoons lemon juice
Dash of pepper and paprika
1½ teaspoons salt
½ teaspoon white sugar

Measure all the ingredients into a large jar; shake until well blended. Let chill until ready to serve. Strain; serve with cheese wafers. 10 servings.

CHAPTER 3

Beverages

FRENCH CHOCOLATE

2 squares unsweetened chocolate
  ½ cup water
1 cup double-strength coffee
  ¼ cup sugar

Dash of salt
Half a dash of cinnamon
2½ cups milk
  ½ cup 18% cream

Combine the chocolate and water in the top of a double boiler. Heat over boiling water till melted; blend well. Have the coffee freshly made and double strength; that is, use 3 tablespoons coffee to 1 cup water. Add the coffee, sugar, salt and cinnamon. Heat the milk and cream separately; add to the chocolate mixture and beat till frothy. Serve hot. Serves 6.

ECONOMY HOT CHOCOLATE

2 squares (2 ounces)
  unsweetened chocolate
½ cup white sugar
2 tablespoons flour

Dash of salt
2 cups boiling water
4 cups of milk

Melt the chocolate in the top of the double boiler; blend in the sugar, flour, and salt. Add the boiling water; stir well. Boil slowly over direct heat for 8 minutes or until thick and smooth. Add the milk; heat to the boiling point. Beat till light and frothy; serve at once. Yield: 8 cups chocolate.

TEA

Scald the tea pot with boiling water; if possible use an earthen pot. Measure 1 teaspoon tea per person into the pot; add 1 additional teaspoon for the pot. Add 1 cup of boiling water for each serving. Let stand 3 to 5 minutes. Pour immediately.

For iced tea make the tea double strength. Pour over cracked ice in tall glasses.

TEA TO SERVE 100

½ pound tea   5 gallons boiling water

Tie the tea loosely in a cheesecloth bag. Place the bag in a kettle of boiling water. Cover tightly; decrease heat so the water will not boil. Infuse for 8 minutes.

Note: 1 gallon of water is sufficient for 24 servings of tea. 1 pound of loaf sugar will serve 100 cups of tea. 1½ quarts of 18% cream will serve 100 cups of tea.

HOT SPICED CIDER

½ teaspoon whole cloves
1-3″ stick cinnamon
3 slices lemon

1 quart cider
⅓ cup brown sugar

Tie the cloves, cinnamon and lemon slices in a cheesecloth bag. Heat the cider and brown sugar to boiling; add the spice bag; let simmer 10 minutes. Take out the bag; serve the cider in mugs with a dash of nutmeg on top. Serves 5.

COCOA SYRUP

1 cup cocoa
2 cups granulated sugar
⅛ teaspoon salt

2 cups hot water
3 teaspoons vanilla

Combine the cocoa, sugar, salt and water. Stir over moderate heat until dissolved; simmer 3 minutes. Add the vanilla; beat with the dover beater. Store in a covered jar. Yield—1 quart of syrup. Use three tablespoons of syrup for each glass milk. Serves 18.

RULES FOR GOOD COFFEE MAKING

1. Start with a clean pot; there should be no stale odor from past brews. Boiling out the coffee pot with household ammonia and water does the trick.

2. Use fresh coffee.

3. Measure both the coffee and water. We use 2 level measuring spoons of coffee to 1 measuring cup of cold water.

Percolator Coffee: Use measurements as above. Use the percolator at full capacity if possible. Percolate 10 minutes; remove coffee grounds.

Steeped Coffee: Use measurements as above. Tie the coffee in a cheesecloth bag. Bring just to the boil; remove the bag and pour.

Demitasse Coffee: Use measurements as above, or if you prefer stronger coffee use 3 level tablespoons to 1 cup cold water. Serve black or with cream and sugar.

Café Au Lait: Make extra strength coffee as above. Measure; heat the same quantity whole milk. Pour the coffee and hot milk simultaneously into warm cups.

Coffee Maker Coffee: Measure the water into the lower bowl of the coffee maker; adjust the upper bowl; measure in coffee as above. Place on the heat; when the water has risen to the top bowl take from the heat; stir; let the coffee stand till it returns to the lower bowl.

BOILED COFFEE TO SERVE 100

2 pounds medium ground coffee   1 teaspoon salt
5 gallons boiling water

Tie the coffee loosely in a cheesecloth bag.   Drop the bag into a kettle of boiling water; add the salt; cover tightly. Keep just under the boiling point for 10 minutes. This amount of coffee requires:

1 pound loaf sugar   2½ quarts 18% cream

ICED COFFEE

Make coffee by any one of the above methods using 3 tablespoons of coffee instead of 2 with each cup of cold water. Fill tall glasses with cracked ice; pour the hot coffee brew over the ice. Allow ⅔ cup hot coffee for each serving.

FRUIT PUNCH TO SERVE 75

1 cup canned pineapple, crushed   3 tablespoons orange rind,
10 cups water   grated
8 cups white sugar   6 cups lemon juice
2 tablespoons lemon rind, grated   4 cups orange juice

Drain the pineapple juice from the pulp. Make a syrup of the water, sugar, pineapple pulp, lemon and orange rinds; boil for 10 minutes. Cool; add the pineapple, orange and lemon juice; strain.   Yield: 4½ quarts syrup. For making up punch, use 1 part syrup to 3 parts water; a few sprays of fresh mint may be added for flavor.

RHUBARB PUNCH

¾ cup white sugar   4 whole cloves
¼ teaspoon cream of tartar   ⅛ teaspoon mace
3 cups water   1 tablespoon orange rind,
2 pounds rhubarb (about 4½   grated
cups), diced   2 tablespoons lemon juice
1-3″ stick cinnamon   ½ cup orange juice

Boil together for 5 minutes the sugar, cream of tartar and 1 cup water; cool. Add the remaining water to the rhubarb; add the spices and grated orange rind. Simmer till tender; strain. Add the cooled syrup and fruit juices. Chill; before serving add the same quantity of ice cold water. This recipe may be multiplied, as the punch will keep in the refrigerator. Serves 8.

GRAPE JUICE

1 six quart basket blue grapes   White sugar

Wash the grapes; pick them from the stems; place in a preserving kettle. Add water until it shows. Heat to boiling; reduce the heat; simmer until the pulp and seeds separate. Press through a colander; strain the juice through a flannel cloth. Measure the juice; to every 4 cups of juice add 1 cup white sugar. Heat to boiling; continue simmering for 20 minutes. Pour into sterile jars; screw the lids down tightly; dip in hot parowax before storing. Yield: 3 pints.

LEMONADE

1 cup cold water   ¾ cup lemon juice
  1 cup white sugar   4 cups cold water
⅛ teaspoon tartaric acid

Measure the water, sugar and tartaric acid into a saucepan; boil 5 minutes without stirring; cool, add the lemon juice and cold water. Chill till ready to serve. Pour over ice cubes; serve with a slice of orange. Serves 8-10.

LEMON AMBROSIA

1 two pound can corn syrup   1 cup lemon juice
  6 cups white sugar   1 ounce citric acid
7 cups hot water   1 ounce tartaric acid
  4 tablespoons grated lemon rind

Make a syrup of the corn syrup, sugar and water; boil for 5 minutes. Cool slightly; pour over the grated rind and juice of the lemons. Add the citric and tartaric acids; stir till dissolved. Store in the refrigerator; dilute as required with ice cold water, using one part syrup to three parts water. Yield: 3½ quarts of syrup, sufficient to make 2 gallons of beverage.

RASPBERRY VINEGAR

4 quarts raspberries   6 cups sugar   2 cups cider vinegar

Pick over and measure 2 quarts raspberries into an enamel bowl (be sure there are no chips in it). Pour the vinegar over the berries; stir gently, without breaking the berries; cover and set aside in a cool place for 24 hours. Strain off and reserve the juice. Measure the second 2 quarts of berries into the bowl; cover with the strained liquid; stir gently; again let stand for 24 hours. Strain off the liquid; heat to boiling; add the sugar and simmer 20 minutes. Store in sterile bottles, which can be tightly corked. Add 2 to 3 tablespoons to 1 glass cold water. Yield: 2 pints.

CHAPTER 4

Breads (Quick and Yeast)

Breads made at home use leavening of two sorts, either quick or yeast; that is why we divide them into those two sections.

QUICK BREADS: These are the hot biscuits, the waffles, the nut loaves, the muffins that delight our families and make a dining table more appealing. Quick breads require a technique all their own.

SUCCESS RULES:

(1) Sift all flour before measuring.

(2) Cut the fat in coarsely.

(3) Add the liquid all at once.

(4) Stir lightly and quickly; beating makes a coarse, hole-y mixture.

(5) Have a pre-heated oven so that baking starts quickly.

FAIRY TEA BISCUITS

Temperature: 450°F.   Time: 12-15 minutes

2 cups sifted all-purpose flour   ¼ teaspoon baking soda
  ½ teaspoon salt   3 tablespoons shortening
3 teaspoons baking powder   ⅔ cup thick sour milk

Sift together the flour, salt, baking powder and baking soda. Cut in the shortening. Add the sour milk all at once. Stir lightly with a knife; turn on a floured board and knead gently for 20 counts. Roll the dough about ½" thick; cut with a floured cutter. Place on an oiled cookie sheet, having the biscuits touching. Bake in a hot oven. Yield: 12 biscuits light as a feather.

FLAKY HOT BISCUITS

Temperature: 450°F.   Time: 12-15 minutes

2 cups sifted all-purpose flour   4 tablespoons shortening
  4½ teaspoons baking powder   1 cup milk
½ teaspoon salt   Flour for kneading

Sift together the flour, baking powder and salt. Cut the shortening in coarsely (it should be about the size of small pea). Make a well in the centre; turn the milk in all at once; stir lightly with a knife. Turn on a floured board; gather the batter into a ball; knead gently for 20 counts. Roll the dough about ½" thick. Cut out with a floured cutter; place the biscuits, touching one another, on an oiled cookie sheet. Bake in a hot oven. Serve hot. Yield: 12 biscuits.

BUTTERSCOTCH BISCUITS

Temperature: 375°F.   Time: 15-20 minutes
¼ cup softened fat   ⅓ cup corn syrup
  ⅓ cup brown sugar   1 batter Flaky Hot Biscuits

Measure the fat, sugar and corn syrup into a bowl; let stand till room temperature; beat till smooth. Drop a teaspoonful of the mixture into 16 muffin tins. Make up the biscuit batter as in the preceding recipe. Roll into a rectangle; spread with the remainder of the butterscotch mixture. Roll up as a jelly roll; cut in ½″ slices. Place a slice in each muffin tin. Bake in a moderate oven till done. Remove from the pan while still warm. Yield: 16 biscuits.

MARMALADE CRESCENTS

Temperature: 450°F.   Time: 12-15 minutes
1 batter Flaky Hot Biscuits   ½ cup orange marmalade
  2 tablespoons softened cream cheese (plain) or butter

Make up a Flaky Hot Biscuit batter. Roll into an oblong ½″ thick. Spread with the softened cream cheese or butter; spread with the marmalade. Cut into 3″ squares, then cut each square into triangles. Roll up each triangle crosswise like jelly roll. Place on an oiled baking sheet; bake in a hot oven. Yield: 16 rolls.

CHELSEA BUNS

Temperature: 425°F.   Time: 15-20 minutes
¼ cup shortening   ½ teaspoon salt
  ⅓ cup brown sugar   ¼ cup shortening
⅓ cup corn syrup   1 cup milk
  2 cups sifted all-purpose flour   ½ cup raisins
4 teaspoons baking powder   ¼ cup nuts, chopped

Cream together the shortening, brown sugar and corn syrup. Drop ¼ teaspoonful of this mixture in the bottom of 16 oiled muffin pans. Sift together the flour, baking powder and salt; cut in ¼ cup of shortening until the mixture is crumbly. Add the milk all at once; stir lightly. Turn the mixture on a well floured board. Gather the batter into a ball; knead lightly for 20 counts. Roll in an oblong 8″ x 12″; spread with the remainder of the butterscotch mixture. Sprinkle with the raisins, which have been washed and drained, and the nuts. Roll up as for a jelly roll. Cut in pieces ¾″ thick. Place, cut side down, in the muffin pans. Bake in a moderate oven till done. Yield: 16 muffins.

Note: Left over buns may be reheated. Place them in a brown paper bag, close bag, heat in a moderate oven till warm.

HANDY BISCUIT MIX

6 cups sifted all-purpose flour   1 tablespoon salt
  4½ tablespoons baking powder   ¾ cup shortening

Measure the flour, baking powder and salt into the sifter; sift 4 times; cut in the shortening until the mixture resembles coarse corn meal. Store in the refrigerator in a covered jar. This mixture will keep about 10 days.

When you want to make a pan of hot biscuits use ¾ cup milk to 2 cups of the mixture. If the batter is mixed, rolled out, spread with strawberry or raspberry jam, rolled up like a jelly roll and cut in slices, you have a delicious fruit biscuit. Use a 450°F. oven; bake 12-15 minutes. Yield: 36 hot biscuits.

WHOLE WHEAT TEA BISCUITS

Temperature: 450°F.   Time: 12-15 minutes
1 cup sifted all-purpose flour   ¼ cup shortening
  4½ teaspoons baking powder   1 cup whole wheat flour
1 teaspoon salt   1 cup milk
  1 tablespoon white sugar

Sift together the flour, baking powder, salt and sugar. Cut in the shortening until the mixture is coarse and crumby. Add the whole wheat flour; blend. Make a well in the centre of the mixture; add the milk all at once. Stir lightly. Turn on a floured board and knead gently for 20 counts. Roll about ½″ thick. Cut with a floured cutter. Place the biscuits on an oiled cookie sheet touching one another. Bake in a hot oven till done. You will have a dozen good sized biscuits that split cleanly across to enclose the butter.

MOLASSES GEMS

Temperature: 350°F.   Time: 30 minutes
3 tablespoons shortening   ½ teaspoon ginger
  2 tablespoons white sugar   1 egg, well beaten
¾ cup molasses   2 cups sifted all-purpose flour
  1 teaspoon cinnamon   ½ teaspoon soda
¼ teaspoon cloves   ½ cup sour milk

Measure the shortening, sugar, ¼ cup of the molasses and the spices into a large saucepan. Place over moderate heat; stir and cook till smooth. Cool to room temperature; add the well-beaten egg; mix well. Add the sifted dry ingredients alternately with the sour milk and the remaining half cup of molasses. Blend lightly; pour into oiled muffin pans. Bake in a moderate oven. Yield: 12 large muffins.

FRESH BLUEBERRY MUFFINS

Temperature: 425°F.   Time: 15-20 minutes

1 cup fresh blueberries
  1 tablespoon flour
1 teaspoon grated lemon rind
2 eggs, well beaten
3 tablespoons melted
  shortening
¾ cup milk
  ¼ cup white sugar
1¾ cups sifted all-purpose
  flour
¾ teaspoon salt
3 teaspoons baking powder

Measure the blueberries, 1 tablespoon flour and the lemon rind in a bag; shake thoroughly. Beat the eggs till very light; add the melted shortening, milk and sugar; beat again till foamy. Sift 1¾ cups flour, the salt and the baking powder together three times; make a well in the centre of the mixture; add the egg mixture all at once. Stir quickly and lightly. Fill oiled muffin tins ⅓ full; sprinkle with the blueberries; fill with batter till the pans are ⅔ full. Bake in a hot oven till firm and golden brown. Let stand in the pans for 5 minutes before removing. Yield: 12 muffins.

QUICK MUFFINS

Temperature: 375°F.   Time: 25 minutes

2 cups sifted all-purpose flour
  3½ teaspoons baking powder
½ teaspoon salt
  1 egg
1 cup milk
  3 tablespoons sugar
2 tablespoons melted
  shortening

Sift together the flour, baking powder and salt. Beat the egg lightly; add the milk and sugar; again beat. Add to the flour mixture all at once; stir with light quick strokes. Add the melted shortening; blend. Fill oiled muffin tins ⅔ full; bake in moderately hot oven till golden brown. Yield: 12 large muffins.

BRAN MUFFINS

Temperature: 400°F.   Time: 25 minutes

2 cups sifted all-purpose
  flour
1½ teaspoons baking
  powder
1 teaspoon baking soda
  1½ teaspoons salt
2 cups baking bran
  1 egg
⅓ cup molasses
  1¾ cups sour milk
3 tablespoons melted
  shortening

Sift together the flour, baking powder, baking soda and salt; stir in the bran. Beat the egg until light; add the molasses, milk and melted shortening. Combine the two mixtures, stirring only enough to mix them. Fill oiled muffin tins two-thirds full. Bake in moderate oven. Yield: 12 large or 18 medium sized muffins.

HOT BISCUIT FOLDOVERS

Temperature: 450°F.

Time: 12-15 minutes

2 cups sifted all-purpose
  flour
1 tablespoon white sugar
3 teaspoons baking powder

½ teaspoon salt
  ¼ cup fat
1 cup rich milk
1 egg, well beaten

Sift together the flour, white sugar, baking powder and salt. Cut in the fat; add the milk and well beaten egg. Mix quickly; knead lightly. Roll into a rectangle ⅓″ thick; brush with melted butter. Cut with a 2½″ cutter; place some jam or marmalade on one side; fold over like a pocketbook. Place on an oiled cookie sheet; let rise for 30 minutes. Bake in a piping hot oven (450°F.) until golden brown. Serve hot. Yield: 15 biscuits.

DATE MUFFINS

Temperature: 375°F.

Time: 20 minutes

½ cup brown sugar
1 egg
1 teaspoon salt
1 tablespoon melted shortening
1 cup date filling

1½ cups bran
1 cup sifted all-purpose
  flour
1 teaspoon baking soda
1 cup sour milk

Measure the brown sugar, egg, salt, shortening and date filling into a bowl. Beat vigorously until smooth; add the bran. Add the flour and baking soda sifted together. Add the sour milk all at once, stirring the batter as little as possible. Pour into muffin pans which have been oiled; let stand 3 minutes. Bake in moderate oven. Yield: 1 dozen large muffins.

Date Filling

1 cup chopped dates
1 cup hot water

½ cup brown sugar
1 teaspoon lemon juice

Mix all ingredients in a saucepan. Simmer gently until smooth and thick.

PRUNE MUFFINS

Temperature: 400°F.

Time: 25 minutes

¼ cup shortening
  ⅓ cup brown sugar or
    molasses
1 egg
  ¾ cup cooked prunes,
    chopped

2 cups sifted all-purpose
  flour
4 teaspoons baking powder
1 teaspoon salt
¼ teaspoon grated nutmeg
  ¾ cup milk

Cream the shortening thoroughly; gradually add the sugar or molasses; beat till light. Add the well-beaten egg and the prunes;

mix well. Sift together the flour, baking powder, salt and nutmeg. Add alternately with the milk to the prune mixture. Fill oiled muffin tins ⅔ full; bake in a hot oven. A half prune pressed into the batter adds to the appearance and taste of the muffins. Yield: 12 large muffins.

GINGER CHEESE MUFFINS

Temperature: 350°F.   Time: 20 minutes

2 cups sifted all-purpose flour   1 egg
   3 teaspoons baking powder   ½ cup milk
¼ teaspoon baking soda   ½ cup corn syrup or molasses
   ½ teaspoon ginger   ¼ cup melted shortening
½ teaspoon salt   ⅔ cup grated cheese

Sift together the dry ingredients two or three times. Beat the egg until light; add the milk, the syrup or molasses. Combine the two mixtures, stirring as little as possible. Add the melted shortening and the cheese; blend. Fill oiled muffin tins ⅔ full; bake in a moderate oven until firm. Cover with a towel and let stand for 5 minutes before removing from pan. Serve hot. Yield: 12 large muffins.

NOTE TO BRIDES: *This batter is stiff but that's the way it should be.*

CREAM SCONES

Temperature: 450°F.   Time: 12-15 minutes

2¼ cups sifted all-purpose   ¼ cup shortening
   flour   2 eggs
3 teaspoons baking powder   ½ cup cereal cream
   ½ teaspoon salt   2 tablespoons sugar

Sift together the flour, baking powder and salt. Cut in the shortening with a dough blender. Beat the eggs until light; add the cream and sugar. Make a well in the centre of the flour mixture; add the egg mixture all at once. Stir lightly, mixing as little as possible; turn on a floured board. Knead lightly until the dough is smooth. Roll to ¾ inch thickness. Cut crosswise in diamonds; brush lightly with the following glaze:

GLAZE

2 tablespoons cold milk   1 tablespoon sugar

Bake in a hot oven; split, butter and serve with raspberry jam. Yield: 18 scones.

CORN MEAL MUFFINS

Temperature: 400°F.   Time: 30 minutes

1½ cups sifted all-purpose flour   ¾ cup yellow corn meal
   3 teaspoons baking powder   1 egg, well beaten
½ teaspoon salt   4 tablespoons melted fat
   2 tablespoons white sugar   1 cup milk

Sift the dry ingredients together 2 or 3 times. To the well beaten egg add the melted fat and the milk; blend well. Make a well in the centre of the flour mixture; add the liquid all at once. Stir quickly and vigorously till the mixture is blended. Don't beat this batter, that makes too many holes; remember, the stirring must be speedy.   Fill oiled muffin tins ⅔ full; bake in a hot oven. Serve warm with jam and butter. Yield: 12 large muffins.

SPICED MOLASSES MUFFINS

Temperature: 400°F.   Time: 20-25 minutes

1 cup sifted all-purpose flour   1 cup whole wheat flour
   4 teaspoons baking powder   1 egg, slightly beaten
1 teaspoon salt   4 tablespoons molasses
   1 teaspoon cinnamon   1 cup milk
½ teaspoon allspice   3 tablespoons melted shortening

Sift together the flour, baking powder, salt, cinnamon and allspice. Add the whole wheat flour; mix well. Slightly beat the egg; add the molasses and milk. Add to the flour mixture, stirring just enough to wet the flour. Add the melted shortening. Stir quickly. Fill oiled muffin tins ⅔ full. Bake in a hot oven till done. This quantity makes 12 good-sized muffins.

NOTE: This same batter can be baked in a loaf pan, sliced and buttered.

CHEESE PINWHEELS

Temperature: 450°F.   Time: 12-15 minutes

2 cups sifted all-purpose flour   ¼ cup shortening
   4½ teaspoons baking   1 cup milk
   powder   Flour for kneading
½ teaspoon salt   1 cup grated cheese

Sift together the flour, baking powder and salt two or three times. Cut the fat in coarsely (until the mixture is like coarse corn meal). Add the milk all at once; stir in lightly with a knife. Flour the board with your hands. Turn out the batter on the floured board; gather it into a ball and knead gently for 20 counts. Roll out the dough ½" thick; sprinkle with the grated cheese;

roll up as for a jelly roll. Cut in ½″ slices; place the biscuits on an oiled sheet, touching one another. Bake in a hot oven.

In place of the cheese, grated carrot may be used or chopped parsley. It is best to brush the batter lightly with melted butter when using carrots or parsley; the biscuits are richer and they also roll better. Yield: 24 pinwheels.

POTATO SCONES

Temperature: 425°F.   Time: 15-18 minutes

1½ cups sifted all-purpose flour	⅓ cup shortening
	1 cup dry mashed potatoes
2 teaspoons baking powder	1 egg, slightly beaten
½ teaspoon salt	6 tablespoons milk

Sift together the flour, baking powder and salt; cut in the shortening until the mixture is like coarse corn meal; rub the mashed potatoes into the mixture (they should be dry and mealy). Slightly beat the egg; add the milk; stir into the potato mixture, mixing very lightly. Turn on a floured board and divide into 3 parts. Roll each part into a round; cut each round into 4 scones. Bake in a quick oven; serve hot with butter and honey. Yield: 12 scones.

COFFEE RING WITH FRUIT FILLING

Temperature: 450°F.-350°F.   Time: 35 minutes

2 cups sifted all-purpose flour	1 cup milk
4½ teaspoons baking powder	1 egg, slightly beaten
½ teaspoon salt	¼ cup brown sugar
1 tablespoon white sugar	¼ cup currants
¼ cup shortening	¼ cup candied cherries, chopped

Sift together the flour, baking powder, salt and sugar. Cut in the shortening until the mixture is the consistency of coarse corn meal. Make a well in the centre; add the milk all at once. Stir lightly and turn on a floured board. Gather into a ball and knead lightly for 20 counts. Roll into an oblong roll about ¼″ thick. Beat the egg slightly; add the brown sugar, currants and cherries; spread on the batter. Roll up as for a jelly roll and place on an oiled pie plate, joining the ends to make a circle. With the scissors, slash at 2″ intervals. Bake in a hot oven for 10 minutes; reduce the heat and continue baking till done, about 25 minutes. If you want the coffee ring to look like a million dollars top it with this glaze:

Simmer together for 3 minutes 2 tablespoons of fat and 2 tablespoons of corn syrup. While the ring is still warm, pour the glaze over it. Yield: 12 slices.

SOUR CREAM SCONES

Temperature: 425°F.   Time: 12-15 minutes

1 teaspoon lemon rind, grated
1 tablespoon lemon juice
2 cups sifted all-purpose flour
½ teaspoon baking powder
½ teaspoon baking soda
½ teaspoon salt
2 tablespoons white sugar
¼ cup shortening
2 eggs, slightly beaten
½ cup thick sour cream

Mix together the grated lemon rind and juice. Sift together the flour, baking powder, baking soda, salt and sugar. Cut in the fat until the mixture is crumbly. Slightly beat the eggs; add the sour cream, the lemon juice and rind. Combine with the flour mixture; stir lightly till all the flour disappears. Turn on a floured board; knead for 20 counts. Roll into a rectangle ½" thick; cut into 4" squares. Cut each square diagonally to make triangles. Brush with rich milk; sprinkle lightly with sugar. Bake in a hot oven till golden brown. Yield: 18 scones.

MARMALADE BREAD

Temperature: 325°F.   Time: 1 hour

2 tablespoons shortening
2 tablespoons white sugar
1 egg, well beaten
¼ cup orange marmalade
1 tablespoon grated orange rind
½ cup milk
1½ cups sifted all-purpose flour
2 teaspoons baking powder
½ teaspoon salt
¼ cup nuts, chopped

Cream together the shortening and white sugar; add the well-beaten egg, marmalade and orange rind; beat till fluffy. Add the milk; blend well. Add the sifted dry ingredients and nuts all at once; stir briskly. Pour into an oiled loaf pan 9" x 5" x 3" which has been lined with oiled paper; let stand 20 minutes; bake in a moderate oven. Serve sandwich fashion with plain cream cheese as the filling.

SPICED CURRANT LOAF

Temperature: 325°F.   Time: 1 hour, 15 minutes

1½ cups sifted all-purpose flour
2¼ teaspoons baking powder
½ teaspoon salt
½ teaspoon cinnamon
¼ teaspoon mace
⅛ teaspoon cloves
¾ cup currants
1 egg, well beaten
½ cup milk
⅜ cup corn syrup or molasses
2 tablespoons melted shortening

Sift together the flour, baking powder, salt and spices; add the currants, which have been plumped in boiling water and drained. Beat the egg till light; add the milk, the corn syrup or molasses and the melted shortening. Combine the two mixtures; stir lightly. Turn into a pan 9″ x 5″ x 3″ which has been lined with waxed paper. Bake in a moderate oven till done. Let stand 24 hours before slicing.

DARK SECRET FRUIT LOAF

Temperature: 325°F. Time: 1 hour

3 tablespoons shortening
  ⅓ cup brown sugar
½ teaspoon salt
  ½ cup prunes, apricots or
    what have you (uncooked),
    chopped
½ cup milk

½ tablespoon lemon juice
1 egg, well beaten
1¼ cups sifted all-purpose flour
  2 teaspoons baking powder
⅛ teaspoon baking soda
  ¼ cup whole wheat flour or
    bran

Mix together the shortening, brown sugar, salt, chopped dried fruit and milk. Heat slowly till the sugar is dissolved; cool to lukewarm. Add the lemon juice and the well beaten egg. Sift together the flour, baking powder and baking soda; add the whole wheat flour or bran and mix. Add the dry ingredients to the fruit mixture. Stir well but do not beat. Pour into an oiled pan 9″ x 5″ x 3″ which has been lined with oiled paper; bake in a moderate oven about 1 hour. Loaf should stand for 24 hours before slicing.

SALLY LUNN

Temperature: 375°F. Time: 45 minutes

½ cup shortening
  ¾ cup white sugar
2 cups sifted all-purpose flour
  2 teaspoons baking powder
½ teaspoon salt
  2 eggs, lightly beaten

1 cup milk
1 tablespoon sifted all-purpose
  flour
1 tablespoon butter
2 tablespoons brown sugar
1 teaspoon cinnamon

Cream together the shortening and white sugar. Gradually work in the 2 cups all-purpose flour until the mixture is crumbly. Measure out ½ cup of this mixture and set aside; to the remainder add the baking powder and the salt. Beat the eggs lightly; add the milk. Add the egg mixture to the flour mixture, stirring lightly and quickly. Pour the batter into an oiled pan 8″ x 12″. To the reserved ½ cup of the shortening mixture add the 1 tablespoon flour, the butter, brown sugar and cinnamon; sprinkle on the top of the uncooked batter. Bake in a moderately hot oven (375°F.) until done. When cool, cut in squares; split and spread with butter. Yield: 12 squares.

STEAMED BROWN BREAD

Steaming: 3 hours

Oven Temperature: 350°F.   Time: 20 minutes

2 cups sour milk or buttermilk
   ¾ cup molasses or brown sugar
1 cup baking bran
   1 cup yellow corn meal

1 cup whole wheat flour
   2 tablespoons white sugar
2 teaspoons baking soda
   1½ teaspoons salt

Combine the sour milk or buttermilk, the molasses or brown sugar and the bran; let stand 15 minutes. Add all the remaining ingredients; stir only enough to mix well; do not beat the mixture. Turn into oiled baking powder cans, filling them only ⅔ full; this mixture will fill 4 cans. Cover with oiled close-fitting lids; steam, tightly covered, for 3 hours. Uncover; bake in a moderate oven for 20 minutes. Serve warm or cold; spread with lemon or marmalade butter.

CHEESE BREAD

Temperature: 375°F.   Time: 50 minutes

2 cups sifted all-purpose flour
   1½ teaspoons baking powder
1 teaspoon baking soda
   1½ teaspoons salt
¼ teaspoon dry mustard

1 cup cheese, grated
   1 egg, well beaten
1 cup sour milk
   2 tablespoons melted
     shortening

Sift together the flour, baking powder, baking soda, salt and mustard. Add the cheese; mix well. Beat the egg until light; add the milk and shortening; blend. Make a well in the centre of the flour mixture; add the egg mixture all at once; mix lightly. Pour into an oiled pan 9″ x 5″ x 3″; let stand 20 minutes; bake in a moderate oven till done. While still warm, brush the crust with melted butter.

HOT CURRANT BREAD

Temperature: 375°F.   Time: 20-25 minutes

¼ cup shortening
   1 cup white sugar
1 egg
   1½ cups sifted all-purpose
     flour
2 teaspoons baking powder

½ teaspoon salt
   ½ cup milk
⅓ cup currants
   1 teaspoon cinnamon
1 tablespoon brown sugar

Cream the shortening; blend in the sugar in 3 additions; beat till creamy. Add the slightly-beaten egg; beat till light. Sift together the flour, baking powder and salt; add alternately

with the milk to the creamed mixture. Mix this batter as lightly
as possible; pour into an oiled pan 8″ x 12″. Wash and dry the
currants; mix with the cinnamon and brown sugar; sprinkle lightly
over the raw batter. Bake in moderate oven; serve hot with
butter. Yield: 16 squares.

DATE AND NUT LOAF

Temperature: 325°F.

Time: 1 hour

1 cup dates, chopped
 ¾ cup brown sugar
1 teaspoon salt
 ½ cup boiling water
1 egg
 1 teaspoon vanilla

1½ cups sifted all-purpose
 flour
1 teaspoon baking powder
 1 teaspoon baking soda
½ cup nuts, chopped
 ¼ cup melted shortening

Measure the dates, brown sugar and salt into a mixing bowl.
Add the boiling water; stir well; let stand till cool. Add the well-
beaten egg and vanilla; add the sifted dry ingredients, stirring with
a few quick, sure strokes. Add the nuts and shortening; blend
lightly. Pour into a loaf pan 9″ x 5″ x 3″ which has been oiled and
lined with heavy brown paper. Bake in a slow oven till done.
Let the loaf stand 24 hours before cutting.

PRUNE LOAF

Temperature: 350°F.

Time: 1 hour

1 cup uncooked prunes
 2 cups sifted all-purpose flour
4 teaspoons baking powder
 ½ teaspoon baking soda
1½ teaspoons salt
 2 tablespoons white sugar

1 cup whole wheat flour
 ¼ cup shortening
2 tablespoons grated orange
 rind
2 eggs, well beaten
 1 cup plus 2 tablespoons milk

Wash the prunes; cover with warm water; cook for 5 minutes.
Remove the pits; chop the prune meat finely. Sift together the
flour, baking powder, baking soda, salt and sugar; add the whole
wheat flour. Cut in the shortening; add the chopped prunes and
the orange rind. Mix together the well-beaten eggs and milk;
add to the flour mixture; stir lightly until blended. Bake in one
long loaf pan or two pans 9″ x 5″ x 3″ which have been lined with
oiled paper. Let the bread stand 24 hours before slicing.

NOTE TO BRIDES: *This bread is the best ever for lunch boxes:
it's especially nice with lemon butter. To make the butter, add 1
tablespoon lemon juice and 1 teaspoon grated lemon rind to ½ cup
butter.*

HONEY FRUIT LOAF

Temperature: 325°F.

Time: 1½ hours

1 cup shortening
1 cup honey
½ cup raw carrot, grated
½ cup apple, peeled and grated
2 eggs, well beaten
3 cups sifted all-purpose flour

3 teaspoons baking powder
1 teaspoon cinnamon
1 teaspoon nutmeg
1 teaspoon cloves
½ teaspoon salt
¾ cup mixed peel, chopped
1 cup raisins, chopped

Cream together the shortening and honey; beat till light; add the grated carrot. Peel, core and grate the apple; add to the mixture. Add the eggs, well beaten. Add the sifted dry ingredients and fruit; blend well. Pour into an oiled loaf pan 9″ x 5″ x 3″. Let stand 10 minutes before baking. Bake in a slow oven till firm. Let stand 24 hours before slicing.

JOHNNY CAKE

Temperature: 400°F.

Time: 1 hour

1⅓ cups sifted all-purpose flour
⅔ cup fine cornmeal
4 teaspoons baking powder
½ teaspoon salt

2 eggs, well beaten
⅔ cup milk
⅓ cup corn syrup
¼ cup melted shortening

Sift the dry ingredients. To the well-beaten eggs add the milk, corn syrup and melted shortening. Combine the two mixtures; beat till smooth; pour into an oiled pan 8″ x 8″ x 2″. Bake in a hot oven; serve hot with butter and corn syrup. Yield: 12 servings.

Pancakes

Use a heavy iron or aluminum frying pan or griddle for baking pancakes. Heat the pan until a few drops of cold water poured into the pan retain their shape a few seconds. If the drops spread out on the griddle, the temperature is too low; if they break up and evaporate immediately, the temperature is too high. Too cool a griddle will produce pancakes which will be thin and tough; too hot a griddle will brown them before the centre is cooked. To prevent the mixture from sticking to the griddle, add a little melted shortening to the pancake batter.

Basic Recipe

1 egg
1¾ cups milk
3 tablespoons sugar
1½ cups sifted all-purpose
   flour

3 teaspoons baking powder
½ teaspoon salt
3 teaspoons melted shortening
¼ teaspoon vanilla

Beat the egg till light; add the milk and sugar. Add the sifted dry ingredients in 3 siftings, beating only enough to make a smooth batter. Stir in the melted shortening and vanilla. Heat the griddle; brush lightly with oil; drop the batter by tablespoonfuls on the griddle. Cook till the pancakes are brown and filled with bubbles. Turn and bake on the other side. Do not turn more than once during cooking. Serve hot with butter and maple syrup. This batter will make 12 good sized pancakes.

DUTCH POTATO PANCAKES

3 pounds uncooked potatoes,
   (8 or 9 medium size)
3 eggs, separated
1¼ cups sifted pastry
   flour

½ teaspoon salt
   Dash of pepper and paprika
1 large tart apple, grated
1 teaspoon onion, finely
   chopped

Peel the potatoes, quarter and let stand in cold water for one hour; grate; drain through a colander. Add the egg yolks, flour, seasonings, grated apple and onion. Lastly fold in the stiffly-beaten egg whites. Have the griddle hot and very lightly greased. Pour out a small quantity as the batter spreads. Bake on both sides, turning only once. Serve with maple syrup and butter. Yield: 12 pancakes.

BLUEBERRY GRIDDLE CAKES

2 cups sifted all-purpose
   flour
3 tablespoons white sugar
½ teaspoon salt
3 teaspoons baking powder
2 eggs

1 cup milk
4 tablespoons melted
   shortening
1 cup blueberries
   Dash of cinnamon, nutmeg
   and mace

Sift together the flour, sugar, salt and baking powder. Beat the eggs till very light; add the milk. Add the milk mixture slowly to the dry ingredients; beat with the dover beater till smooth; add the melted shortening. Fold in the blueberries and spices. Have the griddle pan hot and lightly greased. Drop by tablespoonfuls and turn only once during baking. Serve with butter and honey. Yield: 16 griddle cakes.

SOUR MILK GRIDDLE CAKES

⅞ cup sifted all-purpose
  flour
½ teaspoon baking soda
  ½ teaspoon salt

⅛ teaspoon nutmeg
1 egg
1 teaspoon melted shortening
1 cup sour milk

Sift together the dry ingredients. Beat the egg till very light; add the shortening and sour milk. Add to the flour mixture; stir quickly and lightly. Drop the batter by spoonfuls on the hot griddle; bake 2-3 minutes; when bubbles show up on the surface and begin to break, lift the cakes with the spatula. If the under surface is browned, turn and bake on the other side; turn only once. Serve warm, with butter and syrup. Yield: 8 griddle cakes.

Yeast Breads

Home-made breads or rolls have a fragrance appeal that outdoes the famous Chanel No. 5. Add to the sensory attraction these facts—home-made breads and rolls cost one-third as much as cake; they use one-third the amount of sugar; they give double the bulk and an infinite variety. Don't be afraid to try yeast mixtures; once you've mastered the technique, you'll find them the most satisfactory batter to make.

SUCCESS RULES:

(1) Be moderate in all things. Have the liquid lukewarm, the pans room temperature.

(2) Never put the sponge in direct heat to rise; that is, never directly on the radiator or oven. Indirect heat without draft brings the sponge up evenly.

(3) Use a moderate oven in baking; keep the crust soft by brushing with melted butter.

BROWN BREAD
(*Basic Recipe*)

Temperature: 400°F.-375°F.   Time: 50-60 minutes

2 cakes compressed yeast
  3 tablespoons molasses
4 cups lukewarm liquid, part
  milk and part water

2 tablespoons melted shortening
  4 cups sifted all-purpose flour
1 tablespoon salt
  7 cups whole wheat flour

Dissolve the yeast and molasses in the lukewarm liquid. Add the shortening; add the all-purpose flour, cup by cup. Beat until smooth; add the salt and whole wheat flour. This dough should be stiff enough to handle without sticking. Turn on a floured board; knead until smooth and elastic. Place in an oiled bowl; cover and let rise until light (about 1½ hours) in a warm place. Punch down to release gas bubbles; mould in loaves; place each loaf in an oiled pan 9″ x 5″ x 3″. Cover and let rise until double in bulk (about 1 hour). Bake in a 400°F. oven for 15 minutes; reduce heat to 375°F., and continue baking 35-45 minutes. Makes 3 large loaves, 1½ pounds each.

WHOLE WHEAT BREAD

(*Basic Recipe*)

Temperature: 400°F.-375°F.　　Time: 50-60 minutes

2 cakes compressed yeast	4 tablespoons molasses or corn
¼ cup lukewarm water	syrup
1 teaspoon white sugar	1 tablespoon salt
1 cup milk	3 cups whole wheat flour
1 cup water	2 cups sifted all-purpose flour
⅓ cup shortening	1 tablespoon grated orange rind

Crumble the yeast cakes in the lukewarm water; add the sugar and stir well. Scald the milk; add the water, shortening, molasses or corn syrup and salt; cool to lukewarm. Combine with the yeast mixture. Add the flour, cup by cup, until the mixture can be turned out on a floured board. Sprinkle with the orange rind; knead until smooth. Place in an oiled bowl; brush with oil; cover and let rise in a warm place until double in bulk (about 1¼ hours). Turn on a floured board and knead just enough to release the gas bubbles. Cut in half and roll each half into a ball. Cover and let stand 10 minutes. Shape each half into a loaf; place in an oiled pan 9″ x 5″ x 3″. Let rise till light (about 40 minutes). Bake in a hot oven (400°F.) for 15 minutes; reduce the heat to 375°F.; continue cooking till done (about 35 minutes). If you want a soft crust and no crumbling, brush the loaves with fat just before removing from the oven. Yield: two 2 pound loaves.

NOTE TO BRIDES: *Double the recipe and make in addition a pan of rolls, a cinnamon loaf or a fruit loaf.*

WHITE BREAD
(Basic Recipe)

Temperature: 400°F.-375°F.   Time: 50-60 minutes

2 cakes compressed yeast
  3 tablespoons white sugar
    or corn syrup
4 cups lukewarm liquid
  (Milk, or part milk and part
  water)

2 tablespoons melted
  shortening
12 cups sifted all-purpose
  flour
1½ tablespoons salt

Dissolve the yeast and sugar or corn syrup in the lukewarm liquid. This may be part milk and part water, or instead of the water, use drained potato water. Add the shortening; beat in ½ the flour, cup by cup. Beat until smooth; add the remainder of the flour and the salt. This dough should be stiff enough to handle without sticking. Turn on a floured board; knead lightly until smooth and elastic. Place the batter in an oiled bowl; cover and let rise in warm place until light (about 1½ hours). Knead to release gas bubbles; mould into loaves; place each loaf in an oiled pan 9″ x 5″ x 3″; brush with melted butter. Cover and let rise until double in bulk (about 1 hour). Bake in hot oven, 400°F., for 15 minutes; reduce to moderate oven, 375°F., and finish baking for 35 to 45 minutes. Makes 3 large loaves, 1½ pounds each.

NORWEGIAN CHRISTMAS ROLL

Temperature: 400°-350°F.   Time: 40 minutes

1 cup warm milk
  ½ cup melted shortening
½ cup honey
  2 eggs, well beaten
2 cakes compressed yeast
  ¼ cup warm water
2 teaspoons grated lemon rind

4½ to 5 cups sifted all-purpose
  flour
½ teaspoon salt
  ½ teaspoon cinnamon
½ cup seedless raisins
  ½ cup mixed peel, chopped

Combine in a mixing bowl the warm milk, shortening and honey. Add the well-beaten eggs. Add the yeast, which has been dissolved in the warm water, and the lemon rind. Beat well with the dover beater. Sift in the dry ingredients cup by cup; add the chopped fruit, mix well; turn on floured board and knead lightly. Place in oiled bowl; cover and let rise in warm place until double in bulk (about 1 hour). Turn on floured board and knead to release gas bubbles. Divide into four equal parts; twist each part; place side by side in oiled pan 8″ x 8″ x 3½″. Cover; let rise in a warm place until light (about ¾ hour). Bake in hot oven (400°F.) for 10 minutes; reduce heat to 350°F. and finish baking.

When cool, cover with the following glaze: Simmer together ¼ cup butter, ¼ cup corn syrup for 3 minutes; brush over the bun; glaze. Yield: 24 slices.

PRUNE BREAD

Temperature: 375°F.   Time: 45 minutes

1 cup prunes chopped   1 egg, well beaten
  2 cakes compressed yeast   5 - 5½ cups sifted
1 cup lukewarm milk   all-purpose flour
  ½ teaspoon salt   ¼ cup molasses
1 teaspoon cinnamon   ½ cup cooking bran
  ¼ teaspoon nutmeg   ¼ cup melted shortening

Wash 1½ cups prunes; cover with warm water; simmer 15 minutes. Drain the prunes; remove the pits and chop the meat; There should be 1 cup. Crumble the yeast into the lukewarm milk; add the salt, spices, egg and 1 cup of flour. Beat well; add the second cup of flour; add the molasses, bran, shortening, chopped prunes and the remainder of the flour. Knead lightly; place in an oiled bowl; cover and let rise in a warm place till light (about 1½ hours). Turn on a floured board and knead lightly. Divide the batter in half; shape each half into a loaf. Place in oiled pans; let rise till light. Bake in a moderate oven till done. Brush with melted butter; let cool before slicing. Yield: two 1½ pound loaves

QUICK SALLY LUNN

Temperature: 400°F.   Time: 25 minutes

1 cake compressed yeast   2 eggs
  1 cup milk, scalded and cooled   3 cups sifted all-purpose
2 tablespoons white sugar   flour
  ¼ cup melted shortening   ½ teaspoon salt

Crumble the yeast in the lukewarm milk. Add the white sugar, melted shortening and well-beaten eggs. Sift in the flour and salt. Beat thoroughly until smooth and thick. Pour into two 9″ cake pans which have been oiled. Cover and let rise until double in bulk (about 45 minutes). Sprinkle with Streusel Crumbs; bake in a moderate oven. Serve hot with butter.

STREUSEL CRUMBS

2 tablespoons butter   ¼ cup cake or cookie
  2 tablespoons brown sugar   crumbs
4 tablespoons flour   ½ teaspoon cinnamon

Cream the butter and sugar; add flour, crumbs and cinnamon. Mix together until crumbly; sprinkle on the raised dough.

ALMOND COFFEE RING

Temperature: 375°F.   Time: 25-30 minutes

1 cake compressed yeast   1 teaspoon grated orange rind
  ¼ cup lukewarm water   1 egg, well beaten
½ cup milk   2½ cups sifted all-purpose flour
  ¼ cup white sugar   ½ cup almonds, chopped
¾ teaspoon salt   2 tablespoons brown sugar
  ¼ cup melted shortening   ½ teaspoon cinnamon

Crumble the yeast into the lukewarm water; measure the milk, sugar, salt, melted shortening and orange rind into a mixing bowl; heat to lukewarm. Add the yeast; beat till smooth. Add the well-beaten egg. Add the flour, cup by cup, beating well after each addition. Turn the batter on a floured board and knead lightly. Place in an oiled bowl; cover and let rise until light, about 1 hour. Turn out on the floured board again and knead gently. Divide into 3 parts; roll each part into a rectangle about ¼ inch thick. Sprinkle each rectangle with a mixture of the almonds, brown sugar and cinnamon. Roll each as for a jelly roll, then twist slightly. Lay the 3 rolls on an oiled cookie sheet and braid. Cover and let rise until light (about ¾ hour). Bake in a moderate oven. Yield: 18 slices.

NOTE TO BRIDES: *This is a truly delicious roll, one on which you can build a reputation.*

WHITE ROLLS
(*Basic Recipe*)

Temperature: 375°F.   Time: 15-20 minutes

1 cake compressed yeast   ¾ teaspoon salt
  ¼ cup lukewarm water   ½ teaspoon grated lemon
1 cup milk   rind or dash of mace
2 tablespoons shortening   2½-3 cups sifted all-purpose
2 tablespoons corn syrup or   flour
  sugar

Crumble the yeast into the lukewarm water. Measure the milk, shortening, corn syrup or sugar, salt and flavoring into a large bowl; heat to lukewarm. Beat in the softened yeast. Beat in the flour, cup by cup; this batter should be soft. Turn on a floured board; knead only enough to form into a ball. Place in an oiled bowl; cover; let rise in a warm place (80°-85°F.) until double in bulk, about 1 hour, 15 minutes. Turn out on a floured board; shape into rolls as desired. Place on an oiled cookie sheet; let rise till double in bulk, about 30 minutes. Bake in a moderate oven till golden brown. Yield: 12-14 rolls, depending on the size.

NOTE TO BRIDES: *If the rolls are brushed with cream or rich milk before baking the crust is very tender. If the rolls are brushed with melted butter after baking, the crust does not crumble. To glaze the rolls after baking brush with a mixture of 1 tablespoon white sugar and 2 tablespoons milk. Put the rolls back in the oven again for a minute.*

Variations

Bow Knots: Roll the dough ½″ thick; cut in strips ½″ wide and 4″ long. Knot loosely.

Clover Leaf Rolls: Shape the dough in tiny balls; dip in melted shortening; place 3 in each section of the oiled muffin pans.

Parker House Rolls: Roll the dough ½″ thick; cut in 2½″ rounds. Grease the rounds a little off centre with the dull edge of a coarse knife. Brush the small half with melted butter; fold over and press the edges together.

Whole Wheat Rolls: Follow the recipe for white rolls, substituting molasses for the corn syrup and 1 cup of whole wheat or graham flour for 1 cup white flour.

Sugar Topped Buns: Have ready oiled muffin pans, 2 tablespoons of melted butter in a saucer and 2 tablespoons of white sugar in another saucer. Cut the dough in small balls with the scissors. Roll each ball smooth between palms of the hands. Dip the top first in melted butter, then in granulated sugar. Place, sugar side up, in the oiled muffin pans.

Rich Rolls: With the addition of eggs, more sugar and shortening, the rolls get richer and more cake-like in texture. These rich rolls can double for dessert.

BUTTER HORNS

Temperature: 400°F.   Time: 15 minutes

1 cake compressed yeast	1 teaspoon salt
¼ cup lukewarm water	⅛ teaspoon mace
1 cup scalded milk	3 eggs, well beaten
½ cup shortening	4½ cups sifted all-purpose flour
⅓ cup sugar	2 tablespoons softened butter

Soften the yeast in lukewarm water. Scald the milk in the top of a double boiler; add the shortening, sugar, salt and mace. Cool to lukewarm; beat in the softened yeast. Add the well-beaten eggs; blend well. Add the flour, cup by cup; mix to a smooth dough. Knead lightly on a floured board. Place in an oiled bowl; cover and let rise in a warm place until double in bulk (about 2 hours). Punch down to release gas bubbles; divide the dough into three parts. Roll each third in a pie-shaped 9″ round. Cut each round into 12 pie-shaped wedges; brush each with softened butter. Roll each wedge, starting from the wide end and rolling towards the centre. Place on an oiled cookie sheet; cover and let rise in a warm place till light. Brush with softened butter; bake in a hot oven. Yield: 3 dozen butter horns.

BUTTERMILK ROLLS

Temperature: 400°F.   Time: 15-20 minutes

1 medium potato
  ¼ cup shortening
1 cake compressed yeast
  ¼ cup lukewarm water
2 tablespoons white sugar

½ teaspoon salt
  1 cup buttermilk
1 egg, well beaten
  3½-4 cups sifted all-purpose
  flour

Peel the potato; cook till tender. Press through the ricer; there should be ½ cup. While the potato is still warm, add the shortening; stir till it is melted. Dissolve the yeast cake in the lukewarm water; beat into the potato mixture. Add the sugar and salt to the buttermilk; heat to lukewarm; add to the potato mixture. Add the well-beaten egg; add the flour cup by cup, stirring and beating until the mixture cannot be stirred any longer. Turn on a floured board; knead gently till smooth. Place the sponge in an oiled bowl; cover and let rise in a warm place till light (about 1½ hours). Knead down lightly; shape into rolls. Place them on an oiled cookie sheet; again let rise till light, about 1 hour. Bake in a hot oven; while still warm brush with melted butter. Yield: 24 rolls.

CRUSTY CURLS
(*Unusual*)

Temperature: 400°F.   Time: 15 minutes

1 cake compressed yeast
  ¼ cup lukewarm water
¾ cup milk
  ¼ cup melted shortening
2 tablespoons white sugar
  1 teaspoon salt
1 teaspoon grated lemon rind

2 teaspoons lemon juice
  1 egg, lightly beaten
3-3½ cups sifted all-purpose
  flour
24 oiled clothes pins
  Cream cheese
Mayonnaise

Crumble the yeast into the lukewarm water. Measure the milk, melted shortening, sugar, salt, lemon rind and juice into a mixing bowl. Heat to lukewarm; add the dissolved yeast and beat well. Add the egg and again blend. Beat in the flour, cup by cup; turn the batter on a floured board and knead gently. Place in an oiled bowl; cover and let rise till light, about 1½ hours. Knead down again and roll into a rectangle ½" thick; cut in strips ½" wide. Oil the clothes pins (the knobby kind); wind them with strips of dough from top to bottom. Fasten underneath; place on an oiled cookie sheet to rise, about ½ hour. Bake in a hot oven till golden brown. Take from the oven and brush with melted butter; gently loosen the clothes pins and pull them out. Mix plain cream cheese with a little mayonnaise; fill the ends of the rolls and serve.

HOT CROSS BUNS

Temperature: 375°F.
1 cake compressed yeast
 ¼ cup lukewarm water
1 cup milk
 ⅓ cup corn syrup
½ teaspoon salt

Time: 20-25 minutes
¼ cup melted shortening
 1 teaspoon grated lemon rind
1 egg, well beaten
 ½ cup raisins
3½ - 4 cups sifted all-purpose
 flour

Crumble the yeast into the lukewarm water. Measure the milk, corn syrup, salt, shortening and lemon rind into a mixing bowl; heat until the mixture is lukewarm. Beat in the dissolved yeast and the egg; add the raisins. Beat in 2 cups of flour; stir till smooth. Add the remaining flour; mix well. Turn on a floured board, shape into a ball and knead lightly. Place in an oiled bowl; cover and let rise in a warm place till double in bulk (about 2 hours). Turn on a floured board and knead to release gas bubbles. Shape into medium-sized buns; place on an oiled cookie sheet about 2″ apart. Cover and again let rise (about 1 hour); with the scissors cut a small cross on the top of each bun. Bake 20-25 minutes in a moderately hot oven. Three minutes before baking is completed, remove and brush with 1 tablespoon of sugar dissolved in 2 tablespoons of milk. While still hot, fill the crosses with icing made with icing sugar and hot water. Yield: 18 buns.

HOMEMADE PRUNE ROLLS

Temperature: 400°F.-350°F.
18 cooked prunes
 18 nuts, shelled
2 cakes compressed yeast
 ¼ cup lukewarm water
¾ cup milk, scalded
 ⅓ cup corn syrup

Time: 25 minutes
½ teaspoon salt
 ⅓ cup melted shortening
1/16 teaspoon mace
 1 egg, well beaten
1 cup whole wheat flour
 3 cups sifted all-purpose flour

Remove the pits from the prunes; stuff each prune with a nut. Soften the yeast in lukewarm water, combine it with the scalded milk, the corn syrup, salt, shortening and mace. Add the well beaten egg and the whole wheat flour; mix well. Add the white flour, cup by cup, beating well after each cupful; this dough should not be stiff. Turn into an oiled bowl; cover; let rise in a warm place till double in bulk (1 to 1¼ hours). Turn out on floured board; knead lightly to release gas bubbles. Cut off small pieces of dough; shape into round rolls. Slash the top with scissors and insert a stuffed prune in the opening. Place the rolls in oiled muffin pans; cover; let rise till light (about ½ hour). Bake in hot oven (400° F.) for 10 minutes; reduce the heat to 350°F. and finish baking. Yield: 18 rolls.

HOMEMADE BUNS

Temperature: 400°F.   Time: 15-20 minutes

4 cups mashed potatoes   1 cup hot milk
  1 cup potato water (lukewarm)   1 teaspoon salt
1 cake compressed yeast   1 tablespoon sugar
  4 cups sifted all-purpose   2 tablespoons shortening
    flour   1 egg, well beaten

Cook, drain and mash 6 large potatoes, saving the potato water. Soften the yeast in 1 cup of the lukewarm potato water; add 1 cup of the flour. Beat till smooth; let rise in a warm place until light (about 1 hour). Combine the hot milk, mashed potatoes, salt, sugar, shortening and well beaten egg; mix with the sponge; add the remaining 3 cups of flour, cup by cup. Cover; let rise till light (about 1 hour). Have ready 2 oiled cookie sheets; drop spoonfuls of the batter on the sheets about 2″ apart (do not handle the batter). Let rise until light; bake in a hot oven for 15 to 20 minutes. Yield: 45 buns. Even the crumbs are delicious!

REFRIGERATOR ROLLS

Temperature: 375°F.   Time: 20-25 minutes

1 cake compressed yeast   1 teaspoon salt
  ¼ cup lukewarm water   1 teaspoon grated lemon rind
1 cup milk   1 egg, well beaten
  ¼ cup melted shortening   3-3½ cups sifted all-
¼ cup corn syrup or white sugar   purpose flour

Crumble the yeast into the lukewarm water. Measure the milk, melted shortening, corn syrup or sugar, salt and lemon rind into a bowl; heat to lukewarm. Add the dissolved yeast and the well beaten egg; beat well. Add 1 cup of the flour; blend with the dover beater; add the second cup of flour and again beat. Beat in the remainder of the flour with a spoon. Turn on a floured board and knead lightly; turn into an oiled bowl, cover tightly with waxed paper and place in the refrigerator. When ready to use, turn the dough out on a floured board; knead lightly, then roll to about ½″ thickness. Cut with a 2½″ cutter; place the rolls on an oiled cookie sheet. Let rise till light, about 1 hour; bake in a moderate oven till golden brown. Five minutes before taking from the oven brush the rolls with a mixture of 1 egg yolk beaten lightly with ½ cup cold water; return to the oven to glaze. Yield: 24 rolls.

NOTE TO BRIDES: *This dough will keep for a week. If it rises in the refrigerator don't worry; the gas bubbles can be punched down quite easily. Keep the bowl tightly covered.*

CHAPTER 5

Cakes, Fillings and Frostings

APPLESAUCE CAKE
(*With Meringue*)

Temperature: 350°F.

Time: 1 hour

½ cup shortening
1 cup brown sugar
2 egg yolks, unbeaten
2 cups sifted cake flour
1 teaspoon baking soda

¼ teaspoon salt
1 teaspoon cinnamon
½ teaspoon cloves
½ teaspoon nutmeg
1 cup thick, unsweetened applesauce

Cream together the shortening and the brown sugar; add the egg yolks; blend well. Sift together the flour, baking soda, salt and spices. Add to the creamed mixture alternately with the applesauce. Pour into a pan 8″ x 12″ x 2″ which has been lined with waxed paper and oiled with cooking oil; top with the following meringue:

Meringue

2 egg whites
½ cup brown sugar

½ cup shredded wheat, rolled very fine

Beat the egg whites until stiff; gradually add the sugar; beat again until the mixture peaks. Spread over the raw batter; sprinkle with the finely rolled shredded wheat (measured after rolling). Bake in a moderate oven. Yield: 20 pieces.

BANANA CAKE

Temperature: 375°F.

Time: 30-35 minutes

⅓ cup shortening
¾ cup brown sugar
¾ teaspoon vanilla
1 egg, well beaten
¾ cup mashed bananas

1½ cups sifted pastry flour
1 teaspoon baking powder
⅓ teaspoon salt
½ teaspoon baking soda
2 tablespoons thick sour milk

Cream together the shortening, sugar and vanilla; beat till light. Add the egg, well beaten, and the mashed bananas. Add the sifted dry ingredients alternately with the sour milk; beat quickly and lightly until smooth. Pour into a square pan 8″ x 8″ which has been lined with oiled paper; bake in a moderate oven. This cake is delicious when fresh; it needs no icing. Yield: 12-16 pieces.

FRUIT BIRTHDAY CAKE

Temperature: 350°F.   Time: 25 minutes

½ cup shortening   2 cups sifted pastry flour
 1 cup brown sugar   1 teaspoon baking soda
2 eggs, well beaten   ½ teaspoon nutmeg
 1 orange, chopped   ½ teaspoon cinnamon
1 cup raisins, chopped   ½ cup sour milk

Cream the shortening; gradually add the sugar; beat till fluffy. Add the well beaten eggs. Cut the orange in quarters; put through the food chopper with the raisins; add to the creamed mixture; blend well. Add the sifted dry ingredients alternately with the sour milk. Pour into two 9″ layer cake pans lined with waxed paper and oiled; bake in a moderate oven. When cool, put to-together with Cream Filling and ice with Fruit and Nut Icing. Yield: 16 pieces.

RICH BIRTHDAY CAKE

Temperature: 375°F.   Time: 20-25 minutes

⅔ cup shortening   2 cups sifted pastry flour
 1 cup fine sifted sugar   3 teaspoons baking powder
½ teaspoon vanilla   ¼ teaspoon salt
 2 eggs   ¾ cup milk
2 egg yolks

Cream together until fluffy the shortening and ½ cup of sugar; add the vanilla and blend. Beat the eggs and egg yolks till very light; add the remainder of the sugar and again beat. Add to the creamed mixture; beat with the dover beater until light. Add the sifted dry ingredients alternately with the milk; blend with the dover beater. Bake in two 9″ layer cake pans which have been lined with waxed paper. When cool, put together and frost with Seven Minute Icing made with the two surplus egg whites. Yield: 16 pieces.

CHOCOLATE LAYER CAKE

Temperature: 375°F.   Time: 20-25 minutes

2 squares (2 oz.) unsweetened   2 eggs, well beaten
   chocolate   1½ cups sifted cake flour
½ cup hot coffee infusion   1 teaspoon baking soda
 ½ cup shortening   1 teaspoon baking powder
1¼ cups brown sugar   ½ teaspoon salt
 1 teaspoon vanilla   ½ cup thick sour milk

Measure the chocolate and hot coffee into a saucepan; simmer gently until slightly thickened; cool. Cream together the shorten-ing, brown sugar and vanilla. Add the chocolate mixture; add the well beaten eggs; beat till fluffy. Add the sifted dry ingredients alternately with the sour milk. Stir lightly; divide between two 8" layer cake pans which have been oiled and floured. Bake in a moderate oven till firm; let stand in the pans for 5 minutes. Remove; cool slightly; put together with Chocolate Cream Filling and Sea Foam Frosting. Yield: 12 pieces.

ORANGE CHOCOLATE CAKE

Temperature: 375°F.

Time: 35-40 minutes

3 squares (3 oz.) unsweetened chocolate
4 tablespoons brown sugar
⅔ cup water
1 tablespoon grated orange rind
⅔ cup shortening

1¼ cups brown sugar
3 eggs, separated
2 cups sifted cake flour
3 teaspoons baking powder
½ teaspoon salt
½ cup milk

Combine the chocolate, 4 tablespoons of brown sugar and the water in a saucepan; cook over low heat until thick, stirring constantly. Add the orange rind; let cool. Cream together the shortening and brown sugar; add the unbeaten egg yolks; beat till smooth and light. Add the chocolate mixture; blend thoroughly. Add the sifted dry ingredients alternately with the milk; fold in the stiffly beaten egg whites. Pour into an oiled 8" x 12" pan which has been lined with waxed paper; bake in a moderate oven till done. When cold, frost with a thin icing made by mixing a little icing sugar with hot orange juice. Yield: 20 pieces.

COCOA CAKE
(One Egg)

Temperature: 375°F.

Time: 30-35 minutes

¼ cup cocoa
¼ cup boiling water
⅓ cup shortening
¾ cup brown sugar
1 egg, well beaten

1¼ cups sifted pastry flour
⅓ teaspoon salt
¾ teaspoon baking soda
½ cup sour milk

Measure the cocoa into a mixing bowl; add the boiling water; stir till dissolved. Cream together the shortening and sugar; add the well beaten egg; beat till fluffy. Combine with the cocoa mixture and beat well. Add the sifted dry ingredients alternately with the sour milk. Blend; pour into an oiled pan 8" x 6" which has been lined with waxed paper; bake in a moderate oven until done. This cake is very tender, so let it stand in pan five minutes before inverting to cool. Ice with a plain Butter Icing. Yield: 9 pieces.

CHOCOLATE LIGHTNING CAKE

Temperature: 375°F.

Time: 30-35 minutes

2 squares (2 oz.) unsweetened
  chocolate
1½ tablespoons shortening
  ¾ cup white sugar
1 cup sifted cake flour

2 teaspoons baking powder
  ½ teaspoon salt
2 eggs, unbeaten
  ½ cup milk

Combine the chocolate and shortening in the top of a double boiler; melt over boiling water. Remove from the heat; add, without beating or stirring, all the remaining ingredients. Mix thoroughly, beating quickly and lightly. Pour into a square pan 8″ x 8″ which has been lined with waxed paper; bake in a moderate oven until done. This cake is moist and delicious; ice with thin white icing. Yield: 12-16 pieces.

EGGLESS CHOCOLATE CAKE

Temperature: 375°F.

Time: 40-45 minutes

2 squares (2 oz.) unsweetened
  chocolate
1 cup milk
  ⅓ cup shortening ·
1 cup brown sugar

1 teaspoon vanilla
  2 cups sifted pastry flour
¾ teaspoon salt
  ¾ teaspoon baking soda

Melt the chocolate in the top of the double boiler; add the milk; beat with the dover beater until smooth; cool slightly. Cream together the shortening, sugar and vanilla; add to the chocolate mixture. Sift the flour with the salt and baking soda; fold into the chocolate mixture. Beat till smooth; pour into a loaf pan 9″ x 5″ x 3″ which has been lined with oiled paper. Bake in a moderate oven till done. Yield: 12 slices.

CHRISTMAS CAKE (Dark)

Temperature: 275°F.

Time: 3 hours

1 cup butter
  1¼ cups brown sugar,
    firmly packed
½ cup corn syrup
  4 eggs, well beaten
¼ cup strawberry jam
  ¼ cup candied lemon peel,
    chopped
½ cup candied citron peel,
  chopped
½ cup candied cherries,
  chopped

¼ cup candied orange peel,
  chopped
1 cup seedless raisins, chopped
  1 cup currants, washed and
    dried
½ cup nuts, chopped
  2½ cups sifted pastry flour
½ teaspoon baking soda
  ¼ teaspoon salt
½ teaspoon cinnamon
  ¼ teaspoon cloves
¼ teaspoon mace

Cream the butter; gradually beat in the sugar and corn syrup; add the well beaten eggs. Add the jam, peel, fruit and nuts.

Gradually add the sifted dry ingredients; mix well. Pour the batter into an oiled square pan 8″ x 8″ x 3½″ which has been lined with heavy brown paper; bake in a slow oven until firm and golden brown. To prevent the cake drying out, cover with heavy brown paper after the first half hour of baking. Glaze the cake or ice with Almond Icing. Yield: 4 lbs.

CHRISTMAS CAKE (Light)

Temperature: 325°F.

Time: 1 hour, 45 minutes

1 cup mixed peel, sliced
  1 cup glacé cherries, sliced
1 cup raisins, chopped
  2½ cups sifted all-purpose
    flour
1 cup shortening
  1 cup white sugar

1 tablespoon grated orange rind
  1 teaspoon grated lemon rind
5 eggs, unbeaten
  1 teaspoon baking powder
½ teaspoon salt
  1 tablespoon lemon juice

Slice the peel and cherries; chop the raisins; dredge with ½ cup of flour. Cream together the shortening, sugar, orange and lemon rind. Add the eggs, unbeaten, one at a time; beat thoroughly after each addition. Sift together the remaining flour, baking powder and salt; add to the creamed mixture in 3 additions. Add the lemon juice; add the floured fruit. Line a pan 9″ x 5″ x 3″ with heavy waxed paper. Pour in the batter; bake in a moderate oven until done. Yield: about 3 lbs.

BUDGET FUDGE CAKE

Temperature: 375°F.

Time: 30-35 minutes

2 squares (2 oz.) unsweetened
  chocolate
1 egg, separated
  1 cup milk
2 tablespoons softened butter
  ¾ cup brown sugar

1 teaspoon vanilla
  1½ cups sifted all-purpose
    flour
1 teaspoon baking soda
  ⅛ teaspoon salt

Unfold the paper around the chocolate squares; let them stand on top of the radiator or oven until soft. Beat the egg yolk until light; add the softened chocolate and ½ cup milk; beat until thick. Add the butter and sugar; beat again. Add the remaining ½ cup milk to which the vanilla has been added; add the sifted dry ingredients. Stir lightly until smooth; turn into an oiled pan 8″ x 8″; bake until firm. When cool, frost with this icing:

Measure ¾ cup white sugar into the top of the double boiler; add the egg white, 1 teaspoon corn syrup and 2 teaspoons lemon juice. Cook and beat with the dover beater over boiling water until the mixture peaks. Yield: 12-16 pieces.

CRUMB CAKE

Temperature: 375°F.   Time: 35-40 minutes

2 cups sifted pastry flour   ¾ cup shortening
1 cup brown sugar

Sift together the flour and brown sugar; rub in the shortening with the tips of the fingers. When the mixture is crumbly, take out ¾ cup; to the remainder add all at once and without beating:

¼ teaspoon salt   1 cup raisins, chopped
¼ teaspoon nutmeg   ¾ cup thick sour milk
¼ teaspoon cloves   ¼ cup brown sugar
1 teaspoon cinnamon   1 teaspoon baking soda
1 egg, unbeaten

Beat this mixture until smooth; pour into an oiled pan 8″ x 12″; sprinkle the reserved crumb mixture over the raw batter. Bake in a moderate oven until done. Yield: 20 pieces.

RED DEVIL'S FOOD CAKE

Temperature: 375°F.   Time: 35-40 minutes

⅓ cup shortening   1 teaspoon vanilla
   3 squares (3 oz.) unsweetened   1½ cups sifted cake flour
     chocolate, grated   ¾ teaspoon salt
1¼ cups brown sugar   ¾ teaspoon baking soda
   ¾ cup water   ¾ teaspoon baking powder
2 eggs, unbeaten   ⅜ cup thick sour milk

Melt the shortening in the top of a double boiler; add the grated chocolate; stir until melted. Add the sugar and water; beat until well blended. Remove from the heat; cool to room temperature. Add the eggs, one at a time; beat until light; add the vanilla. Add the sifted dry ingredients alternately with the sour milk. Pour into an oiled pan 8″ x 8″ lined with waxed paper; bake in a moderate oven until done. Yield: 12-16 pieces.

SELF FROSTING FUDGE CAKE

Temperature: 350°F.   Time: 50 minutes

¼ cup boiling water   ½ teaspoon vanilla
   ¼ cup cocoa   1¼ cups sifted pastry flour
⅓ cup melted shortening   ¼ teaspoon salt
   ⅔ cup white sugar   ¾ teaspoon baking soda
2 egg yolks   ⅜ cup sour milk

Pour the boiling water over the cocoa; let stand till slightly cool. Add the melted shortening and sugar; beat well with the dover beater. Add the well beaten egg yolks and vanilla; again beat. Add the sifted dry ingredients alternately with the sour milk. Pour into an oiled 8″ x 8″ pan which has been lined with waxed paper. Spread the raw batter with the following meringue:

2 egg whites, stiffly beaten ¾ cup brown sugar
  ½ teaspoon baking powder   ½ cup chopped nuts

To the stiffly beaten egg whites add the baking powder and sugar. Spread over the raw batter; sprinkle with chopped nuts; bake in a moderate oven until done. Yield: 12-16 pieces.

CANADIAN FRUIT CAKE

Temperature: 300°F.   Time: 2 hours

1 cup diced salt pork   2 teaspoons cinnamon
  1 cup boiling water   4 cups sifted all-purpose
2 teaspoons baking soda   flour
  1 cup dark molasses   1 cup raisins, chopped
1 cup brown sugar   1 cup mixed peel, chopped
  2 eggs, separated   1½ teaspoons lemon flavoring
1 teaspoon cloves   1 teaspoon grated lemon rind

Dice the pork very fine, taking out any bits of lean meat; cover with the boiling water; let stand 5 minutes. Add the baking soda, molasses and sugar; stir until well dissolved; add the well beaten egg yolks. Add the sifted dry ingredients alternately with the chopped fruit. Add the lemon flavoring and grated rind; fold in the stiffly beaten egg whites. Pour into 2 square pans 8″ x 8″ x 3½″ which have been lined with heavy brown paper and oiled; bake in a slow oven. Store 2 weeks before using. Yield: 6 lbs. of cake.

LIGHT FRUIT CAKE

Temperature: 300°F.   Time: 3 hours

1 cup butter   1 cup citron peel, chopped
  2 cups white sugar   1 cup glacé cherries, chopped
4 cups sifted all-purpose flour 1 cup orange and lemon peel,
  2 teaspoons baking powder   chopped
½ teaspoon salt   1 cup nuts, chopped
  1 cup grapefruit juice   1 cup shredded coconut
2 cups sultana raisins, chopped 8 egg whites

Cream together the butter and sugar; add the sifted dry ingredients alternately with the fruit juice. Plump the raisins in skim milk and dry; mix with the chopped fruit and nuts; add gradually to the cake batter. Fold in the stiffly beaten egg whites. Turn into 2 pans 8″ x 8″ x 3½″ which have been lined with heavy brown paper and oiled; bake in a slow oven until firm. Yield: 6 lbs.

ECONOMY FRUIT CAKE

Temperature: 300°F.-280°F.   Time: 2 hours, 15 minutes

1 cup shortening
2 cups white sugar
1 teaspoon grated lemon rind
2 eggs, well beaten
1 teaspoon baking soda
1 cup molasses
4½ cups sifted all-purpose flour
1 teaspoon baking powder
½ teaspoon salt
1 teaspoon cinnamon
1 teaspoon cloves
1 teaspoon nutmeg
1 cup milk
1 cup seedless raisins, chopped
½ cup currants
½ cup mixed peel, chopped
½ cup prunes, chopped
½ cup nuts, chopped

Cream together the shortening and sugar; beat until light. Add the grated lemon rind and the well beaten eggs; beat with the dover beater till smooth. Stir the baking soda into the molasses; add to the creamed mixture. Add the sifted dry ingredients alternately with the milk; with one addition of flour add the chopped fruits, peel and nuts. The raisins and currants should be plumped in hot water; the prunes should be washed, covered with boiling water and let stand until cold. Drain and chop the prunes; crack down the pits and use the nut meats chopped. Blend well; bake in 2 square pans 8″ x 8″ x 3½″ which have been lined with heavy brown paper and oiled. To prevent the cakes drying out cover with a sheet of heavy brown paper; remove for the last half hour of baking. Bake in a slow oven for about 2 hours; when done, let cool in the pans; remove, wrap in waxed paper and store in a crock. Yield: 6 lbs. cake.

HOT WATER GINGERBREAD

Temperature: 350°F.   Time: 50 minutes

½ cup shortening
½ cup brown sugar
1 egg, well beaten
1 cup dark molasses
2½ cups sifted cake flour
1½ teaspoons baking soda
1 teaspoon ginger
1 teaspoon cinnamon
¼ teaspoon nutmeg
¼ teaspoon cloves
½ teaspoon salt
1 cup hot water

Cream together the shortening and sugar until fluffy; add the well beaten egg and molasses; blend well. Sift the dry ingredients three times; add alternately with the hot water to the creamed mixture. Beat until smooth after each addition of flour. Pour into a pan 8″ x 12″ which had been lined with oil paper; bake in a moderate oven until done.

You can serve half the gingerbread hot for dessert with a sauce. Split the remaining half; fill with plain cream cheese moistened with some prune juice—indeed, a mashed up prune or two can often be worked in with the cheese. Cut in squares and serve as a second dessert. Yield for 2 desserts: 20 squares.

CREAMY JELLY ROLL

Temperature: 400°F.   Time: 13 minutes

4 eggs   ¾ cup sifted cake flour
  ¾ teaspoon baking powder   1 teaspoon lemon juice
¼ teaspoon salt   ¼ teaspoon grated lemon
  ¾ cup white sugar   rind

Break the eggs into a mixing bowl; add the baking powder and the salt. Set the bowl in a pan of hot water; beat the mixture until light and fluffy. Gradually add the sugar, beating well until the sugar is dissolved. Remove the bowl from the hot water; fold in the flour which has been sifted three times. Add the lemon juice and rind; turn into a shallow jelly roll pan 9″ x 13″ which has been lined with waxed paper. Bake in a fairly hot oven. As soon as the cake is taken from the oven, turn out on a tea towel dusted with powdered sugar. Remove the paper, trim the edges and roll up quickly and carefully. Cool slightly; unroll. Spread with cream filling and again roll up in a clean towel. Let cool before slicing. Yield: 12 slices.

LEMON CAKE

Temperature: 375°F.   Time: 35-40 minutes

½ cup shortening   3 teaspoons baking powder
  1 cup white sugar   ¼ teaspoon salt
1 teaspoon grated lemon rind   ¼ cup cold water
  2 eggs, separated   ½ cup lemon juice
2 cups sifted cake flour

Cream together the shortening, ¾ cup sugar and the lemon rind. Add the well beaten egg yolks. Add the sifted dry ingredients alternately with a mixture of the cold water and lemon juice. Stiffly beat the egg whites; add the reserved ¼ cup of sugar and beat again. Fold into the cake batter. Pour into a square pan 8″ x 8″ lined with waxed paper. Bake until done. Let stand in the pan for 5 minutes. Invert on a cooling rack; remove the paper and dust lightly with icing sugar. A delicious variation with this cake is to split it, fill it with lemon butter and put together again. Cut in squares; spread each square lightly with lemon filling and roll in shredded coconut. Yield: 12-16 pieces.

PRIZE GINGERBREAD

Temperature: 350°F.   Time: 30 minutes

½ cup shortening
¾ cup brown sugar
½ cup corn syrup or molasses
⅔ cup boiling water
2¼ cups sifted pastry flour
1 teaspoon baking powder
1 teaspoon baking soda
½ teaspoon salt
½ teaspoon cinnamon
½ teaspoon nutmeg
½ teaspoon ginger
2 eggs, well beaten

Cream the shortening; gradually add the brown sugar and syrup or molasses. Add the hot water; let stand until lukewarm. Add the sifted dry ingredients in three additions, beating well after each addition. Add the well beaten eggs; beat with the dover beater (this batter is quite thin). Pour into a pan 8″ x 12″ which has been lined with waxed paper; bake in a moderate oven. When cool, cut in squares. Yield: 20 squares.

GOLD CAKE

Temperature: 375°F.   Time: 25-30 minutes

2 cups cake flour
3 teaspoons baking powder
¼ teaspoon salt
½ cup shortening
⅞ cup white sugar
1 teaspoon grated orange rind
3 egg yolks
¾ cup milk
1 teaspoon lemon juice

Measure the flour, baking powder and salt into the sifter; sift 4 times. Cream together the shortening, sugar and orange rind; beat till fluffy. Beat the egg yolks until light; add to the creamed mixture. Add the sifted dry ingredients alternately with the milk; add the lemon juice. Pour the batter into two 9″ layer cake pans which have been lined with oiled paper. Bake in a moderate oven until done. Put together with Lemon Filling; spread a thin layer of the filling over the top of the cake. Frost the top and sides with Snow Icing. Yield: 16 pieces.

GOLD AND SILVER CAKE

Temperature: 375°F.   Time: 35-40 minutes

⅓ cup shortening
⅔ cup fine sifted sugar
1 tablespoon grated orange rind
1 egg
2 egg yolks
1⅓ cups sifted pastry flour
2¼ teaspoons baking powder
¼ teaspoon salt
½ cup orange juice

Cream the shortening and ⅓ cup of sugar to the consistency of ice cream; add the grated orange rind. Beat the egg and egg yolks till thick and lemon colored; add the remainder of the sugar, beat thoroughly. Add to the shortening mixture; beat with the dover beater. Add the sifted dry ingredients alternately with the orange juice; beat quickly and lightly. Pour the batter into a 9″ oiled tube pan; bake in a moderate oven till done. When cool, cover with Silver Frosting. Yield: 12 pieces.

HONEY RAISIN LOAF

Temperature: 300°F.   Time: 2 hours, 10 minutes

1 cup raisins
  1 cup skim milk
1 cup shortening
1 cup honey
1½ teaspoons vanilla
  ½ teaspoon almond flavoring

4 eggs
  3 cups plus 6 tablespoons
    sifted all-purpose flour
3 teaspoons baking powder
  ½ teaspoon salt
  ½ cup walnuts, chopped

Cover the raisins with skim milk; soak for 15 minutes. Drain and dry; discard the milk. Cut the raisins fine with the scissors. Cream together the shortening and the honey; add the flavorings and the well-beaten eggs. Beat till smooth with the dover beater. Add the sifted dry ingredients in 3 additions. Add the raisins and nuts. Pour into a square fruit cake pan 8″ x 8″ or a loaf pan 9″ x 5″ x 3″, lined with heavy brown paper and oiled. Bake in a slow oven; when cool put away to age for a few days. Yield: 3 lbs.

CHOCOLATE CREAM JELLY ROLL

Temperature: 400°F.   Time: 13 minutes

6 tablespoons cake flour
6 tablespoons cocoa
½ teaspoon baking powder
  ¼ teaspoon salt

4 eggs, separated
  ¾ cup white sugar
1 teaspoon vanilla

Mix and sift the flour, cocoa, baking powder and salt four times. Beat the egg whites until stiff and glossy; gradually add ½ cup of the sugar; beat again until the mixture peaks. Beat the yolks till thick and lemon colored; add the remainder of the sugar and the vanilla; beat again. Combine the whites and the yolk mixture. Carefully fold in the sifted dry ingredients; blend lightly. Line a jelly roll pan 15″ x 10″ with oiled paper; pour in the batter and spread evenly. Bake in a hot oven 13 minutes. Turn on a towel, lightly dusted with powdered sugar. Cut off the edges and remove the paper. Spread with Chocolate Filling and roll. Cool, cut in slices and serve with Mocha Sauce. Yield: 12 slices.

JELLY ROLL

Temperature: 400°F.   Time: 13 minutes

2 eggs, separated
  2 tablespoons cold water
½ cup white sugar
  ¾ cup sifted cake flour

½ teaspoon salt
  1 teaspoon baking powder
¼ teaspoon vanilla
  ¼ teaspoon lemon flavoring

Beat the egg yolks till light and lemon colored; add the cold water and beat again. Gradually beat in the sugar; beat till light. Sift the dry ingredients four times; fold into the egg and sugar mixture; add the flavoring. Fold in the stiffly beaten egg whites. Pour into a shallow pan 9″ x 13″ which has been lined with waxed paper; bake in a hot oven till done. Turn out on a cloth lightly dusted with powdered sugar, trim off the edges and spread with Lemon Filling. Yield: 12 slices.

SPECIAL LOAF CAKE
(*Eggless*)

Temperature: 350°F.   Time: 30 minutes

1 cup sour milk
  1 cup corn syrup
2⅓ cups sifted all-purpose flour
  ½ teaspoon salt
1¾ teaspoons baking soda

2 teaspoons ginger
  1 teaspoon cinnamon
½ teaspoon cloves
  1 cup raisins, chopped
¼ cup melted shortening

Combine the sour milk and corn syrup. Sift in the dry ingredients; stir vigorously; add the chopped raisins and melted shortening; blend well. Pour into loaf pan 9″ x 5″ x 3″ lined with waxed paper and oiled. Bake in a moderate oven. This loaf is moist and inexpensive. Don't let it stand too long; it gets dry.

ONE EGG CAKE

Temperature: 375°F.   Time: 25-30 minutes

3 tablespoons shortening
  ¾ cup fine white sugar
1 tablespoon grated orange
  rind
1 egg, well beaten

1½ cups sifted cake flour
  1½ teaspoons baking powder
⅛ teaspoon salt
  ½ cup milk
¼ cup nuts, chopped

Cream together the shortening, ½ cup of sugar and the orange rind. Beat the egg until light; add the remaining ¼ cup of sugar and beat till the sugar is dissolved; add to the creamed batter. This mixture should be very light. Sift together the dry ingredients four times. Add them alternately with the milk to the creamed mixture. Beat only enough to smooth the batter; pour into a square pan 8″ x 8″ which has been lined with waxed paper.

Sprinkle the finely chopped nuts over the raw batter. Bake in a moderate oven till firm (25-30 minutes). Let stand in the pan for five minutes before turning out on a cooling rack. Eat while fresh. This cake does not require an icing; the nuts are an excellent substitute. Yield: 12-16 pieces.

ORANGE CAKE

Temperature: 350°F.   Time: 35 minutes

1/3 cup shortening   1 teaspoon baking powder
  3/4 cup brown sugar   1/4 teaspoon baking soda
1/2 tablespoon grated orange   1/2 teaspoon salt
  rind   3/8 cup sour milk
1 egg, well beaten   1/4 cup orange juice
  1 cup sifted cake flour   1 tablespoon white sugar

Cream together the shortening, brown sugar and grated orange rind. Add the well beaten egg; beat till light. Add the sifted dry ingredients alternately with the sour milk. Pour into an oiled pan 8″ x 8″; bake in a moderate oven till done. While still warm and before removing from the pan, brush over with a mixture of the orange juice and sugar. This makes a crisp icing top that's tart and yet sweet. Yield: 12-16 pieces.

MAGIC MERINGUE CAKE

Temperature: 350°F.   Time: 40 minutes

1/3 cup shortening   1 teaspoon baking powder
  1/2 cup white sugar   1/3 teaspoon salt
2 eggs, separated   3 tablespoons milk
  1 1/4 cups sifted pastry flour

Cream the shortening; gradually add the sugar. Beat till fluffy. Add the well beaten egg yolks and blend. Add the sifted dry ingredients alternately with the milk. Spread the batter in an oiled pan 8″ x 12″. Cover with the meringue and bake in a moderate oven until meringue shrinks from the sides of the pan and the cake is done.

(*Meringue*)

2 egg whites   1/2 cup shredded coconut
  1/8 teaspoon salt   1/4 cup nuts, chopped
1/2 cup brown sugar   1 teaspoon vanilla

Stiffly beat the egg whites and salt until stiff but not dry. Add all remaining ingredients and beat again. Spread over the raw batter. Bake in a moderate oven. Yield: 20 pieces.

RAISIN-ORANGE CAKE

Temperature: 350°F.

½ cup shortening
  1 cup brown sugar
1 egg, unbeaten
  2¼ cups sifted cake flour
1 teaspoon baking powder
  1 teaspoon baking soda
¼ teaspoon salt
  1 teaspoon cinnamon

Time: 35-40 minutes

1 cup thick sour milk
  ½ cup nuts, chopped
1 cup raisins, chopped
  1 tablespoon grated orange
    rind
⅓ cup orange juice
  ¼ cup white sugar

Cream together the shortening and brown sugar. Add the unbeaten egg; beat till fluffy. Add the sifted dry ingredients alternately with the sour milk. Lastly, fold in the chopped nuts and raisins. Pour into a pan 8″ x 12″ which has been lined with waxed paper. Bake in a moderate oven till done; take the cake from the oven, and while still warm, brush over with a mixture of the orange rind, orange juice and sugar. Let stand in the pan till cool. This cake is always a favourite with the male members of the family.   Yield: 20 pieces.

ORANGE LAYER CAKE

Temperature: 375°F.

1 orange
  1 cup sugar
½ cup shortening
  2 eggs, separated
2 cups sifted pastry flour

Time: 20-25 minutes

½ teaspoon salt
  3 teaspoons baking powder
⅓ cup water
  3 teaspoons lemon juice

Grate the rind from the orange, being careful not to get into the bitter white skin. Squeeze the orange; reserve ⅓ cup juice for the cake. Cream together the rind, ¾ cup of the sugar and the shortening; beat till fluffy. Add the egg yolks, well beaten; blend well. Add the sifted dry ingredients alternately with the mixture of orange juice, water and lemon juice. Fold in the stiffly beaten egg whites to which has been added the reserved ¼ cup sugar. Pour into two 9″ oiled layer cake pans; bake in a moderate oven till done. When baked, let stand in the pans for 5 minutes. Remove to cooling racks; when cool put together and ice with orange icing. Yield: 16 pieces.

ENGLISH POUND CAKE

Temperature: 300°F.

2¼ cups sifted pastry flour
  ½ teaspoon baking powder
1 teaspoon nutmeg
  1 cup butter
1 cup white sugar

Time: 1½ hours

1 teaspoon grated lemon rind
  2 tablespoons lemon juice
2 tablespoons orange juice
  5 eggs, separated

Sift the flour, baking powder and nutmeg three times. Cream the butter; gradually beat in the sugar. Beat this mixture until it's fluffy. Add the lemon rind, the lemon juice and orange juice; add the well-beaten egg yolks. Fold in the stiffly beaten whites. Sift the flour mixture evenly over the egg mixture; fold in very gently. Pour the batter into a loaf pan 9" x 5" x 3", which has been lined with oiled paper. Bake in a slow oven. Store in a box or crock for a week before cutting. Yield: 2½ lbs. cake.

NOTE TO BRIDES: *Cakes like this are bound to crack on top. Also, they do dry out a little. For the last hour of baking cover the cake with brown paper or put a pan of water in the oven. While the cake is still warm brush it with melted butter. It will not crumble when cut.*

HONEY POUND CAKE

Temperature: 300°F.   Time: 2 hours

¾ cup honey   3 eggs, separated
  ¾ cup raisins, chopped   2½ cups sifted pastry flour
1 teaspoon lemon rind   2¼ teaspoons baking powder
  1 tablespoon lemon juice   ¾ teaspoon salt
¾ cup shortening   ½ cup nuts, chopped
  ½ teaspoon vanilla

Measure the honey into a mixing bowl; warm slightly by standing over hot water. Add the chopped raisins, the lemon rind and juice. Cream the shortening; add the vanilla; add the egg yolks one at a time, beating well after each addition. Combine with the honey mixture. Add the sifted dry ingredients and the chopped nuts. Blend well; fold in the stiffly beaten egg whites. Pour into a square pan 8" x 8" x 3½" lined with waxed paper. Bake in a slow oven till done. Do not cut for a week. Yield: 3 lbs.

DUNDEE POUND CAKE

Temperature: 300°F.   Time: 1½ hours

¾ cup shortening   2 cups sifted cake flour
  ½ cup white sugar   ½ teaspoon baking powder
½ cup corn syrup   ½ cup raisins
  1 teaspoon vanilla   ½ cup currants
3 eggs   ½ cup citron peel, chopped
  1 tablespoon grated orange rind

Cream the shortening with the sugar, corn syrup and vanilla. This mixture should be fluffy. Add the eggs, well beaten, and the orange rind. Add the sifted dry ingredients in three additions. Add the fruit; blend lightly. Pour the batter into a loaf pan 9" x 7" x 3" which has been lined with heavy brown paper. Bake in a slow oven until firm and golden brown. Let stand in a crock or breadbox for one week before cutting. Yield: 2 lbs. cake.

POUND CAKE

Temperature: 315°F.   Time: 1 hour

½ cup hot water   4 teaspoons baking powder
  ½ cup butter   1 teaspoon salt
½ cup shortening   ½ cup milk
  2 cups white sugar   ½ cup raisins, chopped
3 eggs, separated   ½ cup currants, chopped
  3 cups sifted all-purpose flour   ½ cup nuts, chopped

Measure the water into a large saucepan; add the butter and shortening; stir until melted. Gradually add 1½ cups sugar; beat till dissolved; remove from the heat and cool slightly. Beat the egg yolks till light; add to the creamed batter. Sift together the flour, baking powder and salt; add to the creamed batter alternately with the milk. Some of the fruit and nuts should be added with each sifting of the flour until all are in. Lastly, stiffly beat the egg whites; add the reserved ½ cup sugar and beat till glossy. Fold into the cake mixture. Pour the batter into 2 loaf pans 9″ x 5″ x 3″ which have been lined with heavy brown paper and well oiled. Bake in a moderate oven for 1 hour. Store in a bread box or tin for at least two days before slicing. Yield: 3 lbs. cake.

WHITE POUND CAKE

Temperature: 315°F.   Time: 1¾-2 hours

1 cup shortening   1 cup glacé cherries (red or green)
  1 cup white sugar   ½ cup mixed peel, sliced
1 teaspoon grated lemon rind 2½ cups sifted all-purpose flour
  1 tablespoon lemon juice   ½ teaspoon salt
5 eggs, unbeaten   1 teaspoon baking powder

Cream together the shortening, sugar, lemon rind and juice; this mixture should be very fluffy. Add the eggs, one at a time; beat well after every addition. Combine the cherries and peel with ½ cup of the flour. Sift the remaining 2 cups of flour with the salt and baking powder. Add in 3 additions to the creamed batter. Add the floured fruit. Put in a square fruit cake pan 8″ x 8″ x 3½″ lined with oiled brown paper. Bake in a moderate oven till done. When cool, wrap in waxed paper; let stand a week before using. Yield: 3½ lbs.

QUICK CAKE

Temperature: 375°F.   Time: 30-35 minutes

4 tablespoons shortening   ¾ cup white sugar
  2 cups sifted cake flour   1 egg or 2 egg yolks, unbeaten
3 teaspoons baking powder   ¾ cup milk
  ¼ teaspoon salt   1 teaspoon vanilla

Measure the shortening into a bowl; let stand till room temperature. Sift the flour, baking powder, salt and sugar 3 times; add to the shortening. Add all the remaining ingredients; beat vigorously till smooth. Pour into a pan 8″ x 12″ which has been lined with oiled paper. Bake in a moderate oven till done. Let stand in the pan 5 minutes; turn on a cooling rack. When cool, cover with Raspberry Whip.

Raspberry Whip

2 egg whites
  1 cup raspberry jam

2 teaspoons lemon juice
  ⅛ teaspoon salt

Measure all ingredients into a deep bowl. Beat with the dover beater until of spreading consistency. Spread thickly over the top and sides of the cake. This whip should be used quickly. Standing doesn't improve it. Yield: 20 servings.

Variations on Quick Cake

Quick Chocolate Cake: Use the recipe for the Quick Cake with these changes: Sift ½ cup cocoa with the flour and decrease the flour by ¼ cup or melt 2 squares unsweetened chocolate in a saucepan large enough to serve as a mixing bowl; proceed with the original recipe.

Quick Spice Cake: Same recipe as the Quick Cake, adding 1 teaspoon nutmeg or mace.

Quick Marble Cake: Use the Quick Cake recipe and divide it in half. To one half add 1 square of unsweetened chocolate, melted. Place alternate spoonfuls of each batter in an 8″ x 8″ pan, which has been lined with oiled paper.

Quick White Cake: Use the same recipe, using 2 egg whites in place of one egg.

SPICED PRUNE CAKE

Temperature: 350°F.

Time: 50 minutes

½ cup shortening
  1 cup brown sugar
2 eggs, separated
  1 cup prune pulp
1½ cups sifted all-purpose flour
  1 teaspoon baking soda

1 teaspoon baking powder
  1 teaspoon cinnamon
¼ teaspoon cloves
  ¼ teaspoon nutmeg
½ teaspoon salt
  ½ cup thick sour milk

Cream together the shortening and ¾ cup brown sugar; beat till creamy; add the well beaten egg yolks and prune pulp; blend well. Add the sifted dry ingredients alternately with the sour milk. Fold in the stiffly beaten egg whites to which has been added the reserved ¼ cup sugar. Pour into a square oiled pan 8″ x 8″ x 3½″; bake in a moderate oven till firm. Yield: 12 squares.

SPICE CAKE

Temperature: 350°F.   Time: 40 minutes

1 cup seedless raisins, chopped
  1 teaspoon lemon juice
½ cup shortening
  1 cup brown sugar
1 teaspoon grated orange rind
  1 egg, unbeaten
2 cups sifted cake flour

½ teaspoon salt
  1 teaspoon cinnamon
¼ teaspoon mace
  ¼ teaspoon cloves
1 teaspoon baking soda
  ⅔ cup thick sour milk

Plump the raisins in hot water; drain and dry; add the lemon juice. Cream together the shortening, sugar and grated orange rind. Add the unbeaten egg; beat till light and fluffy. Add the sifted dry ingredients alternately with the sour milk; add the raisins. Blend lightly; pour into an oiled 8″ x 12″ pan which has been lined with heavy paper. Bake until done. If you can spare the sugar, a thin icing may be added. Use 2 tablespoons of sugar and 2 teaspoons boiling water; pour over the cake while still a little warm. Yield: 20 pieces.

HONEY SPICE CAKE

Temperature: 350°F.   Time: 45 minutes

¾ cup honey
  ½ cup shortening
½ teaspoon vanilla
  ¼ cup brown sugar
1 egg, separated
  1½ cups sifted cake flour

½ teaspoon cinnamon
  ¼ teaspoon cloves
2 teaspoons baking powder
  ¼ teaspoon baking soda
½ cup sour milk

Measure out the honey; let it warm to room temperature. Cream together the shortening, vanilla and sugar; beat in the honey. Add the egg yolk; beat till light. Add the sifted dry ingredients alternately with the sour milk. Lastly, fold in the stiffly beaten egg white. Pour into a loaf pan 9″ x 5″ lined with oiled brown paper. Bake in a moderate oven till firm. Yield: 12 slices.

RAISIN CAKE

Temperature: 350°F.   Time: 1 hour

1 cup seedless raisins
  1 tablespoon lemon juice
1 teaspoon grated lemon rind
  ½ cup shortening
1 cup brown sugar
  1 egg, well beaten
2 cups sifted all-purpose flour

½ teaspoon salt
  1 teaspoon cinnamon
½ teaspoon nutmeg
  ¼ teaspoon cloves
1 teaspoon baking soda
  ⅔ cup thick sour milk

Cut the raisins with the scissors; add the lemon juice and rind. Let stand while mixing the cake. Cream together the shortening and brown sugar; add the well-beaten egg. Add the sifted dry ingredients alternately with the sour milk. Fold in the raisin-lemon mixture. Pour into a loaf pan 9″ x 5″ x 3″ which has been lined with waxed paper. Bake in a moderate oven until done. This cake needs no icing. Yield: 12-14 slices.

NOTE TO BRIDES: *Here's something for the cuff. Thin slices of this cake put together sandwich fashion with cream cheese, then cut in fingers look well, taste even better.*

SPONGE CAKE

Temperature: 325°F.   Time: 45 minutes

1 cup sifted cake flour	1 cup white sugar
1 teaspoon baking powder	6 tablespoons hot milk
½ teaspoon salt	2 teaspoons lemon juice
3 eggs	1 teaspoon grated lemon rind

This cake is easy to make and never varies in quality but the measuring must be very accurate. Sift the flour before measuring. Measure the sifted flour back into the sifter; add the baking powder and salt; sift three times. Beat the eggs until they are thick and very light. Add the sugar and hot milk gradually to the eggs, beating constantly. Add the lemon juice and rind. Fold in the sifted dry ingredients in three additions; beat till smooth. Pour into an ungreased 9″ tube pan; bake in a slow oven till done. Invert and let hang in the pan for one hour, then loosen. The cake will stay moist for two or three days. Yield: 12 pieces.

ANGEL SPONGE CAKE

Temperature: 325°F.   Time: 1 hour

1 cup sifted all-purpose flour	¼ teaspoon salt
1¼ cups white sugar	1 teaspoon cream of tartar
1 cup egg whites	1 teaspoon vanilla
(8 to 10 egg whites)	¼ teaspoon almond flavoring

Sift the flour; measure again into the sifter; add ¼ cup white sugar. Sift four times. Beat the egg whites and salt till foaming. Add the cream of tartar. Beat again till stiff but not dry. Add the remaining cup of sugar by tablespoonfuls, beating constantly. Beat until there is no grit of sugar. Fold in the flavorings. Sift and fold the flour mixture into the egg mixture in four additions. Pour into an ungreased 9″ tube pan; cut the batter gently through with a knife; this will remove air bubbles. Bake in a moderate oven until done. Invert on a cooling rack for one hour; gently loosen and remove from the pan. Yield: 12 slices.

To use up the egg yolks see Custard Sauce.

FAIRY SPONGE CAKE

Temperature: 350°F.   Time: 35-40 minutes

¼ cup shortening   ¼ cup milk
  ½ cup fine white sugar   ⅛ teaspoon salt
4 eggs, separated   1 cup white sugar
  1 cup sifted cake flour   1 teaspoon vanilla
¼ teaspoon salt   ¼ cup chopped nuts
  1 teaspoon baking powder   1 quart strawberries

Cream together the shortening and ½ cup sugar; beat till fluffy. Add the egg yolks, very well beaten; beat till light. Add the sifted flour, ¼ teaspoon salt and the baking powder alternately with the milk. Line a pan 8″ x 12″ with waxed paper; have the paper ½″ above the sides of the pan. This makes for easy removal. Pour the batter into the pan and smooth. Beat the egg whites and salt till stiff and glossy. Add ¾ cup sugar gradually, beating all the time. Add the vanilla and chopped nuts. Spread over the raw batter; bake in a moderate oven till done. Lift out carefully; peel off the paper and let cool slightly. In the meantime, hull the strawberries and sprinkle with the reserved ¼ cup of sugar. Serve the cake in squares heaped with the sweetened berries. Yield: 20 pieces.

HOT MILK SPONGE CAKE

Temperature: 300°F.   Time: 45-50 minutes

2 eggs, separated   1 teaspoon baking powder
  ¾ cup fine sugar   ½ teaspoon salt
1 teaspoon vanilla   ½ cup milk
  1 cup sifted all-purpose flour   1 teaspoon butter

Separate the eggs; beat the yolks till thick and lemon colored; stiffly beat the whites and fold into the yolks. Gradually add the sugar and vanilla; beat until the sugar is dissolved. Sift the dry ingredients 5 times. Fold into the egg mixture. Heat the milk and butter to boiling; add to the cake batter. Pour into an unoiled pan 8″ x 8″. Bake in a slow oven till firm. Yield: 12 squares.

IMPERIAL SPONGE CAKE

Temperature: 300°F.-315°F.   Time: 50-60 minutes

1½ cups white sugar   ¾ teaspoon cream of tartar
  ½ cup water   ¼ teaspoon salt
6 eggs, separated   1 teaspoon vanilla
  1 cup sifted all-purpose flour

Put the sugar and water in a saucepan; cook gently over low heat till dissolved. Boil to 238°F. or until the syrup will spin a thread. Pour the hot syrup slowly over the stiffly beaten egg whites, beating the mixture until cool. Add the egg yolks which have been beaten till thick and lemon colored. Sift the flour once; measure, add the cream of tartar and salt; sift 5 or 6 times. Fold very carefully into the egg mixture. Add the vanilla. Pour into an ungreased tube pan 9″ x 3½″; bake in a slow oven. Invert the pan on cake rack for one hour before removing cake. This cake may be dusted with powdered sugar or filled with Cocoa Cream. The latter method makes a very delicious dessert. Cut the entire top from the cake about one inch down using a saw bread knife. Lift off this top layer. With a pair of sharp scissors, cut the centre from the main part of the cake by cutting down into the cake one inch from outside edge and one inch from middle hole, being careful to leave a 1″ layer of cake at the bottom. Fill the cavity with one third of the cocoa cream filling. Replace the top. Spread the remaining filling over top and sides of cake. Sprinkle with roasted almonds. Chill 2 or 3 hours before serving.

Cocoa Cream Filling

3 cups whipping cream
  6 tablespoons fine white
    sugar
6 tablespoons cocoa

⅛ teaspoon salt
  ⅓ cup roasted almonds,
    chopped

Put cream, sugar, cocoa and salt in a bowl; chill for one hour. Beat with the dover beater till the mixture will hold its shape.

QUEEN'S ORANGE SPONGE CAKE

Temperature: 300°F.   Time: 50-55 minutes

¾ cup sifted all-purpose flour
  ¼ cup corn starch
1½ teaspoons baking powder
  ¼ teaspoon salt
4 eggs, separated

1 cup white sugar
1 tablespoon grated orange
  rind
¼ cup orange juice.

Sift together the flour, corn starch, baking powder and salt 4 times. Beat the egg yolks until they fall in a thick continuous stream over the beater; gradually add ¾ cup of sugar, beating till dissolved. Add the orange rind and juice. Beat the flour mixture into the egg mixture, a little at a time, using a dover beater. This improves the texture of the cake. Beat the egg whites till stiff and glossy; gradually beat in the remaining ¼ cup of sugar. Fold into the batter; pour into an ungreased tube pan 9″ x 3½″. Bake in a moderate oven for 50-55 minutes. Invert on a cake rack for 1 hour; carefully loosen with a spatula and remove from the pan. This cake does not need icing. Yield: 12 pieces.

RICH WEDDING CAKE

Temperature: 275°F.   Time: 3 hours

2 cups butter
  2½ cups brown sugar,
    firmly packed
1 cup corn syrup
  8 eggs, well beaten
½ cup strawberry jam
  ½ cup candied lemon peel,
    chopped
1 cup candied citron peel,
    chopped
1 cup candied cherries,
    chopped

½ cup candied orange peel,
    chopped
2 cups seedless raisins
  2 cups currants, washed and
    dried
1 cup blanched almonds, shredded
  5 cups sifted cake flour
1 teaspoon baking soda
  ½ teaspoon salt
1 teaspoon cinnamon
  ½ teaspoon cloves
½ teaspoon mace

Cream together the butter, sugar and corn syrup; beat till creamy. Add the well beaten eggs; blend with the dover beater. Add the jam, peels, raisins, currants and shredded almonds. Add the sifted dry ingredients; blend well. Divide the batter into two pans 8″ x 8″ x 3½″ which have been lined with heavy brown paper. Bake in a slow oven till done. After the first hour of baking, cover the cake with brown paper to prevent drying out. Cover with almond paste and Ornamental Frosting. Let age four weeks before cutting. Yield: 8 pounds.

TWO EGG CAKE

Temperature: 350°F.   Time: 20-25 minutes

½ cup shortening
  1 cup white sugar
¼ teaspoon salt
  ½ teaspoon lemon flavoring
1 teaspoon grated lemon rind

2 eggs, separated
  2 cups sifted cake flour
3 teaspoons baking powder
  ¾ cup milk

Cream together the shortening and ¾ cup white sugar. Beat till fluffy; add the salt, flavoring and lemon rind; blend well. Beat the yolks of the eggs until light; add to the creamed batter. Sift the dry ingredients 3 or 4 times. Add alternately with the milk to the creamed batter, stirring only until blended. Fold in the stiffly beaten whites of the eggs to which has been added the reserved ¼ cup of sugar. Pour into two 9″ cake pans which have been oiled and lightly floured. With a spoon push the batter up on the sides of the pan as far as you think the cake will rise. That leaves the sides higher than the centre of the batter and means the cake will bake without a hump in the centre. Bake in a moderate oven till golden brown. Remove from the oven but let stand in the pan for 5 minutes. Invert on a cake cooler; when cool put together with lemon filling. Yield: 16 pieces.

SULTANA CAKE

Temperature: 300°F.

Time: 1½ hours

¾ cup shortening
1 cup white sugar
3 eggs
2 teaspoons grated orange rind
½ teaspoon grated lemon rind

1¾ cups sifted all-purpose flour
½ teaspoon baking powder
1 cup sultana raisins, chopped
¼ cup candied citron peel,
chopped

Cream the shortening; gradually add the sugar; beat until light. Add the well beaten eggs, orange and lemon rind. Add the sifted dry ingredients and fruit; mix well. Pour into tube pan 9″ x 3½″ lined with double thickness of wax paper and oiled. Bake in a slow oven. If the surface of the cake is well brushed with melted butter 15 minutes before it is taken out of the oven, the cake will have a tender crust and will cut without crumbling. Yield: 2 pounds.

NOTE: Soak the raisins in skim milk until well plumped (about ½ hour). Drain and dry before adding to the cake mixture. This will prevent the raisins from falling to the bottom of the cake.

WHITE CAKE

Temperature: 350°F.

Time: 45 minutes

2 eggs, separated
⅓ cup white sugar
⅓ cup sifted cake flour

Dash of salt
⅛ teaspoon cream of tartar
½ teaspoon vanilla

Beat the egg whites till stiff and glossy. Beat in the white sugar until the mixture stands in peaks. Beat the yolks till thick and lemon colored; fold into the whites. Fold in the dry ingredients which have been sifted together; add the vanilla. Pour into an oiled 9″ ring mould; bake in a moderate oven. Invert on a cake rack to cool for an hour. Take the cake from the pan and place on a serving dish. Fill the centre with scoops of ice cream. Pour chocolate sauce over both cake and ice cream; serve at once. Yield: 12 slices.

JAM CUP CAKES

Temperature: 375°F.

Time: 10-12 minutes

½ cup brown sugar
½ cup thick sour cream
1 egg
1 cup sifted all-purpose flour
1½ teaspoons baking powder

½ teaspoon cinnamon
¼ teaspoon cloves
⅛ teaspoon salt
⅛ teaspoon baking soda
½ cup firm jam

Combine the brown sugar, sour cream and egg in a mixing bowl; beat till very light. Sift and add in three additions the flour, baking powder, cinnamon, cloves, salt and baking soda. Fold in the jam. Fill the oiled muffin tins two-thirds full. Bake in a moderate oven till done. Yield: about 20 cup cakes.

CINNAMON CUP CAKES

Temperature: 375°F.

Time: 10-12 minutes

⅓ cup shortening
  ¾ cup brown sugar
1 teaspoon cinnamon
  1 tablespoon grated orange
    rind

2 eggs, unbeaten
1½ cups sifted pastry flour
2 teaspoons baking powder
  ½ teaspoon salt
  ⅔ cup orange juice

Cream together the shortening, brown sugar, cinnamon and orange rind; add the unbeaten eggs, one at a time; beat till light and fluffy. Add the flour, baking powder and salt alternately with the orange juice. Fill oiled muffin pans two-thirds full; bake in a moderate oven. Frost with quick icing made by combining icing sugar and boiling water. Yield: about 28 cup cakes.

DARK CUP CAKES

Temperature: 375°F.

Time: 10-12 minutes

⅞ cup brown sugar
  ½ cup shortening
1 egg, well beaten
  1½ cups sifted cake flour
2 teaspoons baking powder

¼ teaspoon salt
  ½ cup cocoa
  ½ teaspoon cinnamon or
    allspice
  ½ cup milk

Cream together the sugar and shortening; beat till fluffy. Add the well beaten egg. Add the sifted dry ingredients alternately with the milk; beat till smooth. Fill oiled muffin tins ⅔ full. Bake in a moderate oven till done. Ice with a thin icing made by combining 2 tablespoons icing sugar with ½ tablespoon boiling water. Pour a little icing on the top of each cake. Yield: about 28 cup cakes.

CUP CAKES

Temperature: 375°F.

Time: 10-12 minutes

¼ cup shortening
  ½ cup white sugar
½ teaspoon vanilla
  1 egg, well beaten

1 cup plus 2 tablespoons sifted
  pastry flour
1¾ teaspoons baking powder
  ¼ teaspoon salt
  ½ cup milk

Cream together the shortening and sugar; beat till fluffy. Add the vanilla and well beaten egg. Add the sifted dry ingredients alternately with the milk. Rub small muffin tins with salt, then brush with melted shortening; fill ⅔ full of cake mixture. Bake in a moderate oven. When cool, coat lightly with peanut butter, cover with fluffy Seven Minute icing. Yield: 18-1½″ cakes.

SMALL ICED CAKES

Temperature: 375°F.

Time: 12-15 minutes

½ cup shortening
⅞ cup white sugar
1 tablespoon grated orange rind
4 eggs, separated

2 cups sifted cake flour
3 teaspoons baking powder
½ teaspoon salt
¾ cup orange juice

Cream together the shortening, sugar and orange rind; beat till fluffy. Put 2 whole eggs in a bowl with 2 egg yolks. (Reserve the 2 egg whites for frosting.) Beat the eggs and egg yolks till very light. The mixture should fly in a thick, continuous stream over the beater. Add to the creamed mixture and blend well. Add the sifted dry ingredients alternately with the orange juice. Beat lightly. Fill small oiled muffin pans ⅔ full with the batter. Bake till golden brown. When cool, frost with Seven Minute Frosting. Yield: 36 small cakes.

SPICE CUP CAKES

Temperature: 375°F.

Time: 10-12 minutes

½ cup brown sugar
¼ cup shortening
½ teaspoon vanilla
1 egg, unbeaten
1 cup sifted cake flour
1 teaspoon baking powder

⅓ teaspoon baking soda
⅛ teaspoon salt
¼ teaspoon cinnamon
¼ teaspoon cloves
½ cup thick sour milk

Cream together the sugar, shortening and vanilla; add the egg; beat till very light. Sift in the cake flour, baking powder, baking soda, salt, cinnamon and cloves alternately with the sour milk. Beat till smooth; fill oiled muffin tins ⅔ full of batter. Bake in moderate oven. Serve hot and fresh without icing. Yield: 18 cup cakes.

CUSTARD CREAM
(*Cream Puffs*)

1 cup white sugar
½ cup all purpose flour
⅛ teaspoon salt
3 cups scalded milk

3 eggs, well beaten
2 teaspoons vanilla
1 cup heavy cream

Mix together the sugar, flour and salt with a little hot milk. Stir into the scalded milk; cook over boiling water till the mixture is smooth and thick (about 15 minutes). Pour the hot mixture over the well beaten eggs; mix well and return to the double boiler. Cook another 5 minutes. Cool; add vanilla; fold in cream which has been stiffly whipped. This will fill 18 cream puffs generously.

BUTTERSCOTCH FILLING

1¾ cups scalded milk
4 tablespoons corn starch
Speck of salt
¼ cup cold milk

3 tablespoons butter
½ cup brown sugar
1 egg, lightly beaten
1 teaspoon vanilla

Scald the milk in the top of the double boiler.   Mix the corn starch, salt and cold milk to a paste; stir into the hot milk; cook and stir till smooth and thick. Cover; continue cooking for 10 minutes, stirring occasionally. In the meantime, melt the butter in a heavy iron frying pan; add the brown sugar; stir and cook till the mixture is brown and bubbling but not burned. Add the caramel mixture to the hot starch mixture; blend till dissolved. Mix a little of the mixture with the beaten egg; add to the filling; blend well and continue cooking for 3 minutes. Remove from the heat; add the vanilla and beat with the dover beater till smooth. Cool before spreading.   Will fill a 9″ x 13″ jelly roll.

CHOCOLATE FILLING

1 cup scalded milk
2 tablespoons cocoa
½ cup brown sugar
2 tablespoons corn starch
⅛ teaspoon salt

2 tablespoons cold milk
1 egg, lightly beaten
1 teaspoon butter
½ teaspoon vanilla

Scald the milk in the top of a double boiler; add the cocoa and brown sugar; stir over boiling water until well blended. Make a paste of the corn starch, salt and cold milk; stir into the cocoa mixture; stir and cook till smooth and thick. Cover and continue cooking for 10 minutes. Lightly beat the egg; add to the hot mixture. Blend with a dover beater; continue cooking for 3 minutes. Remove from the heat; add the butter and vanilla; beat till creamy. Will fill a 9″ layer cake.

CREAM FILLING

1 cup milk
¼ cup white sugar
1½ tablespoons corn starch
⅛ teaspoon salt

1 egg yolk
½ teaspoon almond flavoring
½ tablespoon butter

Scald the milk in the top of the double boiler. Mix together the sugar, corn starch and salt; pour the hot milk over this mixture; stir and cook over boiling water until thick. Cover; continue cooking for 15 minutes, stirring occasionally. Pour the hot mixture over the slightly beaten egg yolk; blend. Return to the double boiler; continue cooking for 3 minutes. Remove from the heat; add the almond flavoring and butter. Cool before spreading between the layers of the cake. Will fill a 9″ layer cake.

DATE FILLING

1 cup dates, chopped	½ cup brown sugar
1 cup water	1 teaspoon lemon juice

Measure the ingredients into a saucepan. Simmer gently till smooth and thick. Will fill a 9″ layer cake.

FRUIT FILLING

1 cup raisins, chopped	¼ cup brown sugar
⅓ cup hot water	2 teaspoons butter
1 teaspoon grated lemon rind	⅛ teaspoon salt
1 tablespoon lemon juice	

Put the raisins, water, lemon rind, lemon juice and sugar into a saucepan; simmer slowly till thick. Remove from the heat; beat in the butter and salt. Chill; use as filling for oatmeal cookies. Will fill 2 dozen cookies.

LEMON FILLING

2½ tablespoons corn starch	3 tablespoons lemon juice
½ cup white sugar	1 teaspoon grated lemon rind
¾ cup boiling water	1 teaspoon butter
1 egg, beaten	

Blend together the corn starch and white sugar; add the boiling water, stirring all the time. Cook over boiling water till clear, about 10 minutes. Beat the egg; add the lemon juice and rind; stir into the starch mixture; cook three minutes. Beat in 1 teaspoon butter; cool before using. Will fill a 9″ layer cake.

NOTE TO BRIDES: *Use this filling to top an 8″ x 12″ light cake; cover again with Seven Minute Icing. It's a party dessert.*

ALMOND ICING

3 sweet potatoes	1 teaspoon almond flavoring
3 cups icing sugar	½ cups ground almonds

Peel the sweet potatoes; cut in pieces; boil until tender; shake dry. Mash; add sufficient icing sugar to make a spreading paste. Add almond flavoring and, if desired, ground almonds. Will ice a 4-pound cake.

BOILED ICING

1 cup white sugar
⅓ cup water
1 teaspoon cider vinegar

2 egg whites
¼ teaspoon almond flavoring

Combine the sugar, water and vinegar in a deep saucepan. Stir over a hot burner till dissolved. Reduce the heat; boil without stirring till the mixture spins a thread. Have the egg whites stiffly beaten. Pour the hot syrup over them, beating constantly. Beat until the icing holds its shape. Add the almond flavoring. Will fill and frost a 9″ layer cake.

BUTTER ICING

2 tablespoons butter
2 tablespoons honey

2 tablespoons orange juice
1 teaspoon grated orange rind

Measure all ingredients into a bowl; beat till smooth and light. This icing is thin, spreads easily but is quite firm when cold. Will frost a cake 8″ x 8″.

CARAMEL ICING

1 cup brown sugar
1 tablespoon butter
¼ cup cream

1 tablespoon strong coffee
2-2½ cups icing sugar

Mix together the sugar, butter and cream in a heavy saucepan. Stir gently until the sugar is dissolved; increase the heat and bring to a rapid boil. Cook exactly 2 minutes after mixture comes to full rolling boil. Remove from the heat; add the coffee; cool slightly. Beat in the sifted icing sugar until the icing is of spreading consistency. Will frost a 9″ layer cake.

BITTERSWEET CHOCOLATE ICING

1 square (1 oz.) unsweetened
  chocolate
½ cup milk
1 cup white sugar

1½ tablespoons corn syrup
1 tablespoon butter
½ teaspoon vanilla

Put the chocolate, milk, sugar and corn syrup in a saucepan. Cook and stir over low heat until dissolved. Increase the heat; bring the mixture to a full, rolling boil; continue cooking until a bit of the mixture dropped in cold water forms a soft ball (238°F.) Remove from the heat; add the butter and vanilla. Let cool to lukewarm; beat until soft and creamy. Ice the cake before the mixture begins to set. If the icing should stiffen before the cake is iced, let it stand over hot water to soften. Will frost an 8″ x 12″ cake.

CHOCOLATE CREAM ICING

2 squares unsweetened chocolate   3 tablespoons hot milk
   one 4 oz. package cream cheese   ⅔ cup icing sugar

Unfold the paper around the chocolate; let it soften on the paper on top of the oven or radiator. In the meantime, add the hot milk to the cream cheese; blend well; add the melted chocolate and icing sugar. Beat till smooth; spread with a hot knife. Will frost a cake 8″ x 12″.

GLAZE FOR CHRISTMAS CAKE

¾ cup white sugar   1 tablespoon corn syrup
   ¼ cup water

Measure the ingredients into a saucepan. Cook over moderate heat to 220°F. or not quite the soft ball stage. Pour while warm over fruit cake; when cool, store away. If the cake is decorated with peel set it in place while the glaze is still warm. Will glaze two 4 pound cakes.

MAPLE FROSTING

¾ cup maple syrup   1 egg white, stiffly beaten
   ¼ cup white sugar

Cook the maple syrup and sugar together until it spins a thread. Pour this syrup over the stiffly beaten egg white, beating constantly. Frost the cake when the icing is cool enough to keep its shape. Will frost an 8″ x 12″ cake.

ORANGE ICING

1½ cups icing sugar   1 tablespoon melted butter
   1/6 cup orange juice   1 tablespoon grated orange rind

Measure all ingredients into the top of a double boiler. Place over boiling water; cover and let stand 10 minutes. Remove from the heat. Beat the icing until cool and of good spreading consistency. Will fill and frost a 9″ layer cake.

PINK FROSTING

1 egg white   ½ cup strawberry jam
   Speck of salt

Beat the egg white till stiff but not dry. Add the salt and jam, spoon by spoon. Beat till fluffy and the right consistency to spread. Will frost an 8″ x 8″ cake.

ORNAMENTAL ICING

2 egg whites, unbeaten   ¼ teaspoon cream tartar
1 cup sifted icing sugar

Put the egg whites into a bowl; add ½ cup icing sugar; beat vigorously for 7 minutes. Add the remaining ½ cup icing sugar and again beat. Add the cream of tartar and enough additional icing sugar to make the icing spread easily. Tint pastel shades with vegetable colorings; use to decorate the tops of the small cakes. Will frost 60 small cakes.

SEA FOAM ICING

2 egg whites, unbeaten   5 tablespoons cold water
1½ cups brown sugar   1 teaspoon vanilla
Dash of salt   1 teaspoon baking powder

Combine all the ingredients except the vanilla and baking powder in the top of the double boiler; beat until blended. Cook over boiling water, beating constantly with the dover beater, until the frosting is fluffy and holds it shape. This takes about seven minutes. Remove from heat; add the vanilla and baking powder. Beat again until mixture peaks. Use to fill and ice the cake. Fills and frosts a 9″ layer cake.

SEVEN MINUTE ICING

(*Snow or Silver*)

2 egg whites   4 tablespoons cold water
1½ cups white sugar   ½ teaspoon vanilla
1 tablespoon corn syrup   1 teaspoon baking powder

Combine all the ingredients except the vanilla and baking powder in the top of a double boiler; stir until blended. Cook over boiling water, beating constantly with the dover beater, until the frosting is fluffy and holds its shape (this takes about 7 minutes). Remove from the heat; add the vanilla and baking powder; beat again until the mixture peaks. Will fill and ice a 9″ layer cake.

NOTE: For *Snow* or *Silver* Icing substitute lemon juice for the water.

THIN WHITE ICING

This is an icing we use frequently for buns, cakes and hot breads. Measure ½ cup icing sugar into a bowl; add a few drops of boiling water; stir till dissolved. Will ice an 8″ x 8″ cake.

CHAPTER 6

Candies

TEST FOR CANDY

If you make any quantity of candy, a candy thermometer is needed. Without a thermometer, use cold water tests:

Cold Water Test	Thermometer
Soft Ball	236°F.–238°F.
Firm Ball	246°F.–248°F.
Hard Ball	265°F.
Crack	290°F.–300°F.
Brittle	300°F.–310°F.

ALMOND CREAM

2 cups brown sugar
1 tablespoon corn starch
1 tablespoon baking powder
⅛ teaspoon salt
¼ cup milk

¼ cup corn syrup
3 tablespoons butter
⅓ cup roasted almonds, finely chopped
1 teaspoon vanilla

Put the sugar, corn starch, baking powder and salt into a saucepan; mix thoroughly. Add the milk, corn syrup and butter. Stir over low heat until dissolved; boil more rapidly to the soft ball stage. (238°F.). Remove from the heat; let stand 3 minutes. Beat until smooth and thick; add the nuts and flavoring. Blend; pour into an oiled 6″ x 6″ pan. Cut in squares while still warm. Yield: 1 pound candy.

CARAMEL CANDY

2 cups white sugar
¾ cup corn syrup
½ cup butter

2 cups light cream or very rich milk
1 teaspoon vanilla

Place the sugar, corn syrup, butter, and 1 cup of the cream in a saucepan. Cook and stir until the sugar is dissolved and the mixture boils. Add the remaining cup of cream gradually, never letting mixture stop boiling. Cook over low heat till the syrup separates into threads which are hard but not brittle when tested in cold water (248°F.). Remove from the heat; add the nuts and vanilla. Turn into an oiled pan 8″ x 8″ x 2″. While still warm crease in squares; wrap each square in waxed paper. Yield: 2¾ pounds candy.

BUTTERSCOTCH TAFFY

2 cups brown sugar	¼ teaspoon salt
¼ cup corn syrup	⅓ cup butter
1 cup water	¼ teaspoon vanilla

Put the sugar, corn syrup, water and salt into a pan; cook and stir over low heat until the sugar is dissolved. Cook to the firm-ball stage (246°F.). Add the butter. Continue cooking until the candy becomes brittle when dropped into cold water. Remove from the heat; add the vanilla. Pour into an oiled pan 6″ x 6″. While still warm crease into 1″ squares. When cold break into pieces. Yield: 16 pieces.

CHOCOLATE FUDGE

2 cups white sugar	⅛ teaspoon salt
⅔ cup rich milk	2 tablespoons corn syrup
2 squares (2 oz.) unsweetened chocolate, grated	2 tablespoons butter
	1 teaspoon vanilla

Mix together the sugar, milk, grated chocolate, salt and corn syrup in a saucepan. Stir over low heat until the chocolate has melted and the sugar is dissolved. Increase the heat; let the mixture boil until it reaches the soft ball stage—236°F. Stir just enough to prevent scorching. Remove from the heat; add the butter. Let cool to lukewarm(110°F.) without stirring. Add the vanilla; beat until the candy has just lost its gloss and becomes thick enough to hold its shape. Pour immediately into an oiled pan; mark in squares before the candy is firm. Yield: 1 pound candy.

VARIATION: For chocolate nut fudge add ⅓ cup chopped nuts just before pouring.

MARSHMALLOW NUT FUDGE

3 squares (3 oz.) unsweetened chocolate	Pinch of salt
1 tablespoon corn syrup	½ teaspoon orange juice
2 cups white sugar	½ teaspoon vanilla flavoring
1 tablespoon butter	1 cup marshmallows, quartered
1¼ cups rich milk	½ cup walnuts, chopped

Melt the chocolate in a pan over low heat; add the corn syrup, sugar, butter, milk and salt. Stir until dissolved; boil to the soft-ball stage (238°F.). Cool slightly; add the flavorings; beat until stiff and creamy. In the meantime oil a 6″ x 8″ pan; spread on it the quartered marshmallows and chopped nuts. Pour the fudge over them. Mark in 1″ squares before quite cold. Yield: 24 pieces.

NOTE TO BRIDES: *Fudge must not be cooked too quickly. It should also be partially cooled before beating.*

CREAMY FUDGE

1 cup granulated sugar
  1 cup brown sugar
½ cup cocoa
  2 teaspoons corn syrup

¾ cup milk
  1 tablespoon butter
1 tablespoon vanilla

Measure the sugar, cocoa, corn syrup, milk and butter into a saucepan; heat gently, stirring until the sugar is dissolved. Boil, without stirring, to the soft ball stage (238°F.). Remove from the heat; cool gradually; beat until creamy (5 minutes). Add the vanilla; pour into an oiled pan 6″ x 6″. Mark in squares before it hardens. Yield: 16 pieces.

DIVINITY FUDGE

2⅓ cups white sugar
  ⅔ cup corn syrup
½ cup water

¼ teaspoon salt
  2 egg whites
½ teaspoon vanilla

Measure the sugar, corn syrup, water and salt into a saucepan; cook and stir over low heat until dissolved. Increase the heat until the mixture boils; cook, without stirring, to the very hard ball stage (265°F). During this cooking the crystals which form on the sides of the pan should be wiped down with a damp cloth wrapped around the tines of a fork. Have the egg whites stiffly beaten; gradually pour the hot syrup over them. Add the flavoring. Pour into an oiled pan 8″ x 8″. While still warm, cut in squares. Yield: 1¼ pounds.

VARIATIONS: For Orange Divinity, add 3 tablespoons grated orange rind in place of the vanilla; for Almond Divinity, add ⅓ cup almonds which have been blanched and finely chopped.

TAFFY APPLES

¾ cup white sugar
  ½ cup corn syrup
⅜ cup warm water

10 red apples
10 wooden skewers

Measure the sugar into a saucepan with the corn syrup and water. Stir till dissolved; cook over low heat until the syrup is very brittle when tested in cold water (300°F.). Take the saucepan off the heat and place over warm water. Have the apples wiped and on skewers; plunge them in the hot syrup and twirl round until the syrup covers the apple. Stand in milk bottles until the syrup hardens. Oil the top of the milk bottle and the hardened apples won't stick. Yield: 10 taffy apples.

MAPLE CREAM

3 cups light brown sugar
⅓ cup corn syrup
⅓ cup milk
2 tablespoons butter

⅛ teaspoon salt
½ cup nuts, chopped
½ teaspoon vanilla

Measure the sugar, corn syrup, milk, butter and salt into saucepan; stir gently over low heat until dissolved. Boil, without stirring, to the soft ball stage (238°F.). Remove from the heat; cool; beat until creamy and thick. Add the nuts and vanilla. Pour into an oiled pan 8″ x 8″; mark in squares while warm. Yield: 1¼ pounds candy.

SCARECROWS

1 cup corn syrup
1 cup white sugar
2 tablespoons cider vinegar

2 tablespoons butter
6 cups puffed rice

Measure the corn syrup, sugar and vinegar into a saucepan; cook until very brittle when tested in cold water (300°F.). Remove from the heat and add the butter; allow bubbling to die down; pour over the puffed rice. Mix well with a spoon; when slightly cool, form into balls. Have one ball for the body, another for the head; use toothpicks or wooden skewers for arms and legs. Work quickly because the mixture hardens rapidly. Yield: about 24 scarecrows.

REAL CHRISTMAS TOFFEE

1 cup white sugar
¾ cup corn syrup
¾ cup thin cream

1/16 teaspoon salt
1½ teaspoons butter
½ teaspoon vanilla

Measure the sugar, corn syrup, cream and salt into a heavy saucepan; cook and stir until the sugar is dissolved. Continue cooking until a little of the syrup dropped into cold water forms a rather firm ball (248°F.). Add the butter; continue cooking to the hard ball stage. Add the vanilla; pour into an oiled pan 6″ x 6″. While still warm, crease into 1″ squares. Yield: 1 pound candy.

SPICED NUTS

Temperature: 300°F.
1 tablespoon cinnamon
¼ cup white sugar

Time: 30 minutes
1 cup blanched almonds
2 teaspoons egg white

Mix together the cinnamon and sugar. Place the almonds in a bowl; add the egg white; work between the fingers until all the nuts are coated and begin to feel sticky. Add the sugar and cinnamon mixture; stir until every nut is coated. Shake the coated nuts in a sieve to remove excess sugar. Spread on a baking sheet which has been oiled; bake in a slow oven. Yield: ½ pound nuts.

SALTED ALMONDS

Temperature: 300°F.

½ pound almonds   1 teaspoon salt
  1 tablespoon oil

Blanch the almonds by covering the nuts with boiling water; let stand for 5 minutes. Place in cold water until the skins slip off easily. Dry the nuts and place in a bowl; add the oil; toss lightly with a fork. Spread on a cookie sheet; sprinkle with salt. Crisp in a slow oven; they should be stirred from time to time so that they may brown evenly. Yield: ½ pound nuts.

CHAPTER 7

Canning and Pickling

PREPARATION OF VEGETABLES FOR CANNING

The essential thing to watch is the quality of the vegetables. They should be fresh, firm and free from scab or spots. A good rule is to have them in the jars and on their way to canning within four hours after picking. Once picked, sort them over, reserving only the best. Wash and shell or snip the peas and beans. The beets, of course, are scrubbed and you will notice by the chart, we can the beet greens separately; if you have spinach, it may be done in the same way.

Precooking

We have found precooking one of the secrets of successful canning, particularly where canning is done in the hot bath or in the oven. As you know, we cannot get the same intense heat in the bath or oven as we get in a pressure cooker, so the vegetables are boiled for varying lengths of time before canning. Cover closely during cooking and have the vegetables covered with water but not drowned; drain and pack while hot into sterile jars. Add ½ teaspoon salt to each jar and with the peas and tomatoes add ½ teaspoonful of sugar also. The jars should then be filled with boiling water to within ¼ inch of the top. Put on the rubber, the glass and zinc top and screw down tightly, then turn back a quarter turn. The vegetables are now ready for canning.

Hot Bath Canning

You need a large kettle or wash boiler. The jars should be placed on a rack and not touching one another. The racks are inexpensive, handy and don't tip the jars. However, a simple wooden rack can be made from slats. Have the water hot before the jars are put in and time from the moment the water breaks into the boil. When the time is up, lift the jars out carefully and let stand out of the draft; a cold breeze will crack them and there is all that work for nothing. Screw down the tops and invert to test for leaks. Then store for winter use.

Notes

Small whole tomatoes may be canned for salads; instead of filling the jars with boiling water, use hot tomatoes. That way you have salad tomatoes and tomatoes for soup.

Small whole carrots canned with the peas make a colorful and delicious combination.

Green Lima beans canned with the corn gives you a ready-made succotash. For a large family quart jars are more suitable than pints.

Oven Canning

If you decide to oven-can your vegetables, prepare them in exactly the same way, even to loosening the jar ring. Pack the jars on a large tray and place in the oven. No water is needed in the tray. Cook for the specified time, making certain that at no time does the temperature go over 275°F. I frequently turn off the heat for the last half hour and let the jars stay in the oven till cool.

PREPARATION OF FRUITS FOR CANNING

Blanching: This consists of placing peaches or tomatoes in steam or boiling water for 15 to 60 seconds and then dipping in cold water. This sets the colour and loosens the skins so that they will slip off easily. Blanch only sufficient fruit for two or three containers at a time. A wire basket, large strainer or a square of cheesecloth simplifies handling. Rhubarb may be blanched to reduce the acid flavor, set the color and shrink fruit for a closer pack.

Preventing Discoloration: (Brine Bath). As soon as peeled, drop such fruits as peaches, pears and apples in a brine of 1 teaspoon salt to 1 quart cold water. Put in brine only sufficient fruit to fill two or three containers; long standing in brine gives a definitely salty taste. Change the brine as it discolors.

Precooking: Fruits may be simmered before packing. This is recommended for peaches, pears, apples and cherries, particularly when processed in the oven.

SYRUPS FOR OVEN CANNING

Very Thin Syrup—1 cup sugar to 2 cups water gives 2½ cups syrup.

Thin Syrup   —1 cup sugar to 1 cup water gives 1½ cups syrup.

Medium Syrup —1½ cups sugar to 1 cup water gives 1¾ cups syrup.

Heavy Syrup   —2 cups sugar to 1 cup water gives 2 cups syrup.

Boil sugar and water for 5 minutes. For large fruits allow ¾ to 1 cup syrup for each pint jar. For small fruits allow ½ to ¾ cup syrup for each pint jar.

1 cup sugar reduces to ½ cup syrup.

APPROXIMATE YIELDS OF CANNED FRUITS

Kind of Fruit	Type of Standard Container (Box, Basket, etc.)	Weight of Fruit *Pounds*	Approx. No. Qts. Canned Fruit *Quarts*
Berries, including Currants	12-1 qt. boxes	15	12
	24 pt. boxes	15	12
Crab Apples	6 qt. basket (flat)	7	4
	11 qt. basket (flat)	14	9
Cherries	6 qt. basket (flat)	8	5
Peaches	6 qt. basket (heaped)	10	5
Pears	6 qt. basket (heaped)	11	5
	11 qt. basket (flat)	15	7
Plums	6 qt. basket (flat)	8	4
	6 qt. basket (heaped)	11	6

TIME CHART FOR CANNING FRUITS

FRUITS	SYRUP	OVEN CANNING Temperature	OVEN CANNING Time Pts.	OVEN CANNING Time Qts.	HOT BATH CANNING Time Pts.	HOT BATH CANNING Time Qts.
Blackberries	Medium	275°F.	25	30	15	20
Blueberries	Very Thin	275°F.	25	30	15	20
Cherries	Medium	275°F.	25	30	20	25
Crab Apples	Medium	275°F.	25	30	20	25
Gooseberries	Medium	275°F.	25	30	20	25
Peaches (Hot Pack)	Thin	275°F.	30	40	15	20
Pears (Hot Pack)	Thin	275°F.	30	40	15	20
Plums (Hot Pack)	Medium	275°F.	30	35	20	25
Raspberries	Medium	275°F.	25	30	10	15

CHART FOR HOT WATER BATH AND OVEN CANNING

Vegetable	Amount needed to fill 1 pint jar	Preparation	Pre-Cooking	Hot Water Bath in Wash Boiler	Oven Canned Temperature 275 F.
GREEN PEAS	Approx. 2 pounds	Shell and wash	Cover with boiling water; cook 5 minutes.	4 hours	4 hours
GREEN BEANS	Approx. 1 pound	Wash; snip; cut in 1 inch pieces	Cover with boiling water; cook 5 minutes.	3 hours	3½ hours
WAX BEANS	Approx. 1 pound	Wash; snip; cut in 1 inch pieces	Cover with boiling water; cook 5 minutes.	3 hours	3½ hours
BEETS (topped)	Approx. 1¼ pounds	Scrub	Cook till tender, slip off skin.	3 hours	3 hours
BEET GREENS	Approx. 1 pound	Wash; drain; trim	Add very little water. Cook till wilted.	4 hours	3½ hours
CORN	Approx. 6 ears	Husk; remove silk; slice kernels from cobs	Use ½ cup boiling water to 1 cup corn; heat to boiling.	4 hours	4 hours
TOMATOES	1 quart jar—Approx. 3 pounds	Scald; remove core and green spots; slip off skin; quarter	Heat to boiling; add no water.	35 minutes	45 minutes

METHODS OF CANNING

Fruit may be canned cold pack, hot pack or open kettle.

Cold Pack: means that the fruit is packed raw and cold into the jars, then covered with hot syrup.

Hot Pack: means that the fruits are pre-cooked before packing in the jars.

Open Kettle: means that the fruits are simmered in boiling syrup on top of the stove.

CANNING FRUIT WITHOUT SUGAR

Fruit may be canned without sugar and sweetened when used. Wash the fruit; heat to boiling in a heavy saucepan. Pack in sterile jars; oven can at a temperature of 275°F. Pints require 25 minutes, quarts require 35 minutes. Loosely adjust the tops before canning, tighten on removal from the oven. Invert to test for leaks.

CANNED BLUEBERRIES

6 quarts blueberries
1½ cups water
¼ teaspoon salt

1 tablespoon lemon juice
4 cups sugar

Pick over and wash the blueberries; put in a preserving kettle with the water and salt. Cover; simmer gently 5 minutes; add the lemon juice and the sugar. Again bring to the boil; let simmer 3 minutes. Seal at once in sterile jars, filling them to overflowing and screwing down the lids quickly. For winter use as sauce, thicken slightly and serve with fresh warm cake, with blanc mange and with gelatine puddings. It's a delicate fruit for batter puddings and roly poly's. Yield: 7 pints.

CANNED BLUEBERRIES FOR WINTER PIES

Temperature: 275°F.
Time: 35 minutes

1 11-quart basket blueberries
3 cups white sugar
5 cups water

¼ teaspoon salt
½ cup lemon juice

Pick over the berries; place in a large preserving kettle. Add all the remaining ingredients. Bring the mixture to the boil; simmer gently for 5 minutes. Fill sterile quart jars to within ¼" of the top. Adjust the rubber, glass and zinc tops and screw down tightly; loosen back ¼ turn to allow for bubbling. Place the jars on a rack, not touching; oven bake 35 minutes; the oven should never go above 275°F. Remove the blueberries from the oven and invert for 24 hours; this gives you a check on leaking jars and also spaces fruit evenly through syrup. Yield: approximately 8 quarts.

CANNED CHERRIES—HOT PACK

6-quart basket sour cherries   4 cups sugar
  4½ cups water

Wash and pit the cherries. Make a syrup of the sugar and water; boil for 5 minutes; add the cherries. Simmer the cherries for 3 minutes; remove from the heat. Fill sterile jars to within ¼″ of the top with the hot fruit and syrup; adjust the rubbers, the glass and zinc tops. Screw down tightly; turn back ¼ turn. Place jars on a rack in a boiler of hot water, with the water 2″ over the tops of the jars; process for 25 minutes. Remove from the water; tighten down the tops. The amount of sugar may be decreased if desired. Yield: 8 pints.

OVEN-CANNED PEACHES

For a 6-quart basket of peaches make a syrup of 3 cups sugar and 3 cups water. Simmer for 5 minutes; skim.

Scald and skin the peaches; cut in half and remove the stones. Simmer gently in the syrup for 5 minutes. Pack in sterile jars; fill each jar with boiling syrup to within ½″ of the top. Adjust the rubber, glass and zinc tops and screw down tightly; loosen back ¼ turn to allow for bubbling. Place the jars on a rack, not touching; oven bake 35 minutes for pints, 45 minutes for quarts; the oven should never go above 275°F. Remove the peaches from the oven and invert the jars for 24 hours; this gives you a check on leaking jars and also spaces the fruit evenly through the syrup. Yield: approximately 8 pints.

OVEN-CANNED PEARS

For a 6-quart basket of pears make a syrup of 2 cups sugar and 3 cups water. Simmer for 5 minutes; skim.

Peel and core the pears; cut in half. Let stand in brine (1 teaspoon salt to 4 cups water) so that they will not discolor. Drop into the syrup; cook gently for 5 minutes. Pack in sterile jars; fill each jar with boiling syrup to within ½″ of the top. Adjust the rubber, glass and zinc tops and screw down tightly; loosen back ¼ turn to allow for bubbling. Place the jars on a rack, not touching; oven bake 35 minutes for pints, 45 minutes for quarts; the oven should never go above 275°F. Remove the pears from the oven and invert for 24 hours; this gives you a check on leaking jars and also spaces the fruit evenly through the syrup. Yield: approximately 8 pints.

CANNED PINEAPPLE

1½ quarts pineapple   1 cup sugar
  1½ cups water

Peel the pineapple; dice. Combine the water and sugar; boil 5 minutes; add the diced pineapple. Simmer till tender, about 8 minutes. Place the fruit in sterile jars; adjust the rubbers and fill to overflowing with the boiling syrup. Tighten the tops and invert to test for leaks. Yield: 5 pints.

OVEN-CANNED RASPBERRIES

Pick over the berries; pack them in sterile pint or quart jars. Tap down smartly as the fruit is being packed so that the berries will not be floating in the syrup when done.

When the jars are filled, place on a rack in the oven, temperature 300°F. Do not put on the rubbers or tops; do not have the jars touching. When the fruit is hot through and through and the juice has begun to draw out (about 25 minutes), remove the jars from the oven and fill to overflowing with boiling syrup. Adjust the rubbers, glass and zinc tops, screw down tightly and invert to test for leaks.

(Syrup)

1 cup white sugar   2 cups water

Measure the sugar and water into a saucepan; simmer for 5 minutes.

RHUBARB FOR WINTER PIES

Use tender, fresh rhubarb; wipe; cut in 1″ lengths. Crush cup by cup in sterile jars; a wooden potato masher is ideal for this crushing. The rhubarb should not be bruised but crushed only until the juice flows. Fill sterile jars to overflowing; screw on the lids; wrap each jar in newspaper to exclude the light. Sweeten when used.

PRESERVED STRAWBERRIES

4 quarts strawberries   2½ cups water
  2 cups sugar   Juice of 1 lemon

Wash the berries, then hull them. Make a syrup of the sugar, water and lemon juice; boil for four minutes. Add the strawberries; simmer three minutes. Let stand in the syrup overnight; this plumps them so that they don't rise to the top of the jars after canning. In the morning bring quickly to the boiling point, using the hottest element. Pack in hot, sterile jars to within ¼″ of the top; adjust the jar rings and the tops. Tighten, then loosen tops ¼ turn. Place in a pan of hot water and oven bake for 25 minutes, using a 275°F. oven. Remove the jars from the oven, tighten the tops and wrap each jar before storing. Yield: 6 pints.

STRAWBERRY PRESERVES

4 pounds strawberries   1 tablespoon lemon juice
2 pounds white sugar

Wash and hull the strawberries; weigh after hulling. Place alternate layers of fruit and sugar in an enamel bowl; sprinkle with the lemon juice. Cover the bowl with a damp cloth then with a bath towel; let stand over-night. In the morning, drain off the juice without crushing the strawberries. Bring it to a rolling boil; skim. Add one layer of berries; let them come to the boil. Place the fruit in sterile jars; fill the jars to overflowing with the boiling syrup. Seal; invert to test for leaks. When cool, wrap in newspaper and store. The fruit retains its color, flavor and shape. Yield: 6 pint jars.

TOMATOES CANNED IN GLASS JARS

Scald and skin the tomatoes; pack them in sterile jars, adding 1 teaspoon salt and 1 teaspoon sugar to each quart jar. Fill the jars to within ¼" of the top with boiling hot tomato juice, made from large tomatoes. Now release the air bubbles by running a knife around the edge of the jar. Adjust the rubber, glass and zinc tops; screw down, then back ¼ turn to allow for bubbling. Bake in slow oven (275°F.) 35 minutes for pint jars, 45 minutes for quarts. Remove from the oven, screw down the tops and invert to test for leaks.

GRAPE CONSERVE

8 pounds grapes   4 pears
  4 tart apples   2 oranges, sliced
  4 peaches   Sugar

Wash and stem the grapes; weigh. Separate the pulp from the skin. Place the pulp in a preserving kettle; add the apples which have been cored and diced (do not peel). Cook the grapes and apples gently until soft; press through a sieve. To this pulp add the grape skins, the peaches and pears which have been peeled and diced, the oranges which have been thinly sliced and quartered. Simmer gently until soft; measure. For each cup of fruit pulp add ¾ cup white sugar. Stir until dissolved; cook slowly until thick. Yield: 8-8 oz. jars.

PEACH CONSERVE

12 cups peaches, finely chopped
2 oranges
12 maraschino cherries, chopped

1 teaspoon grated lemon rind
Juice of 1 lemon
9 cups white sugar

Cover the peaches with boiling water for 1 minute; blanch, skin and finely chop. Put the oranges through the food chopper; add to the peaches. Add the chopped cherries, the lemon rind and juice. Add the white sugar; stir and let stand for 2 hours. Simmer for 1 hour or until clear and transparent. Seal in sterile jars. Yield: 12-6 oz. jars.

NOTE TO BRIDES: *The quickest way to chop the peaches is this. Hold the peach in your hand and criss-cross with the paring knife right to the stone; all the fruit can be pressed off at once.*

PINEAPPLE CONSERVE

4 cups rhubarb, diced
1 pineapple, diced
3 oranges, sliced
2 lemons, sliced

¼ pound almonds, blanched and
    chopped
7 cups granulated sugar

Wipe and dice the rhubarb; peel and core the pineapple and dice. Slice the oranges in thin slices and cut in eighths; slice the lemons in thin slices and cut in quarters. Blanch and chop the almonds. Combine all the ingredients, including the sugar, in the preserving kettle; mix well and let stand overnight. In the morning simmer gently until the mixture is thick. Seal in sterile glasses; top with parowax. Yield: 8-8 oz. jars.

GRAPE JELLY

3 pounds ripe grapes
½ cup water

7 cups white sugar
½ cup commercial pectin

Wash and stem the grapes; weigh, then crush. Add ½ cup of water and heat to boiling. Cover; simmer ten minutes. Strain through a jelly bag. Measure the juice into a preserving kettle (there should be four cups). Heat the juice to boiling; add the sugar slowly, stirring continuously. Bring to a rapid boil as quickly as possible. When boiling all over, add the commercial pectin. Stir and again bring to a boil. Cook for thirty seconds, timing from the moment the mixture breaks into a rolling boil. Remove from the heat, skim and pour into sterile jars. Cover with hot parowax. Yield: approximately 8-8 oz. jars.

GOLDEN JAM

2 lemons
  3 oranges
3 cups water

4 tart apples
1 can crushed pineapple
6 cups white sugar

Wipe the lemons and oranges; cut in eighths without peeling; run through the food chopper. Add the water; cook slowly till the fruit is tender and the mixture quite thick (1½ hours). Add the apples, pared, cored and finely chopped, the pineapple and juice and the sugar. Simmer gently until transparent. Seal in sterile jars. Yield: 8-8 oz. jars.

GRAPE JAM

4 pound purple grapes   5 cups white sugar

Wash and stem the grapes; weigh. Separate the pulp from the skins. Cook the pulp gently until soft; press through a sieve. Mix the sieved pulp and the skins in a preserving kettle; cook exactly 5 minutes. Add the sugar slowly, stirring until it is completely dissolved. Simmer gently until thick (about 15 minutes). Pour into sterile glasses; cover with hot parowax. Yield: approximately 5-8 oz. jars.

RASPBERRY JAM

6 cups raspberries   ⅓ cup lemon juice
  4 cups white sugar

Measure the raspberries (well packed) and the sugar into a preserving kettle and let stand until the sugar is dissolved; stir frequently. Place on a hot burner and bring to a rapid boil. Boil for 5 minutes, timing from the minute the mixture breaks into a rolling boil. Add the lemon juice and continue boiling for 5 minutes. Seal at once in hot sterile jars. This is a delicious jam for batter puddings, muffins or roly-poly desserts. Yield: 6-8 oz. jars.

STRAWBERRY JAM

6 cups sliced strawberries   ½ cup strained lemon juice
  5 cups white sugar

Wash and hull the strawberries; slice and pack firmly in the cup. Measure into an enamel pan; add the sugar and stir well. Let stand till the sugar is entirely dissolved. Place on a hot burner; bring to a full rolling boil as quickly as possible. Boil hard for 5 minutes. Take from the heat and stir in the lemon juice; boil again for 3 minutes. Pour into hot sterile jars and seal. This jam is soft, yet firm enough to have some character. Yield: 6-8 oz. jars.

STRAWBERRY AND RHUBARB JAM

4 cups rhubarb, diced
  4 cups strawberries, crushed
6 cups white sugar

1/16 teaspoon baking soda
1 teaspoon grated lemon rind
1 tablespoon lemon juice

Wipe the rhubarb; dice without peeling. Hull the berries and crush with a potato masher. Measure the two fruits into a preserving kettle. Add the sugar; stir thoroughly and let stand overnight. In the morning put on a hot burner and bring to the boil. Add the baking soda, lemon rind and juice and continue boiling until thick enough to jar. Pour into hot sterile jars, and while warm cover with hot parowax. Yield: approximately 8-8 oz. jars.

SLICED STRAWBERRY JAM

4½ cups strawberries, sliced
  7 cups white sugar
1/16 teaspoon salt

1 tablespoon lemon juice
½ 8-oz. bottle commercial
  pectin

Hull two quarts ripe strawberries; slice crosswise. Measure into the preserving kettle; there should be 4½ cups well packed. Add the sugar and salt; stir well and let stand overnight. In the morning add the lemon juice. Put on a hot burner; bring to a full rolling boil. Let boil three minutes, timing from the moment the mixture is boiling all over; stir constantly. Remove from the heat; stir in the pectin. Stir and skim for five minutes. Pour into hot sterile jars and cover with hot parowax. Yield: approximately 8-8 oz. jars.

CARROT AND ORANGE MARMALADE

6 medium sized carrots
  3 medium sized oranges

1 lemon, juice and grated rind
White sugar

Scrape and dice the carrots; cook in a small quantity of water until tender; drain. Slice the oranges thinly; combine the fruit with the carrots and measure. For each cup of the mixture add ⅔ cup sugar. Stir well; let stand overnight. Boil rapidly until clear; pour into sterile jars. Yield: 4 pints.

QUICK·ORANGE MARMALADE

3 large oranges
  (about 1¾ pounds in all)
2 lemons

3 tablespoons lemon juice
  5 cups water
6 cups sugar

Choose fresh juicy oranges and good lemons; wipe; cut each orange and lemon into 8 sections. Scoop out the pulp; remove all seeds; place in preserving kettle. Slice the rinds paper thin; add to the pulp. Add the additional lemon juice and water. Bring to the boil; reduce the heat; simmer, uncovered, for 1 hour. Add the sugar; again bring to the boil; simmer about 50 minutes more. Test by dropping a spoonful of the hot liquid on a cold plate and chilling in the refrigerator; if not set, continue simmering for a few minutes and test again. Yield: 3 pints.

APPLE BUTTER

12 cups tart apples
2 cups cider vinegar
Brown sugar
2 teaspoons cinnamon
1 teaspoon cloves
½ teaspoon allspice
Grated rind and juice of
1 lemon

Quarter and core the apples; cook slowly until soft in the cider vinegar. Press through a sieve; measure; to each cup of pulp add ½ cup brown sugar. Add the spices, lemon juice and rind. Cook slowly till thick. Yield: 3 pints.

TOMATO BUTTER

8 pounds ripe tomatoes
(approximately 6-quart basket)
3 cups brown sugar
¼ cup salt
½ cup mixed pickling spices
(tied in a bag)
3 cups cider vinegar
½ teaspoon hot red pepper

Scald and skin the tomatoes; cut in pieces; put in a preserving kettle. Add the remaining ingredients; cook gently, uncovered, until thick (about 3 hours), stirring frequently. Seal in sterile jars. Yield: approximately 4 pints.

TOMATO CATSUP

1 peck ripe tomatoes
(15 pounds)
7 tablespoons salt
3 red peppers (sweet)
1 red pepper (hot)
3 large onions
6 stalks celery and leaves
2 cups brown sugar
1 tablespoon celery seed
2 teaspoons mustard seed
1 tablespoon mixed pickling
spice
2-5″ sticks cinnamon
3 cups cider vinegar

Wipe and chop the tomatoes; sprinkle with 3 tablespoons of the salt; let stand 3 hours. Drain off the liquid; put the tomatoes in a large preserving kettle. Add the peppers, seeded and chopped; the onions, peeled and chopped and the chopped celery. Cook until tender; strain through a sieve to remove all the seeds. Cook this strained liquid for 20 minutes; add the remaining salt, brown sugar and spices, tied loosely in a cheesecloth bag. Boil slowly until thick; add the vinegar and continue cooking another 10 minutes. Yield: approximately 4 pints.

APPLE CHUTNEY

8 cups onion, chopped
  6 cups tart apples, chopped
4 cups brown sugar
  2 cups raisins, chopped
2 teaspoons cinnamon
  1 teaspoon powdered cloves

1 teaspoon ginger
1 teaspoon mace
1 tablespoon salt
3 tablespoons dark molasses
. Dash of cayenne pepper

Peel and chop the onions; measure after chopping; there should be 8 cups. Peel, core and dice the apples; there should be 6 cups. Add all the other ingredients and simmer slowly without a cover till thick; this takes about 2 hours. Seal in sterile jars. Yield: 4 pints.

TOMATO CHUTNEY

15 ripe red tomatoes
  3 cups tart apples, chopped
3 onions, finely chopped
  2 cups cider vinegar
2 tablespoons salt
  2 cups brown sugar
1 cup raisins

1 teaspoon cinnamon
1 teaspoon dry mustard
$\frac{1}{2}$ teaspoon cayenne
$\frac{1}{2}$ teaspoon allspice
1 teaspoon cloves
$\frac{1}{2}$ cup mixed pickling
  spice (tied in a bag)

Scald, skin and chop the tomatoes into a preserving kettle, Add the apples, peeled, cored and finely chopped; add the onions. peeled and chopped; add all the remaining ingredients. Stir well and let stand one hour before boiling. Cook slowly till thick, about 2 hours. Seal in sterile jars. Yield: approximately $4\frac{1}{2}$ pints.

TOMATO PASTE

Blanch tomatoes for 2 minutes in boiling water; plunge into cold water, remove the skins and cut into pieces. Put in a double boiler and cook slowly over boiling water to the consistency of apple butter; sieve; fill sterile quart jars; add a teaspoon of salt to each quart. Fill the jars to within $\frac{1}{4}$" of the top. Now release the air bubbles by running a knife around the top of each jar. Put on the rubber rings, the glass tops and screw down, then turn back $\frac{1}{4}$ turn to allow for bubbling. Bake in slow oven (275°F.) for 35 minutes for pint jars. 45 minutes for quarts. Remove from the oven, screw down the tops; invert to test for leaks.

BREAD AND BUTTER PICKLES

6 quarts cucumbers, sliced
  8 tablespoons salt
Water to cover
  8 cups cider vinegar

$1\frac{1}{2}$ tablespoons celery seed
3 tablespoons mustard seed
3 teaspoons curry powder
4 cups white sugar

Choose smooth, green cucumbers, definitely not ripe. Wipe dry; slice thinly and evenly. Put in an enamel preserving kettle, sprinkling each layer with salt; barely cover with water and weight down overnight. In the morning, drain and rinse well. Combine all the remaining ingredients and heat to boiling. Add the cucumber slices and cook for 4 minutes. Keep the mixture just below boiling all that time; boiling will soften and toughen the pickles. Stir constantly; seal in hot sterile jars. Yield: approximately 5 pints.

UNCOOKED CRANBERRY CONSERVE

2 cups cranberries	½ lemon
1 apple, peeled and cored	1¼ cups white sugar
1 orange	

Put the cranberries and apple through the chopper. Quarter the orange and remove the seeds; put orange and lemon through the chopper. Mix all the fruits with the sugar. Store in a covered jar in the refrigerator; let age for 2 days before using. Yield: 1 pint.

NOTE TO BRIDES: *This conserve is delicious with cold ham or turkey.*

RIPE CUCUMBER PICKLE

3 large, ripe cucumbers	½ cup water
2 onions	⅓ cup white sugar
2 green peppers	⅓ cup dry mustard
4 stalks celery, chopped	⅓ cup flour
½ cup salt	1 teaspoon turmeric
3 cups cider vinegar	1 tablespoon salad oil

Peel and quarter the cucumbers; remove the seeds and dice; place in preserving kettle. Add the onions which have been peeled and thinly sliced. Remove the seeds from the peppers, cut in thin strips and add; add the chopped celery and the salt. Let stand 1 hour; strain. Add the vinegar; cook 10 minutes. Make a paste of all remaining ingredients. Mix smooth with some of the hot liquid. Add slowly to the pickle; simmer for 20 minutes. Seal in sterile jars. Yield: 3½ pints.

DILL PICKLES

50 large cucumbers	Dill
Mustard seed	5 quarts cold water
Celery seed	1 cup salt
Bay leaves	2 cups cider vinegar
Whole pickling spice	

Wipe the cucumbers and pack in hot sterile jars. To each quart jar add ½ teaspoon mustard seed, ½ teaspoon celery seed, 1 bay leaf, ½ teaspoon pickling spice and 1 large piece of dill. Heat the water, salt and vinegar to the boiling point; fill the jars to overflowing; seal. These may be used after standing 1 week.

END OF THE SEASON PICKLE

36 medium green tomatoes
  6 medium onions
2 sweet green peppers
  2 sweet red peppers
1 hot red pepper
  1 cup water

2 cups cider vinegar
6 cups brown sugar
5 teaspoons salt
5 teaspoons curry powder
5 teaspoons celery seed

Put the tomatoes, onions and peppers through the coarse knife of the chopper. Put in the preserving kettle; add 1 cup water; simmer gently for 15 minutes. Drain well, pressing out all the liquid. Add the vinegar, brown sugar, salt and spices. Bring to a boil; simmer gently for 5 minutes; pour into sterile jars and seal. Yield: approximately 9 pints.

MIXED SWEET PICKLES

2 quarts cucumbers
  2 quarts silver skin onions
2 quarts cauliflower

1½ cups salt
  2 quarts boiling water
Vinegar solution
Alum

Wipe the cucumbers and cut in pieces; measure after cutting. Cover the onions with boiling water; let stand for 5 minutes; skin. Break the cauliflower into flowerlets. Combine the 3 vegetables in a large preserving kettle; sprinkle with the salt and add the 2 quarts boiling water. Cover tightly and let stand till morning. Drain; simmer the vegetables in a weak solution of vinegar (1 pint vinegar to 2 pints water) for 1 hour. After the first ½ hour of cooking, add a piece of alum the size of a walnut; at the end of the hour's cooking, drain and discard this liquid. Dry the pickles with a soft cloth; pack in sterile jars. Fill the jars to overflowing with the following syrup poured on boiling hot:

3 cups cider vinegar
  3 cups brown sugar
1½ teaspoons mustard seed

⅛ teaspoon hot red pepper
3 tablespoons whole mixed
  pickling spice (tied in a bag)

Seal at once. Let the pickles stand for 3 weeks before using. Yield: about 8 pints.

MUSTARD PICKLES

1 quart silver skin onions
  1 quart green tomatoes
1 quart cucumbers

1 quart cauliflower
4 cups celery, diced
6 sweet green peppers

Have the onions as uniform as possible; peel them and leave them whole. Do not peel the tomatoes; cut them in thick slices and then dice. Peel the cucumbers; remove the seeds and dice. Break the cauliflower into small flowerlets. Dice the celery. Remove the stems and seeds from the green peppers; cut in narrow strips. Place all these ingredients in boiling salted water and cook till tender; drain thoroughly.

In the meantime, prepare the following dressing:

4 tablespoons corn starch	6 cups cider vinegar
4 tablespoons dry mustard	3 cups brown sugar
1½ teaspoons turmeric	1 egg
1 teaspoon salt	1 tablespoon salad oil

Make a paste with the corn starch, mustard, turmeric, salt and 1 cup vinegar. Combine the remaining 5 cups of vinegar with the brown sugar and heat to boiling. Stir in the paste; cook and stir till smooth and thick. Add the drained vegetables; continue cooking 5 minutes. Beat the egg slightly with the salad oil; stir into the pickle mixture; continue cooking 3 minutes. Seal in sterile jars. Yield: 6 pints.

QUEEN'S PICKLE

8 large green tomatoes	6 cups cold water
3 green peppers	6 cups cider vinegar
1 red pepper	2 cups brown sugar
3 cups small silver skin onions	2 teaspoons celery seed
4 cups cauliflower pieces	1 cup pastry flour
4 cups cucumbers, sliced	1 egg
4 cups very small whole cucumbers	1 cup dry mustard
	1½ teaspoons turmeric
1 cup salt	2 tablespoons salad oil

Thinly slice the tomatoes; seed the peppers and dice. Pour boiling water over the onions, let stand 5 minutes and skin. Break the cauliflower in small flowerlets. Slice the cucumber without peeling; use the small cucumbers whole. Mix all the vegetables in a small preserving kettle; sprinkle with the salt and add 4 cups water. Let stand overnight. In the morning, bring to a boil in the same water, then drain and rinse. In the meantime, heat the vinegar and brown sugar to boiling; mix the celery seed, flour, egg, mustard, and turmeric to a paste with the remaining 2 cups water. Stir into the hot vinegar mixture; cook and stir till smooth and thick; add the salad oil. Add the well drained vegetables and cook 20 minutes, stirring constantly. Pour into sterile jars and seal. Yield: about 10 pints.

NINE-DAY PICKLES

Wash 4 quarts cucumbers; cut in generous pieces. Cover with a strong brine (⅔ cup salt to 1 quart water); let stand for 3 days; drain and wash. Cover with cold water and let stand 24 hours. Drain; repeat this process the 2 following days. On the seventh day, place the cucumbers in a large preserving kettle; cover with weak vinegar solution (1 pint vinegar to 2 pints water). Simmer for 3 hours; at the end of the first hour add a piece of alum the size of a whole walnut. At the end of 3 hours drain, rinse and put the cucumbers in a crock. Make the following syrup; simmer 5 minutes.

6 cups white wine vinegar	2-3″ sticks whole cinnamon
4 cups white sugar	2 tablespoons celery seed
2 tablespoons mixed pickling spices	

Pour the boiling syrup over the pickles; let stand 24 hours. Drain and re-heat the syrup to boiling; pour over the pickles. Repeat for 3 consecutive days in all. On the ninth day seal in sterile jars or store in a crock.

SACCHARIN PICKLES

Gherkins or small, firm cucumbers	1 cup salt
1 gallon cider vinegar	¼ pound white mustard seed
3 cups white sugar	¼ pound ground mustard
2 drams saccharin	1 oz. celery seed
(120 1-grain tablets)	1 oz. curry powder
	1 oz. turmeric

Heat the vinegar to boiling; add the white sugar and stir till dissolved. Cool to lukewarm; add all remaining ingredients; pour into a large crock. Wash and wipe the gherkins; drop them as gathered into the vinegar solution. The large cucumbers should be cut in gherkin-size pieces. These pickles should not be used until they have been in the solution 3 weeks. Be sure to keep the crock in a cool place.

PICKLED BEETS

6-quart basket small beets	½ cup water
1½ cups cider vinegar	1 cup brown sugar

Scrub the beets and top them; cook in boiling salted water till tender. Drain and plunge in cold water; rub off the skins; drop the beets in sterile jars. In the meantime, make a pickling syrup of the vinegar, water and sugar; let the syrup boil 5 minutes; fill the jars with the beets; add syrup to overflowing. Place 3 whole cloves in each jar; screw down the tops and invert each day for a week. Do not use for at least 3 weeks. Yield: 5 pints.

PICKLED GREEN TOMATOES

30 small, firm green tomatoes
60 whole cloves
1½ cups cider vinegar
½ cup water
2¼ cups brown sugar

2-3″ sticks cinnamon
1 tablespoon root ginger
2 tablespoons mixed pickling
spices
½ lemon, thinly sliced

Select firm tomatoes, uniform for size. Peel them, then cook in boiling salted water till tender, about 10 minutes. Drain; let stand overnight and in a single layer; this draws all liquid from them. In the morning, stick each tomato with two whole cloves. Make a syrup with all the remaining ingredients and boil 5 minutes. Add the tomatoes, one layer at a time; simmer for 10 minutes, spooning the syrup over the tomatoes occasionally. Lift the tomatoes carefully into sterile jars; fill to overflowing with the boiling syrup. Yield: approximately 2½ pints.

BEAN RELISH

4 quarts green or wax beans
6 tablespoons flour
⅓ cup dry mustard
1½ teaspoons powdered
turmeric

1 teaspoon celery seed
⅛ teaspoon dry curry powder
1 teaspoon salt
3 cups cider vinegar
3 cups brown sugar

Wash and tip the beans; cut in 1½″ pieces; there should be 4 quarts after cutting. Cook in boiling salted water till tender. Make a paste of the flour, mustard, turmeric, celery seed, curry powder, salt and 1 cup of the cider vinegar. Mix the remainder of the vinegar and the brown sugar in a preserving kettle; heat to boiling. Slowly stir in the spice paste; cook and stir till smooth and thick. Add the drained beans to the hot sauce; cook gently for 10 minutes. Remove from the heat and seal in sterile jars. Yield: approximately 8 pint jars.

CHOPPED BEET RELISH

4 cups cooked beets, chopped
4 cups cabbage, finely chopped
2 cups apples, finely chopped
1 cup cider vinegar

2 cups horse-radish
1 cup white sugar
1 tablespoon salt
½ teaspoon pepper

Combine the chopped beets, cabbage and apples, add the vinegar and stir well. Let stand 1 hour; drain; discard the vinegar. Add the horseradish, sugar, salt and pepper. Heat to boiling; seal in sterile jars. Yield: 5 pints.

PICKLED WATERMELON RIND

1½ quarts watermelon rind, diced
3 tablespoons salt
3 quarts water
4 cups brown sugar
1 cup cider vinegar
2 tablespoons mixed pickling spice
3-3″ sticks cinnamon

After the pink flesh is cut off and used, peel off the green skin from the rind. Dice and measure—you should have 1½ quarts. Soak overnight in a mixture of 1 quart of water and the salt. In the morning, drain and rinse; cover with 1 quart cold water and simmer till tender; drain till no moisture remains. Make a syrup of the remaining 1 quart of water, the sugar and vinegar. Add the spices, tied loosely in a bag; simmer 5 minutes. We use the minimum of syrup in the recipe to save the sugar, so add only half the watermelon cubes to the syrup. Simmer, tightly covered, till clear (about 45 minutes). Remove from the syrup, place in sterile jars and add the remaining half of the raw cubes to the syrup. Again, cook till transparent and place in sterile jars. There should be enough syrup left to fill jars. Seal at once. Yield: 3 pint jars.

CHILI FRUIT RELISH

24 large ripe tomatoes
6 peaches
6 pears
6 apples
6 onions
2 red peppers (sweet)
2 green peppers (sweet)
½ cup whole pickling spice (tied in a bag)
2 tablespoons salt
3 cups white sugar
4 cups cider vinegar

Scald and skin the tomatoes; cut in pieces; put in a large preserving kettle. Scald, skin and dice the peaches; peel, core and dice the pears and apples. Peel and finely chop the onions; seed and dice the peppers. Add all the fruits and vegetables to the tomatoes; mix well. Add the spices tied loosely in a bag, the salt, sugar and vinegar. Let stand for 2 hours before boiling; simmer gently till thick (about 2 hours). Yield: approximately 8 pints.

UNCOOKED RELISH

3 hot red peppers
12 large green tomatoes, unpeeled
12 MacIntosh Red apples, cored and unpeeled
1 large onion, skinned
2 cups cider vinegar
2 cups brown sugar
5 tablespoons salt
¼ cup lemon juice
1 tablespoon mustard seed

Remove the seeds and stems from peppers. Put the peppers, tomatoes, apples and onion through the food chopper, using the coarse knife. Heat the vinegar sufficiently to dissolve the brown sugar. Add the salt, lemon juice and mustard seed. Stir in the chopped vegetables and mix thoroughly. Let stand in a crock for 3 days, stirring 4 or 5 times a day. Seal in sterile jars. Yield: approximately 5 pints.

CHILI SAUCE

30 large, ripe tomatoes	3 cups cider vinegar
8 medium onions	3 tablespoons salt
3 sweet green peppers	2½ cups brown sugar
2 sweet red peppers	6 tablespoons mixed pickling
2 cups celery, diced	spice (tied in a bag)

Use only firm, ripe, bright red tomatoes. Scald, skin and cut them up into a large preserving kettle. Peel and dice the onions; remove the stems and seeds from the green and red peppers, cut in strips; dice the celery. Add to the tomatoes; add all the remaining ingredients. Bring to a rapid boil; simmer, uncovered, until thick, about 3 hours. Pour into sterile jars and seal at once. Yield: approximately 8 pints. This recipe may be cut in half or one half may be spiced. When almost thick enough to jar, divide the chili sauce in half. Continue cooking the first half till thick. To the second half add 1½ teaspoons cinnamon, ½ teaspoon cloves, ¼ teaspoon ginger. Cook till thick, then seal. Yield: approximately 7 pints.

SPICED PEARS

30 large pears	1 teaspoon grated lemon rind
60 whole cloves	¼ cup mixed pickling spices
2 cups cider vinegar	(tied in a bag)
½ cup water	1 tablespoon root ginger
3 cups brown sugar	2-3″ cinnamon sticks
½ lemon, thinly sliced	

Peel the pears, cut in half and core; stick each half with a whole clove. Let the pears stand in brine (1 teaspoon salt to 1 quart cold water) to prevent discoloration. Make a syrup of the vinegar, water, brown sugar, lemon and lemon rind; add all the spices tied in a bag. Simmer for 10 minutes. Drain the pears and drop them into the syrup. Simmer slowly till tender. Place carefully in sterile jars; fill to overflowing with the syrup. Seal at once. Yield: approximately 5 pints.

NOTE TO BRIDES: *This same recipe may also be used for peaches, Tolman Sweet apples, prunes or plums.*

CHAPTER 8

Cookies

ANNE'S COOKIES

Temperature: 375°F.   Time: 12-15 minutes

⅓ cup shortening
 ⅔ cup brown sugar
½ teaspoon vanilla
 1 egg, well beaten
1½ cups sifted pastry flour

¼ teaspoon baking soda
 ¾ teaspoon baking powder
¼ teaspoon salt
 4 tablespoons sour milk
½ cup raisins, chopped

Cream together the shortening, sugar and vanilla; add the egg, well beaten. Add the sifted dry ingredients alternately with the sour milk; add the chopped fruit. Drop by spoonfuls on an oiled cookie sheet; bake in a moderate oven till done. Yield: about 40 cookies.

APPLESAUCE COOKIES

Temperature: 400°F.   Time: 10 minutes

½ cup shortening
 1 cup brown sugar
1 egg
 2 cups sifted cake flour
1½ teaspoons baking powder
 ¼ teaspoon baking soda

½ teaspoon cinnamon
 ¼ teaspoon cloves
1 teaspoon salt
 1 cup thick, unsweetened
  applesauce
½ cup raisins, chopped

Cream together the shortening and the brown sugar; add the unbeaten egg; blend till light. Add the sifted dry ingredients alternately with the applesauce. Add the raisins. Drop by spoonfuls on an oiled cookie sheet. Bake on the top rack of a fairly hot oven. Keep in a tin box for a day or two till the spice flavor is all through the cookies. Yield: about 60 cookies.

RICH BROWN COOKIES

Temperature: 375°F.   Time: 12-13 minutes

½ cup shortening
 ½ cup molasses
1 egg, well beaten
 2¼ cups sifted all-purpose
  flour

1 teaspoon ginger
 1 teaspoon cinnamon
⅛ teaspoon mace
 ½ teaspoon baking soda
½ teaspoon salt

Cream together the shortening and molasses. Add the well beaten egg; beat until light. Add the sifted dry ingredients and mix well. Chill the dough for two hours. Roll on a floured board;

cut with a floured cutter. Place on an oiled cookie sheet; bake in a moderately hot oven on the top rack. Yield: 5 dozen 2″ cookies.

BILL'S BROWNIES

Temperature: 350°F. Time: 30-35 minutes

1½ ozs. unsweetened chocolate (1½ squares)
3 tablespoons fat
1 cup white sugar
½ cup milk

1 cup sifted pastry flour
2 teaspoons baking powder
2 eggs, unbeaten
1 teaspoon vanilla
1 tablespoon grated orange rind

Melt the unsweetened chocolate and fat together; blend well. Measure into a bowl the sugar, milk, flour, baking powder and unbeaten eggs; add the melted chocolate mixture. Beat vigorously with the dover beater till the mixture is smooth and thick. Add the vanilla and orange rind. Pour into an oiled pan 8″ by 8″ by 2″; bake in a moderate oven till firm. Immediately upon removing from the oven cut in squares. Cool slightly and lift from the pan. If desired, frost with a thin coating of your favorite chocolate icing. Yield: 24 bars.

BUTTERSCOTCH FINGERS

Temperature: 400°F.
        350°F.

Time: 12-15 minutes
        35 minutes

1 cup sifted all-purpose flour
½ teaspoon salt
½ cup shortening
1 tablespoon cold water
2 eggs, well beaten
1 cup brown sugar
½ cup nuts, chopped

¼ cup maraschino cherries, chopped
1 teaspoon vanilla
2 tablespoons sifted all-purpose flour
½ teaspoon salt
¼ teaspoon baking powder

Sift together 1 cup all-purpose flour and the salt; cut in the shortening until the mixture is crumbly. Add the cold water and blend. This dough is very stiff. Press the batter into an oiled pan 8″ x 12″. Bake in a hot oven (400°F.) for 12 - 15 minutes. Remove from the oven and spread the following mixture over the partly cooked base. Beat the eggs till very light; add the brown sugar; beat again until the sugar is dissolved. Add the chopped nuts, cherries, vanilla, 2 tablespoons of flour, the salt and baking powder. Blend lightly; spread this mixture over the partly cooked batter. Bake in a moderate oven for 35 minutes. Cut in finger-lengths while still warm. Yield: about 44 bars.

BUTTERSCOTCH COOKIES

Temperature: 400°F. Time: 10 minutes

¾ cup brown sugar
 ½ cup shortening
1½ teaspoons vanilla
 2 eggs, well beaten

1 tablespoon sour cream
 3 cups sifted all-purpose flour
2 teaspoons baking powder
 ½ teaspoon salt

Pack the brown sugar firmly in the cup when measuring. Cream it with the shortening and vanilla till light and fluffy. Add the well beaten eggs and sour cream; blend well. Add the sifted dry ingredients, stirring till smooth after each addition. Shape into a roll; wrap in waxed paper and chill. Slice with a sharp knife; place the slices on an oiled cookie sheet. Bake in a hot oven (400°F). This quantity will make about 50 cookies.

CARAMEL SQUARES

Temperature: 350°F. Time: 25 minutes

¾ cup brown sugar
 ¼ cup corn syrup
 ¼ cup shortening
  1 egg
1 cup sifted cake flour

1 teaspoon baking powder
 ¼ teaspoon salt
 ⅓ cup nuts, chopped
 ⅓ cup dates, chopped
 ½ teaspoon vanilla

Measure the sugar, corn syrup and shortening into a saucepan. Stir over low heat until the shortening is melted and the mixture well blended. Remove from the heat; cool; add the unbeaten egg. Beat until light. Sift together the dry ingredients; add to the first mixture. Add the nuts, dates and flavoring. Blend thoroughly. Spread on an oiled pan 8″ x 12″. Bake in a moderate oven; cut in squares while still warm. Roll the squares in powdered sugar. Yield: about 60 bars.

CHOCOLATE CHIP COOKIES

Temperature: 375°F. Time: 8-10 minutes

½ cup shortening
 ¼ cup brown sugar
¼ cup white sugar
 ½ teaspoon vanilla
1 egg, well beaten
 1 cup plus 2 tablespoons
  sifted all-purpose flour

½ teaspoon salt
 ½ teaspoon baking soda
 ½ cup nuts, chopped
 ½ cup semi-sweet chocolate,
  slivered

Cream together the shortening, brown sugar, white sugar and vanilla; add the egg and beat until fluffy. Add the sifted dry ingredients in three additions. Add the nuts and slivered chocolate; blend well and chill. Drop by spoonfuls on an oiled cookie sheet; bake in a moderate oven till done. Yield: about 24 cookies.

CINNAMON COOKIES

Temperature: 375°F. Time: 12-15 minutes

½ cup shortening	2 cups sifted pastry flour
½ cup white sugar	1½ tablespoons sour cream
1 teaspoon vanilla	1 teaspoon cinnamon
1 egg, separated	2 tablespoons white sugar

Cream the shortening; gradually add the sugar and vanilla. Blend well; add the unbeaten egg yolk; again blend. Add the sifted flour and sour cream; mix thoroughly. Chill well; turn on a floured board and roll to ⅛" thickness. Cut with a floured cookie cutter; brush with egg white; sprinkle with a mixture of cinnamon and 2 tablespoons white sugar. Place on an oiled cookie sheet and bake in a fairly hot oven. Yield: about 2 dozen 2" cookies.

COCONUT CRISPS

Temperature: 325°F. Time: 12-15 minutes

½ cup shortening	⅞ cup sifted pastry flour
½ cup brown sugar	⅛ teaspoon salt
1 egg, unbeaten	1 teaspoon baking powder
¾ cup rolled oats	⅛ teaspoon baking soda
½ cup coconut	

Cream the shortening; gradually beat in the sugar. Add the unbeaten egg; beat until fluffy. Add the rolled oats and coconut. Sift together the dry ingredients; add to the creamed mixture; chill. Drop by spoonfuls about 2" apart on an oiled cookie sheet; press flat with the tines of a fork. Bake in a slow oven until crisp; remove from the pan while hot. Yield: 30 cookies.

CRISP COOKIES

Temperature: 325°F. Time: 15 minutes

¾ cup sifted pastry flour	¼ cup nuts, chopped
⅛ teaspoon salt	¾ cup rolled oats
⅛ teaspoon baking soda	½ cup shortening
1 teaspoon baking powder	½ cup brown sugar
⅜ cup baking bran	1 egg, lightly beaten

Sift together the flour, salt, baking soda and baking powder; add the bran, chopped nuts and rolled oats; blend well. Add the shortening; blend with the fingers until the mixture is crumbly. Combine the sugar and lightly beaten egg; beat until fluffy. Blend the two mixtures. Chill the batter; take off small pieces and roll until round. Place on an oiled cookie sheet; press flat with the tines of a fork. Bake in a moderate oven. Yield: approximately 48 small cookies.

CORNFLAKE COOKIES

Temperature: 325°F.
Time: 15-20 minutes
¼ cup oatmeal, toasted
1 egg white
⅛ teaspoon salt
4 tablespoons white sugar
¼ teaspoon vanilla
1 cup cornflakes

Oven toast the oatmeal until the flakes are golden brown. Mix together the egg white and salt; beat until stiff but not dry. Add the sugar gradually, spoonful by spoonful, beating all the time; add the vanilla. Fold in the cornflakes and the toasted oatmeal flakes; drop by spoonfuls on an oiled cookie sheet. Bake in a moderate oven until done. Yield: 20 cookies.

GOLDEN FANCIES

Temperature: 375°F.
Time: 12 minutes
1 cup shortening
1 cup brown sugar
1 egg, well beaten
3 cups sifted pastry flour
1 teaspoon baking soda
¼ cup hot water

Cream together the shortening and sugar; beat until light; add the well beaten egg. Add the sifted flour and baking soda alternately with the hot water, mixing well. Chill the batter; place spoonfuls of batter on an oiled baking sheet about 2″ apart; press flat with the tines of a fork. Bake in a moderate oven. Yield: about 100 cookies. They're particularly good put together with strawberry jam just before serving.

HONEY-OATMEAL HERMITS

Temperature: 350°F.
Time: 15-18 minutes
1 cup sifted pastry flour
1 teaspoon baking soda
¼ teaspoon salt
½ teaspoon allspice
½ teaspoon cinnamon
1¼ cups rolled oats
½ cup shortening
1 cup honey
2 eggs, well beaten
3 tablespoons sour milk
1 cup raisins, chopped
¼ cup nuts, chopped
8 maraschino cherries, chopped
1 tablespoon lemon juice
1 teaspoon grated lemon rind

Sift together the flour, baking soda, salt and spices; add the rolled oats; blend. Cream together the shortening and honey; beat till light. Add the well beaten eggs and the sour milk; add the sifted dry ingredients. Mix lightly; add the chopped fruit and nuts, the lemon juice and rind. Chill the batter; drop by spoonfuls on an oiled cookie sheet. Bake in a moderate oven till done. Yield: about 50 spicy fruit drops. Store them in a tin cookie box, for additional flavor leave a couple of prunes in with cookies.

HERMITS

Temperature: 375°F.

Time: 15 minutes

½ cup shortening
½ cup white sugar
1 teaspoon vanilla
1 egg, well beaten
½ cup nuts, chopped
1 cup raisins, chopped
1½ cups sifted pastry flour

2 teaspoons baking powder
½ teaspoon salt
½ teaspoon cloves
1 teaspoon cinnamon
1 teaspoon allspice
¼ cup sour cream

Cream together the shortening and sugar; beat until light. Add the vanilla and well beaten egg; add the chopped nuts and raisins. Add the sifted dry ingredients alternately with the sour cream; mix well. Chill; drop by spoonfuls about 2″ apart on an oiled cookie sheet. Bake in a moderate oven. Yield: about 48 2″ cookies.

CRISP HONEY COOKIES

Temperature: 350°F.

Time: 12-15 minutes

1 cup butter
1 cup honey
3¾ cups sifted pastry
flour

2 teaspoons baking soda
½ teaspoon cinnamon
½ teaspoon cloves
½ teaspoon allspice

Measure the butter and honey into a saucepan. Heat until dissolved; boil 1 minute; cool. Add the sifted dry ingredients in 3 additions; this batter should be a soft dough. Chill well; roll thin; cut with a floured cutter. Place on an oiled cookie sheet; bake in a moderate oven. These cookies are thin and burn easily; if you want to be especially careful, cut heavy brown paper to fit the cookie sheet, bake the cookies on the paper. Yield: 100 cookies.

FILLED OATMEAL CRISPS

Temperature: 350°F.

Time: 10-12 minutes

1¼ cups sifted pastry flour
¼ teaspoon baking powder
¼ teaspoon salt
1¼ cups rolled oats

½ cup shortening
1 teaspoon grated lemon rind
⅓ cup brown sugar
1 egg, well beaten

Sift together the flour, baking powder and salt; add the rolled oats. Add the shortening and lemon rind; work till the mixture is crumbly. Add the sugar and well beaten egg. Chill the batter; roll very thin; cut with a 2″ cutter. Bake on an oiled cookie sheet till crisp. Put together in pairs with Date Filling. Yield: 2 dozen cookies.

MINCEMEAT COOKIES

Temperature: 425°F. Time: 10-12 minutes

¾ cup shortening
 ¾ cup brown sugar
½ teaspoon vanilla
 1 egg, well beaten
2¾ cups sifted pastry
 flour

½ teaspoon baking soda
 ½ teaspoon baking powder
½ teaspoon salt
 1 teaspoon cinnamon
½ cup thick sour milk
½ cup mincemeat

Cream together the shortening, sugar and vanilla; beat this mixture until it is creamy and fluffy. Add the egg, well beaten; add the sifted dry ingredients alternately with the sour milk. Chill the batter; take out small pieces of batter, roll thinly on a lightly floured board, cut with a 2″ cutter. Put together in pairs, moistening the edge of the undercrust and using a half teaspoon of mincemeat as filling. Pinch the edges together and place on an oiled cookie sheet; bake in a hot oven. Yield: about 24 pairs of cookies. Jam, jelly or apple butter may be used to vary the flavor.

OATMEAL MACAROONS

Temperature: 350°F. Time: 10-12 minutes

1 egg, lightly beaten
 ⅓ cup white sugar
2 teaspoons melted butter
 ¾ cup rolled oats

¼ cup shredded coconut
 ¼ teaspoon salt
½ teaspoon vanilla

Beat the egg until light; gradually beat in the sugar; stir in all the remaining ingredients. Let stand for 5 minutes; place spoonfuls of the mixture on an oiled baking sheet. The easiest way to spoon out cookie mixtures is to oil 2 spoons; use one to spoon out the mixture, the second to push it on the pan. If the spoons are kept oiled the bowl of the spoon doesn't fill up. Bake the macaroons on the top shelf in a moderate oven till delicately browned. While still warm, remove from the pan with a spatula or thin-bladed knife. Yield: 20 good sized macaroons.

OATMEAL SPICE COOKIES

Temperature: 375°F. Time: 10 minutes

½ cup shortening
 1¼ cups brown sugar
1 egg, well beaten
 1¼ cups rolled oats
1¾ cups sifted pastry flour

½ teaspoon salt
 1 teaspoon baking soda
½ teaspoon ginger
 ½ teaspoon cinnamon
¼ teaspoon mace or nutmeg

Cream together the shortening and brown sugar; add the well beaten egg; beat till fluffy. Add the rolled oats; blend well; let stand 5 minutes. Add the sifted dry ingredients in three additions. This batter is quite stiff. Take out small pieces; roll between the palms of the hands; place 2″ apart on an oiled cookie sheet. Flatten with the tines of a fork. Bake in a moderate oven till golden brown. Yield: 100 small cookies.

OATMEAL SQUARES

Temperature: 400°F.	Time: 20-25 minutes
1 cup brown sugar	½ teaspoon cinnamon
1¼ cups fine rolled oats	¾ cup shortening
1½ cups sifted all-purpose flour	2 cups Date Filling
½ teaspoon salt	1 egg yolk
	1 tablespoon water

Measure the sugar, rolled oats, flour, salt and cinnamon into a mixing bowl; rub in the shortening until the mixture is crumbly. Spread half the mixture in a shallow pan 8″ x 12″; press down level. Spread with the Date Filling; add the remaining half of the crumb mixture; press flat with a spoon. Brush with a mixture of egg yolk and water. Bake in a moderate oven till done. When cool, cut in squares. Yield: 24 squares.

DELICIOUS NUT BARS

Temperature: 350°F.	Time: 40 minutes

PART I

¼ cup shortening	1 cup sifted all-purpose flour
½ cup brown sugar	

Cream the shortening; gradually add the brown sugar; blend well. Sift in the flour, stirring with a fork until the mixture is crumbly. Pat into an oiled pan 8″ x 12″; bake in a moderate oven for 12 to 15 minutes. Watch that the edges do not brown too much.

PART II

2 eggs, slightly beaten	½ teaspoon baking powder
1 cup brown sugar	1 cup shredded coconut
1 teaspoon vanilla	½ cup raisins, chopped
1 tablespoon corn starch	½ cup nuts, chopped
¼ teaspoon salt	

Mix together the slightly beaten eggs, sugar and vanilla. Add the remaining ingredients; mix well. Pour over the partly baked shortbread foundation; return to the oven and continue cooking for 25 minutes. While still warm cut in bars. Yield: 30 bars.

ORANGE DROP COOKIES

Temperature: 350°F. Time: 8 minutes

⅔ cup brown sugar ¼ cup orange juice
6 tablespoons shortening 1½ cups sifted pastry flour
1 egg, well beaten ⅓ teaspoon baking soda
1 teaspoon grated orange rind ⅔ teaspoon baking powder

Cream together the sugar and shortening; add the well beaten egg; beat till fluffy. Add the orange rind and juice; add the sifted dry ingredients; blend well. Chill the batter; drop by spoonfuls on an oiled cookie sheet about 2″ apart. Bake in a moderate oven till done. The recipe may be doubled and the batter stored in the refrigerator until needed. Yield: 30 cookies.

ORANGE SQUARES

Temperature: 350°F. Time: 40-45 minutes

½ cup shortening 2 cups sifted all-purpose flour
⅞ cup white sugar 1 teaspoon baking powder
1 egg, well beaten ½ teaspoon salt
1 cup thick sour milk 1 teaspoon baking soda
1 cup cooked prunes, chopped 1 tablespoon warm water
½ cup seedless raisins, chopped ⅓ cup orange juice
1 tablespoon grated orange rind ¼ cup white sugar

Cream together the shortening and ⅞ cup white sugar; mix till light. Add the egg, well beaten; blend again. Add the sour milk, fruit and grated orange rind. Sift together the flour, baking powder and salt; add in three additions to the first batter. Dissolve the baking soda in the warm water and add; blend lightly; pour into an oiled pan 8″ x 12″. Bake in a moderate oven till firm. While still hot, brush with a mixture of the orange juice and ¼ cup white sugar. Cut into squares while still warm. Yield: 30 squares.

PEANUT BUTTER COOKIES

Temperature: 375°F. Time: 12-15 minutes

½ cup peanut butter 2 teaspoons grated lemon rind
¼ cup shortening 1 cup sifted all-purpose flour
½ cup brown sugar ¼ teaspoon salt
1 egg, unbeaten ½ teaspoon baking soda
2 tablespoons lemon juice

Cream together the peanut butter, shortening and sugar; beat till light. Add the unbeaten egg, lemon juice and grated lemon rind; mix thoroughly. Stir in the sifted dry ingredients; mix well. Shape into 2 rolls; roll in waxed paper and chill overnight in the refrigerator. Cut in thin slices with a sharp knife; bake on an oiled cookie sheet. Yield: 48-1½″ cookies.

PUMPKIN COOKIES

Temperature: 400°F.

Time: 15 minutes

½ cup shortening
  1¼ cups brown sugar
1 teaspoon vanilla
  2 eggs, well beaten
1½ cups cooked pumpkin
  2½ cups sifted pastry flour

4 teaspoons baking powder
  ½ teaspoon salt
¼ teaspoon ginger
  ½ teaspoon nutmeg.
  ½ teaspoon cinnamon
1 cup dates or raisins, chopped

Cream together the shortening, sugar and vanilla; beat till light. Add the eggs, well beaten, and the pumpkin. Sift the dry ingredients three times; add in three additions to the first mixture. Add the chopped fruit; let chill for half an hour. Drop by spoonfuls on an oiled cookie sheet; the cookies spread a little, so place them about 2" apart. Bake in a moderate oven. Yield: 72 cookies.

SHORTBREAD COOKIES

Temperature: 325°F.

Time: 20 minutes

1 cup butter
  ½ cup corn starch
½ cup icing sugar

½ teaspoon salt
  2 cups sifted all-purpose
  flour

Beat the butter until creamy but not oily. Sift the dry ingredients four times; add to the butter a little at a time. Work in with a spoon as long as possible, then turn the mixture on a floured board and knead till the mixture cracks slightly. Pat gently to ⅓" thickness and cut with fancy cutters or roll into small balls and press flat with a fork. Bake in a moderate oven. Yield: about 100 small cookies.

SPICED REFRIGERATOR COOKIES

Temperature: 350°F.

Time: 12-15 minutes

½ cup shortening
  ½ cup white sugar
¼ cup molasses
  1 egg, well beaten
2½ cups sifted pastry flour

½ teaspoon baking soda
  1½ teaspoons ginger
½ teaspoon salt
  ½ teaspoon cinnamon

Cream together the shortening, sugar and molasses; beat till creamy; add the well beaten egg. Add the sifted dry ingredients in three additions. Turn this mixture on a floured board; knead lightly until firm. Roll into 2 long rolls; wrap in waxed paper and let chill in the refrigerator for 24 hours. Slice the cookies, making them as thin as possible; bake on an ungreased cookie sheet till firm. Yield: 90 cookies.

CHAPTER 9

Desserts and Dessert Sauces

BAKED APPLES

Temperature: 350°F.   Time: 1 hour

6 tart apples   1 tablespoon grated orange
  1 cup mincemeat   rind
6 tablespoons brown sugar   6 tablespoons water
  6 tablespoons orange juice   One 4 oz. package plain cream
                                 cheese

Core the apples; scoop out some apple from each one. Dice; mix with the mincemeat, the brown sugar, the orange juice and grated rind. Fill the apples and place on a baking dish. Add the cold water; bake in a moderate oven till done, basting frequently. Chill; serve with small balls of cream cheese rolled in orange juice and grated orange rind. Yield: 6 servings.

GLAZED BAKED APPLES

Temperature: 375°F.   Time: 30 minutes

6 firm, tart apples   ¾ cup water
  ½ cup white sugar   1 tablespoon white sugar

Core the apples; peel about one third of the way down; place in a baking dish. Boil together for 5 minutes the ½ cup of sugar and the water; pour the syrup over the apples. Bake uncovered in a moderate oven till the apples are almost tender, (about 30 minutes), basting frequently. Take from the oven; drain off the syrup. Sprinkle each apple with a little sugar and put back on the top rack of the oven till the sugar melts. Pour a little syrup over the apples and return to the oven. Repeat 2 or 3 times until the apples are glazed. Chill and serve with the rich syrup plus a little cream. Serves 6.

GREEN APPLE SAUCE

12 green apples   ½ cup sugar
  ½ cup water

Wash, core and quarter the apples; do not peel. Put in a saucepan with the water; cover and simmer gently for 15-20 minutes. Press through a sieve; add the sugar; stir well till dissolved. When the applesauce is cold, a stiffly beaten egg white folded in makes a delicious light dessert. Yield: 6 servings.

PARADISE APPLES

Temperature: 400°F.   Time: 1 hour

¾ cup white sugar   4 large tart apples
  1 cup water   4 tablespoons raspberry jam
2 teaspoons lemon juice

Combine the sugar and water; boil for 5 minutes; add the lemon juice. In the meantime, cut the apples in half crosswise and core each half; be careful not to break the skin. Place the apples in a shallow baking dish. Place ½ tablespoon jam in each half; pour the syrup over all. Cover and bake in a fairly hot oven till tender. Lift the apples to a serving dish. Boil down the syrup a little; pour over the apples and chill. Serves 4.

APPLE CRISP

Temperature: 375°F.   Time: 30-35 minutes

6 large tart cooking apples   ½ cup brown sugar
  ⅛ teaspoon salt   ¼ cup shortening
1 teaspoon grated lemon rind   ¼ teaspoon salt
  1 tablespoon lemon juice   ½ teaspoon cinnamon
½ cup sifted all-purpose flour

Pare, core and slice the apples in thin slices; place in an oiled pan 8″ x 8″. Sprinkle with the ⅛ teaspoon salt, the lemon rind and juice. Blend together till crumbly the flour, sugar and shortening; add the salt and cinnamon. Sprinkle over apples; bake in a moderate oven till apples are tender. Serve warm with cream. Serves 6.

UPSIDE DOWN APPLE PUDDING

Temperature: 350°F.   Time: 40 minutes

3 tart apples   1 cup sifted all-purpose flour
  ¼ cup butter   1 teaspoon baking powder
¾ cup brown sugar   ¼ teaspoon baking soda
  ⅛ teaspoon nutmeg   ½ teaspoon salt
¼ cup shortening   1 teaspoon ginger
  ⅓ cup white sugar   ½ teaspoon cinnamon
¼ cup molasses   ⅓ cup boiling water
  1 egg, well beaten

Peel and core the apples; cut in ½″ rings. Melt the butter in a round fireproof baking dish; add the brown sugar and nutmeg; let bubble for 1 minute. Press the apple rings into the butterscotch mixture. Cream the shortening with the sugar and molasses; add the well-beaten egg. Add the sifted ingredients. Add the boiling water and mix quickly. Pour over the apples; bake in a moderate oven till done. Serve with cream. Serves 6.

FAR HILLS APPLE DUMPLING

Temperature: 450°F.　　　　　　　Time: 12-15 minutes
　　　　　　350°F.　　　　　　　　　　30 minutes

6 tart apples　　　　　　　　Dash of ground cloves
　Puff paste　　　　　　　　　1 egg yolk
½ cup white sugar　　　　　　1 tablespoon milk
　⅛ teaspoon ground cinnamon　1 tablespoon fine sugar

Peel and core the apples; place each in the centre of a square of puff paste. Fill the centres of the apples with a mixture of the sugar and spices. Moisten the ends of the pastry corners with a mixture of the egg yolk and milk; fold the four corners of the paste over the apple, enclosing it entirely. Place in an oiled baking dish, upside down; brush over with the egg and milk mixture; sprinkle with a little fine white sugar. Bake in a hot oven (450°F.) for 12 to 15 minutes. Reduce the heat to 350°F. continue baking until the apples are cooked and the paste is beautifully browned, about 30 minutes. Serve hot with apricot or butterscotch sauce. Serves 6.

Puff Paste

¼ cup shortening　　　　　　⅛ teaspoon salt
　1½ cups sifted all-purpose　　⅝ cup ice cold water
　flour　　　　　　　　　　　½ cup butter

Rub the shortening into the flour; add the salt and, very gradually, the water. Roll out into a square ½" thick. Spread ¼ cup butter in small pieces over half the square. Fold over; seal the ends and sides to keep the air enclosed. Roll out again to ½" thickness; fold two ends of the square to the middle, making an oblong, then fold two ends of the oblong to the middle (this makes a square). Fold this square in half and seal the sides and ends to enclose the air; chill in the refrigerator for 1 hour. Repeat the procedure twice until all the butter is used, chilling 1 hour between each rolling and folding. Roll the paste thin; cut in 4" squares and proceed with the dumplings. Serves 6.

BLUEBERRY SQUARES

Temperature: 350°F.　　　　　　Time: 45 to 50 minutes

⅓ cup shortening　　　　　　2½ teaspoons baking powder
　1 cup white sugar　　　　　　¼ teaspoon salt
1 teaspoon vanilla　　　　　　⅔ cup milk
　1 egg, unbeaten　　　　　　　1½ cups fresh blueberries
2 cups sifted cake flour　　　1 teaspoon grated lemon rind

Cream together the shortening and ¾ cup sugar. Add the vanilla and the egg; beat till fluffy. Add the sifted dry ingredients alternately with the milk. Pour half the batter into an oiled pan 9″ x 9″. Cover with a mixture of the blueberries, the remaining ¼ cup sugar and the lemon rind. Pour the remainder of the batter over the berries. Bake in a moderate oven till done. Cut in squares; dust with powdered sugar; serve hot with or without cream. Serves 6.

DUTCH APPLE PIE

Temperature: 375°F.   Time: 40-45 minutes

¼ cup shortening
  ¼ cup white sugar
1 teaspoon grated lemon rind
  1 egg
2 cups sifted cake flour
  2½ teaspoons baking
    powder

¼ teaspoon salt
  ¾ cup milk
Green apples, pared, cored and
  cut in eighths
Melted butter
  ¼ cup brown sugar
  ½ teaspoon cinnamon

Cream together the shortening, sugar and lemon rind. Add the egg; beat until the mixture is fluffy. Add the sifted dry ingredients alternately with the milk; beat until smooth. Pour into an oiled pan 8″x 8″. Peel, core and cut the green apples in eighths. Press into the batter in a regular pattern; brush lightly with melted butter, using as much or as little as you can spare. Sprinkle with a mixture of the brown sugar and cinnamon. Bake in a moderate oven until done. Serve warm with cream or hot from the oven with vanilla ice cream. Serves 6.

QUEEN OF PUDDINGS

Temperature: 350°F.   Time: 50 minutes

1½ cups soft bread crumbs
  3 cups milk
1 egg, well beaten
  2 egg yolks
4 tablespoons white sugar
  Dash of salt

¾ teaspoon vanilla
  2 tablespoons melted butter
Strawberry Jam
  2 egg whites
3 tablespoons white sugar
  1 teaspoon corn starch

Soak the bread crumbs in the milk; beat till smooth. Beat the whole egg and 2 egg yolks till lemon-colored. Add the 4 tablespoons sugar and salt; beat till very light; add to the bread mixture. Add the vanilla and melted butter. Blend well; pour into an oiled 1½ quart baking dish. Bake in a pan of hot water in a moderate oven till the custard sets (about 50 minutes). Spread with strawberry jam. Cover the jam with a meringue made by stiffly beating the 2 egg whites, then beating in the 3 tablespoons white sugar and corn starch. Bake the meringue till golden brown; serve the dessert either warm or cold. Serves 6.

SPICED APPLE ROLL

Temperature: 350°F.

Time: 40 minutes

2 cups sifted all-purpose
flour
4 teaspoons baking powder
¾ teaspoon salt
⅛ teaspoon mace
¼ cup shortening
1 egg
½ cup milk
1 tablespoon melted butter

2 cups apples, peeled and
finely chopped
2 tablespoons white sugar
¼ cup raisins, chopped
1 teaspoon cinnamon
¼ teaspoon cloves
¾ cup molasses
¼ teaspoon nutmeg
2 tablespoons butter
1 cup hot water

Sift together the flour, baking powder, salt and mace; cut in the shortening until the mixture is crumbly. Beat the egg lightly; add the milk. Add to the flour mixture and stir quickly; turn on a floured board and knead gently till smooth. Roll in an oblong ¼″ thick and brush with the melted butter. Mix together the chopped apples, sugar, raisins, cinnamon and cloves. Spread on the batter; roll up like a jelly roll. Place in an oiled baking dish, shaped into a circle. Mix together the molasses, nutmeg, butter and hot water. Pour over roll; bake in a moderate oven till done. Serves 6.

NOTE TO BRIDES: *Here's a dessert with a sauce ready-made.*

REFRIGERATOR CHEESE CAKE

1½ cups graham cracker
crumbs
2 tablespoons white sugar
6 tablepoons melted butter
2 tablespoons gelatine
½ cup cold water
2 eggs, separated

½ cup white sugar
½ cup milk
1 teaspoon salt
1½ cups cream cheese
1 teaspoon grated lemon rind
3 tablespoons lemon juice
1 cup cream

Roll the cracker crumbs very fine before measuring. Add 2 tablespoons white sugar and the melted butter. Blend well; reserve ½ cup of this mixture; press the remainder on the bottom and sides of a deep 9″ pie pan; chill. Soak the gelatine in the cold water for 5 minutes. Combine the 2 egg yolks, lightly beaten, with ½ cup white sugar, the milk and salt. Cook over boiling water till the mixture is like custard. Add the soaked gelatine; stir till the mixture begins to thicken. Mix the cream cheese with the lemon rind and juice; add to the custard mixture. Add the cream and blend well. Fold in the stiffly beaten egg whites. Pour into the chilled crust. Sprinkle the top with the reserved ½ cup of crumbs. Chill for 6 to 8 hours before using. It's rich and delicious. Yield: 8 pieces.

CHERRY SQUARES

PART I

Temperature: 350°F. Time: 12 minutes

1 cup sifted pastry flour 4 tablespoons shortening
  ¾ teaspoon baking powder 1 egg yolk
⅛ teaspoon salt

Sift together the flour, baking powder and salt. Cut in the shortening; add the egg yolk; blend well. Press this mixture into an oiled pan 12″ x 8″.

PART II

2 egg whites 1 teaspoon corn starch
  5 tablespoons brown sugar 10 maraschino cherries
½ teaspoon baking powder

Beat the egg whites until stiff and glossy. Add the sugar, baking powder and corn starch; again beat until stiff. Cover the shortbread batter with this mixture. Cut the cherries in half and distribute over the meringue. Bake in a moderate oven (350°F.) for 25-30 minutes. Cut in squares; serve cold. Serves 6.

BAKED CUSTARD

Temperature: 325°F. Time: 20 to 30 minutes

2 eggs or 4 egg yolks 2 cups hot milk
  3 tablespoons white sugar ½ teaspoon vanilla or
¼ teaspoon salt dash of nutmeg

Beat the eggs slightly; add the sugar and salt; add the hot milk slowly. Blend well; add the flavoring; strain into oiled custard cups. Place in a pan of hot water; bake in a moderate oven till firm. Serves 6.

FOR THE BRIDE: *Too much beating of the eggs makes the custard separate. When eggs are scarce and expensive, substitute 1 tablespoon corn starch for 1 egg. The mixture will bind just as well, and has not the same tendency to break apart.*

COFFEE CUSTARD

Scald one tablespoon finely ground coffee with the milk; strain through cheesecloth and then proceed as plain custard.

CHOCOLATE CUSTARD

Melt ¼ oz. unsweetened chocolate and add to the scalded milk. Proceed as in plain custard.

BAKED BUTTERSCOTCH CUSTARD

Temperature: 325°F.   Time: 45 minutes

¼ cup white sugar   ½ teaspoon vanilla
  3 cups milk, scalded   ¼ cup roasted peanuts,
4 eggs   chopped
  ⅓ cup white sugar

Measure ¼ cup white sugar into a heavy saucepan; stir over low heat till the sugar is carmelized. Divide amongst 6 hot oiled custard cups; roll the syrup around the custard cups until coated. Scald the milk. Lightly beat the eggs; add ⅓ cup white sugar and the vanilla; add the scalded milk and blend well. Fill the custard cups; sprinkle with the chopped nuts. Set in a shallow pan of hot water. Bake until firm; test with silver knife. Chill and unmould just before serving. The caramel runs down like a sauce. Serves 6.

NOTE TO BRIDES: *Marshmallows cut in half may be used in the bottom of the custard cups instead of the caramel.*

CHERRY SHORTBREAD

Temperature: 375°F.   Time: 40-45 minutes

4 cups cherries, pitted   1 egg, unbeaten
  ¾ cup brown sugar   1 cup sifted cake flour
¼ teaspoon mace   1½ teaspoons baking powder
  3 drops almond flavoring   ⅛ teaspoon salt
¼ cup shortening   1 tablespoon lemon juice
  ½ cup white sugar   1 teaspoon grated lemon rind

Pit the cherries; mix with the brown sugar, mace and almond flavoring; place in a 1½ quart oiled casserole. Cream together the shortening and white sugar; add the unbeaten egg and beat till fluffy. Add the sifted dry ingredients and blend; add the lemon juice and rind. Drop by spoonfuls on the cherries. Bake in a moderate oven till done. Serve warm with cream. Serves 6.

HOT FUDGE DESSERT

Temperature: 350°F.   Time: 50-55 minutes

1 cup sifted cake flour   ½ cup warm milk
  2 teaspoons baking   2 tablespoons melted
  powder   shortening
¼ teaspoon salt   ½ cup brown sugar
  ½ cup white sugar   4 tablespoons cocoa
2 tablespoons cocoa   2 cups hot water

Sift together 3 times the cake flour, baking powder, salt, sugar and 2 tablespoons cocoa; add the warm milk and stir vigorously (don't beat); add the melted shortening. Pour into a square oiled pan 8″ x 8″. Mix together the brown sugar and the 4 tablespoons cocoa; sprinkle over the raw batter. Pour on 2 cups hot water. Bake in a moderate oven till done, 50-55 minutes. Cut in squares; serve hot with Fluffy Sauce. Serves 6.

CHOCOLATE SOUFFLE

Temperature: 325°F.   Time: 50-60 minutes

2 squares unsweetened chocolate   1 cup hot milk
  3 tablespoons hot water   ⅓ cup white sugar
3 tablespoons butter   ⅛ teaspoon salt
  3 tablespoons sifted all-purpose flour   3 eggs, separated

Dissolve the unsweetened chocolate in the hot water. Melt the butter in a saucepan. Slowly mix in the flour; let bubble over low heat for 3 minutes. Add the hot milk; cook and stir till smooth and thick. Remove from the heat; add the chocolate mixture, sugar and salt. Let cool slightly. Stir in the well beaten egg yolks; fold in the stiffly beaten egg whites. Pour into an oiled 2 quart casserole; bake in a moderate oven. Serve with Mocha Sauce. Serves 6.

NOTE TO BRIDES: *Straight from the oven to the table for this dish. It takes some timing, but that's the way to do it.*

CREAM PUFFS

Temperature: 450°F. for 10 minutes
               400°F. for 25 minutes

1 cup boiling water   1 cup sifted all-purpose flour
  ¼ cup butter   ½ teaspoon salt
¼ cup shortening   4 eggs, unbeaten

Have the water rapidly boiling in a heavy saucepan. Add the butter and shortening; stir till melted. Add the flour and salt, all at once; stir vigorously till blended. Continue stirring and cooking until the mixture leaves the sides of the pan in one mass. Remove from the heat and cool one minute. Add the eggs, unbeaten, one at a time; beat till smooth after each addition. Brush a tablespoon with oil and use it to dip out spoonfuls of the batter on an oiled cookie sheet. Place them 2″ apart; round them and shape them up with the spoon. Bake in a hot oven (450°F.) for 10 minutes. Reduce the heat to 400°F.; continue baking for 25 minutes. Do not open oven door while baking. Cool; cut a slit in the side and fill with vanilla ice cream or Cream Custard. Serves 8.

GOLD PUDDING

Temperature: 300°F. Time: 3 hours

¼ cup yellow corn meal
  ½ teaspoon salt
½ teaspoon ginger
  ¼ teaspoon cinnamon

3 cups milk
  ⅓ cup brown sugar
½ cup cold milk

Mix the corn meal, salt, ginger and cinnamon in the top of double boiler; add the milk and the brown sugar. Cook over boiling water for 30 minutes, stirring occasionally. Pour the mixture into an oiled 2 quart baking dish; bake uncovered in slow oven for 30 minutes, stirring two or three times during this baking. Pour the ½ cup cold milk over the pudding; bake, without stirring, for an additional 1 to 1½ hours. This is a delicious pudding when slowly baked. Serves 4 to 6.

BAKED LEMON PUDDING

Temperature: 375°F. Time: 40 to 45 minutes

2 tablespoons butter
  ¾ cup white sugar
¼ cup sifted pastry flour
  ⅛ teaspoon salt
3 tablespoons lemon juice

1 tablespoon grated lemon
  rind
3 eggs, separated
  1½ cups milk
¼ cup brown sugar

Cream the butter; gradually add the white sugar. Add the sifted flour and salt, lemon juice and rind. Beat the egg yolks until thick and lemon colored; add the milk. Combine the two mixtures. Fold in stiffly beaten egg whites to which has been added the brown sugar. Pour into an oiled 2-quart casserole; bake in a moderate oven till firm. Place a cookie sheet on the top rack of the oven during the last 15 minutes of baking to prevent the top crust from cooking too rapidly. Serves 6.

LEMON SOUFFLE

Temperature: 325°F. Time: 1 hour, 20 minutes

¼ cup butter
  2½ tablespoons corn starch
¼ teaspoon salt
  1 cup hot milk

3 eggs, separated
  ⅓ cup white sugar
3 tablespoons lemon juice
  1 tablespoon lemon rind,
    grated

Melt the butter in the top of the double boiler over boiling water; blend in the corn starch and salt; stir and cook for five minutes. Add the hot milk slowly; cook and stir until thickened; let the mixture cool. Beat the egg yolks till thick and lemon colored; add the sugar, lemon juice and rind; add to the corn starch mixture. Fold in the stiffly beaten egg whites. Pour the batter into a 1½ quart casserole, oiled lightly on the bottom but not at all on the sides. Set in a pan of hot water and bake in a moderate oven till firm. Test with a silver knife. When the knife comes out clean, the souffle is done. Serve at once with cream. Serves 6.

NOTE TO BRIDES: *If the sides of the casserole are oiled, the souffle slips as it rises. A souffle can't be a clinging vine and be successful.*

MAPLE DELIGHT

Temperature: 375°F.   Time: 30-35 minutes

1½ cups maple syrup   1½ cups sifted pastry flour
  1½ tablespoons shortening   3 teaspoons baking powder
4 tablespoons white sugar   ¼ teaspoon salt
  2 eggs, well beaten   1 cup milk

Heat the maple syrup to boiling; pour into a 1½ quart oiled baking dish. Cream together the shortening and sugar; add the well beaten eggs; beat till fluffy. Sift together the flour, baking powder and salt; add alternately with the milk to the creamed batter. Pour into the hot syrup; bake in a moderate oven till golden brown. Serve hot with cream. Serves 6.

COOKED PRUNES

Wash the prunes; cover with warm water; let stand overnight. For flavor, add 1 stick cinnamon or 1 teaspoon grated lemon rind or 1 tablespoon grated orange rind. If you use the cinnamon, take it out before simmering the prunes. The fruit rinds are simmered with the fruit. Simmer gently until tender; no sugar is needed.

PRUNE DELIGHT

Temperature: 350°F.   Time: 40 minutes

¾ cup brown sugar   1 teaspoon baking soda
  ⅓ cup shortening   1 teaspoon cinnamon
1 egg, unbeaten   ½ teaspoon cloves
  ¾ cup cooked prune pulp   ⅓ teaspoon salt
1 cup plus 2 tablespoons sifted ⅜ cup thick sour milk
  all-purpose flour

Cream together the sugar and shortening; add the egg; beat till light and fluffy. Add the prune pulp; add the sifted dry ingredients alternately with the sour milk. Pour the batter into a well oiled tube pan; bake till firm. Unmould; serve hot with Lemon Sauce. Serves 6.

PEACH UPSIDE-DOWN CAKE

Temperature: 350°F.   Time: 40-45 minutes

3 tablespoons butter
⅓ cup brown sugar
6 or 8 peach halves
¼ cup shortening
½ cup white sugar
¼ teaspoon almond flavoring

1 egg, unbeaten
1 cup sifted pastry flour
1½ teaspoons baking
    powder
¼ teaspoon salt
⅜ cup milk

Melt the butter in the bottom of an oiled pan 8″ x 8″. Add the brown sugar; blend well; press the peach halves into the mixture. Cream together the shortening, white sugar and flavoring. Add the unbeaten egg; beat till light and fluffy. Add the sifted dry ingredients alternately with the milk. Beat lightly; pour over the peach halves. Bake in a moderate oven till done. While still warm invert on a cake cooler. Cut into squares; serve hot with Nutmeg Sauce. Serves 6.

PINEAPPLE UPSIDE-DOWN CAKE

Temperature: 325°F.   Time: 35-40 minutes

8 slices fresh pineapple
¼ cup butter
½ cup brown sugar
8 maraschino cherries
1 cup sifted cake flour
1 teaspoon baking powder

¼ teaspoon salt
4 eggs, separated
1 cup white sugar
1 tablespoon melted
    butter
½ teaspoon vanilla

Slice the pineapple; remove the core and skin. Melt ¼ cup butter in a 9″ square pan; add the brown sugar; stir over gentle heat till dissolved. Press the pineapple slices into this mixture; insert a cherry in each core. Sift together the flour, baking powder and salt. Beat the egg yolks till light and lemon colored; gradually beat in half the white sugar. Add 1 tablespoon of melted butter and the vanilla. Beat the egg whites till stiff; gradually beat in the remaining ½ cup of white sugar. Combine the two mixtures. Fold in the sifted dry ingredients. Pour over the pineapple mixture; bake in a fairly moderate oven till done. Invert on a large platter; serve warm. Serves 8.

PRUNE UPSIDE-DOWN CAKE

Temperature: 350°F.   Time: 40-45 minutes

2 tablespoons melted butter
¼ teaspoon cinnamon

3 tablespoons brown sugar
8 to 10 cooked prunes

Oil a square pan 8″ x 8″ well. Melt the butter in it; blend in the cinnamon and brown sugar, spreading well over the bottom of the pan. Cut the prunes in half; take out the pits; press the prune halves into the sugar mixture. Let stand while mixing the batter.

Batter

¼ cup shortening
½ cup brown sugar
1 egg, well beaten
1 cup sifted cake flour
¼ teaspoon salt

1½ teaspoons baking powder
¼ teaspoon allspice
¼ teaspoon cinnamon
⅜ cup milk

Cream together the shortening and sugar; beat till fluffy; add the well beaten egg. Add the sifted dry ingredients alternately with the milk; beat till smooth. Pour over the prunes; do not push the batter quite to the edges of the pan. Bake in a moderate oven until done. Let stand in the pan 5 minutes; invert on a flat plate. This dessert may be served without a sauce or with a sauce made from the juice in which the prunes were cooked. Serves 6.

SURPRISE DESSERT

Temperature: 375°F.   Time: 25 minutes

1 pint jar raspberries
  (or 15-ounce can)
2 tablespoons shortening
¼ cup white sugar
1 egg, well beaten

1 cup sifted pastry flour
1½ teaspoons baking powder
¼ teaspoon salt
⅜ cup milk

Drain the raspberries; save the juice for the sauce. Cream together the shortening and sugar; add the well beaten egg. Add the sifted dry ingredients alternately with the milk. Lastly, add ½ cup drained raspberries; blend well. Fill well oiled muffin tins ⅔ full. Bake in a moderate oven. Serve hot with Raspberry Sauce. Serves 6.

Raspberry Sauce: Add sugar to taste to the juice; thicken slightly with 1 teaspoon of corn starch; beat in 1 teaspoon of butter.

BAKED RHUBARB

Temperature: 350°F.   Time: 30 minutes

4 cups rhubarb, cut in 1″ pieces
⅛ teaspoon salt
⅔ cup sugar

¼ teaspoon cinnamon
2 tablespoons water
2 tablespoons butter

Mix together the rhubarb and salt; let stand half an hour. Add the sugar, cinnamon and water. Stir well; pour into an oiled 2-quart casserole; dot with the butter. Bake, covered, in moderate oven till the rhubarb is tender (about half an hour). Chill; serve with Custard Sauce. Serves 6.

RHUBARB BROWN BETTY

Temperature: 375°F.   Time: 25 minutes

4 cups rhubarb, diced   4 tablespoons shortening
  ⅛ teaspoon salt   1 cup sifted pastry flour
¾ cup brown sugar   ¼ teaspoon cinnamon or mace

Dice the rhubarb; mix with the salt. Let stand a half an hour; put in a shallow baking dish; sprinkle with ¼ cup brown sugar. Bake in the oven for 5 minutes. In the meantime, cream together the remaining ½ cup of brown sugar and the shortening; add the flour and spice; blend till crumbly. Sprinkle on top of the rhubarb; return to the oven. Continue baking till the rhubarb is tender (about 20 minutes). Serves 6.

This pudding is delicious served hot with Custard Sauce.

RHUBARB DELIGHT

Temperature: 400°F.   Time: 15 minutes

5 cups rhubarb, diced   4 cups dry crumbs
  ⅙ teaspoon salt   3 tablespoons melted fat
1 cup white sugar   ½ teaspoon cinnamon or mace

Mix together the rhubarb and salt; let stand half an hour. Add the sugar; stir well; simmer gently for 5 minutes. Combine the crumbs and the melted fat. Heat in a shallow pan in the oven, stirring until a golden brown. Place a layer of the rhubarb in an oiled casserole, then a layer of the crisped crumbs. Repeat till the dish is almost full, topping with the crumbs. Sprinkle with the cinnamon or mace. Bake in a fairly hot oven for 15 minutes. Serve hot with cream. Serves 6.

OLD FASHIONED RICE PUDDING

Temperature: 325°F.   Time: 1 hour, 10 minutes

⅔ cup uncooked rice   1 teaspoon vanilla
  8 cups boiling water   2 eggs, lightly beaten
1 teaspoon salt   ⅓ cup raisins
  1⅓ cups milk   ½ teaspoon grated lemon
⅛ teaspoon salt   rind
  3 tablespoons brown sugar   1 teaspoon lemon juice
1 tablespoon softened butter   ½ cup dry crumbs

Cook the rice in the boiling water to which has been added the 1 teaspoon salt. When tender (about 25 minutes) drain and rinse with cold water. Combine the milk, ⅛ teaspoon salt, the sugar, butter, vanilla and eggs; beat well. Add the cooked rice, raisins, lemon rind and juice. Butter a 1½-quart baking dish; cover the sides and bottom with the dry crumbs. Pour in the rice mixture. Place in a pan of warm water; bake till the custard is set. That pudding is good either hot or cold. It should be creamy as custard. Serves 6.

NOTE TO BRIDES: *Save the rice water; it's a grand starch for thin curtains, collars and cuffs.*

STRAWBERRY SHORTCAKE

Temperature: 450°F.   Time: 15 minutes

2 cups sifted all-purpose flour
1 teaspoon baking powder
½ teaspoon baking soda
½ teaspoon salt
2 tablespoons shortening
1 cup thick sour cream
¼ cup white sugar
4 cups ripe strawberries, chopped

Sift together the flour; baking powder, baking soda and salt; cut in the shortening. Make a well in the centre; pour in the sour cream. Mix lightly; turn on a floured board. Knead for 20 counts; divide the batter in half. Roll each half to ½″ thickness, cut with a ½″ cookie cutter. Brush one half the biscuit lightly with butter; top with the remaining biscuit. Place touching one another on a lightly oiled cookie sheet. Bake in a hot oven till golden brown. Add the sugar to the chopped berries, saving a few of the choice berries for the top. Split the biscuit (the top lifts off quite easily); butter and cover with berries. Add the top biscuit, a few more berries; serve warm with cream. Serves 6-8.

FRUIT SOUFFLE

Temperature: 350°F.   Time: 1 hour

4 tablespoons butter
5 tablespoons sifted pastry flour
¼ teaspoon salt
1 cup rich milk
3 eggs, separated
⅓ cup white sugar
3 tablespoons orange juice
1 tablespoon lemon juice
1 tablespoon grated orange rind

Melt the butter in a saucepan; blend in the flour and salt; let bubble for 3 minutes over direct heat. Add the milk slowly; cook and stir till smooth and thick; cool slightly. Beat the egg yolks till light; add the sugar; stir into the milk mixture. Fold in the stiffly beaten egg whites, the fruit juices and rind. Pour into a 1½-quart casserole oiled only on the bottom. Bake in a pan of hot water in a moderate oven for 1 hour; serve as soon as it comes from the oven. Serves 6.

BUTTERSCOTCH RICE

1 tablespoon gelatine	2 cups hot milk
¼ cup cold water	1½ cups cooked rice
½ cup brown sugar	2 egg whites

Soak the gelatine in the cold water for 5 minutes. Carmelize the brown sugar in a saucepan over moderate heat. Slowly add the hot milk; stir until the sugar is dissolved. Remove from the heat; add the gelatine; stir till dissolved. Add the rice; chill until it begins to set. Beat the egg whites; fold into the rice mixture. Turn into a lightly oiled mould; let chill till set. Unmould on a clear glass plate; serve with Fruit Sauce. Serves 6.

FLUFFY RICE

Use 1 cup of rice for 6 servings. Wash the rice until there is no loose starch left. Have ready two quarts of rapidly boiling water with 3 teaspoons of salt added; drop the rice into it, bit by bit, without letting the water come off the boil. Let it cook until it's tender, between 12 and 25 minutes. Don't stir it, just lift it from time to time with a fork. The rice is tender when a grain pressed between the fingers is soft. When the rice is tender turn it into a colander and drain it. Cover the colander closely with a clean cloth; place it over a pan of hot water on the back of the stove. The separate grains of cooked rice will swell and keep separate.

NOTE TO BRIDES: *A tablespoon of lemon juice added to the boiling water keeps the rice snowy white.*

CARAMEL CREAM

Temperature: 350°F.	Time: 12 minutes
1¼ cups brown sugar	½ cup cold milk
2 tablespoons butter	2 eggs, separated
½ cup hot coffee	½ teaspoon vanilla
2 cups hot milk	3 tablespoons white sugar
4½ tablespoons corn starch	2 tablespoons nuts, chopped
¼ teaspoon salt	

Measure the brown sugar and butter into a heavy saucepan or iron frying pan; caramelize over low heat till brown and bubbly but not burned. Slowly add the hot coffee; simmer until smooth and thick. Scald the milk in the top of the double boiler. Mix the corn starch, salt and cold milk to a paste; stir into the hot milk; cook and stir till smooth and thick. Add the caramel; stir till blended. Cover and continue cooking for 10 minutes. Beat the egg yolks till light; blend a little of the hot caramel with them; stir into the caramel mixture and continue cooking another three minutes. Remove from the heat; add the vanilla. Pour into an oiled baking dish. Cover with a meringue made by combining the stiffly beaten egg whites with the white sugar. Sprinkle with the chopped nuts; brown in a moderate oven. Serves 6.

CHERRY DELIGHT

1¾ cups juice from canned red cherries (heavy syrup)
4 tablespoons corn starch
¼ cup white sugar
1/16 teaspoon salt
¼ cup cold cherry juice
2 tablespoons lemon juice
1 cup canned cherries, drained

Heat the cherry juice to boiling in the top of a double boiler. Mix the corn starch, sugar and salt to a paste with the ¼ cup cold cherry juice. Stir slowly into the hot juice; cook and stir until smooth and thick. Cover; continue cooking over boiling water for 10 minutes, stirring occasionally. Remove from the heat; beat well with the dover beater. Add the lemon juice and drained cherries. Turn into a serving dish; chill thoroughly. Serve with cream. Serves 6.

BLANC MANGE

2 cups milk, scalded
4 tablespoons corn starch
¼ cup white sugar
⅛ teaspoon salt
¼ cup cold milk
½ teaspoon vanilla
2 egg whites (optional)

Scald the milk in the top of the double boiler. Mix the corn starch, sugar and salt with the cold milk; add slowly to the hot milk, stirring constantly till thick. Cover; continue cooking for 10 minutes, stirring occasionally. Remove from the heat; add the vanilla. Fold in the stiffly beaten egg whites if desired. Pour into a glass serving dish and chill. Serve with jam, jelly, canned or fresh fruit, cream, or Lemon Custard Sauce. Serves 6.

CHOCOLATE BLANC MANGE

2 cups milk, scalded
¼ cup white sugar
⅛ teaspoon salt
3 tablespoons corn starch
4 tablespoons cocoa
¼ cup cold milk

Scald the milk in the top of a double boiler. Make a paste of the sugar, salt, corn starch, cocoa and ¼ cup cold milk. Pour slowly into hot milk, stirring constantly until smooth and thick. Cover and cook for 15 minutes, stirring occasionally. Turn into a serving dish. Serve cold with cream. Serves 6.

FLOATING ISLAND

2 eggs, separated
5 tablespoons white sugar
2 cups milk, scalded

2 tablespoons corn starch
⅛ teaspoon salt
1 teaspoon vanilla

Separate the eggs; beat the whites and yolks separately. To the stiffly beaten whites add 1 tablespoon of white sugar; beat again until the mixture peaks. Drop the meringue by spoonfuls on top of the scalded milk. Poach gently; lift off the spoonfuls of meringue and drain. Make a paste of the remainder of the sugar, the corn starch, salt and a little of the hot milk; stir into the hot milk. Cook and stir over boiling water till smooth and thick; cover and continue cooking another 10 minutes. Mix a little of the hot mixture with the well-beaten egg yolks; stir back into the starch mixture. Stir and cook for another three minutes; add the vanilla. Pour into a clear glass serving dish; top with the white meringue. Garnish with flecks of jelly. Serve very cold. Serves 4-5.

BAVARIAN CREAM

1 tablespoon plain gelatine
¼ cup cold water
3 eggs, separated
Pinch of salt
⅓ cup white sugar

1¼ cups hot milk
½ teaspoon vanilla
Green vegetable coloring
Plain sponge cake

Soak the gelatine in the cold water for 5 minutes. Beat the egg yolks until light; add the salt, sugar and hot milk. Cook over boiling water till the mixture coats the spoon. Remove from the heat; add the vanilla and just enough green vegetable coloring to tint the cream a delicate green. Add the dissolved gelatine; chill until the mixture begins to set. Fold in the stiffly beaten egg whites. Line a mould or loaf pan with thin slices of the sponge cake. Spoon the gelatine mixture into the mould; chill till set. Unmould; serve with Vanilla Ice Cream or Custard Sauce. Serves 6.

MINT PUDDING

2 cups hot milk
4 tablespoons corn starch
4 tablespoons white sugar
⅛ teaspoon salt
¼ cup cold milk

1 tablespoon gelatine
¼ cup cold milk
1 or 2 drops oil of peppermint
Green vegetable coloring
¼ cup nuts, chopped

Scald the milk in the top of a double boiler. Make a paste of the corn starch, sugar, salt and cold milk; stir into the hot milk; cook and stir till smooth and thick. Cover and continue cooking for 10 minutes, stirring occasionally. Soak the gelatine in the cold milk for 5 minutes. When the cooked pudding is removed from the heat, add the soaked gelatine; stir till dissolved. Add the drop or two of oil of peppermint if you like the flavor; almond flavoring makes a nice alternative. Add just enough coloring to tint an apple green. Oil an 8″ ring mould; sprinkle the bottom with the chopped nuts. Pour on the pudding mixture; let set till firm; unmould on a clear glass plate; serve with Mocha Sauce and crisp cookies. Serves 6.

BURNT ALMOND BAVARIAN CREAM

1 tablespoon gelatine	3 tablespoons white sugar
¼ cup cold water	1/16 teaspoon salt
2 cups milk, scalded	1½ teaspoons vanilla
6 tablespoons brown sugar	¼ cup almonds, blanched,
3 eggs, separated	chopped and roasted

Soak the gelatine in the cold water for five minutes. Scald the milk in the top of a double boiler. Caramelize the brown sugar over low heat in a heavy frying pan; when brown and bubbly, add slowly to the hot milk; stir till dissolved. Beat the egg yolks lightly with the white sugar and salt; stir into the milk mixture. Cook over hot water (just under boiling) till the mixture coats the spoon, 3 to 4 minutes. Remove from the heat; add the soaked gelatine; stir till dissolved; chill till the mixture begins to set. Fold in the stiffly beaten egg whites, the vanilla and the chopped almonds. Chill till ready to serve. Serve with cream. 6-8 servings.

CHOCOLATE CHARLOTTE

2 tablespoons gelatine	1 cup white sugar
½ cup cold water	⅛ teaspoon salt
3 cups scalded milk	1/16 teaspoon cinnamon
3 squares (3 oz.) unsweetened	1 teaspoon vanilla
chocolate	2 egg whites

Soak the gelatine in the cold water for 5 minutes. Measure the milk and unsweetened chocolate into the top of the double boiler; heat to scalding over boiling water. Blend with the dover beater. Add the sugar, salt, cinnamon and gelatine; stir till dissolved. Remove from the heat; chill until the mixture begins to set. Add the vanilla; fold in the stiffly beaten egg whites. Turn into an oiled ring mould; chill till firm. Unmould; fill the centre with Custard Sauce. Serves 6.

NOTE TO BRIDES: *Use the 2 egg yolks for the sauce. If you want it superlatively smooth, beat with the dover beater just before serving.*

FEATHER SQUARES

1 tablespoon gelatine
  4 tablespoons cold water
1 cup boiling water
  ⅔ cup sugar
Dash of salt

1 tablespoon lemon juice
1 tablespoon grated lemon
  rind
3 egg whites
1 cup oatmeal cookie crumbs

Soak the gelatine in the cold water for 5 minutes. Add the boiling water; stir until dissolved. Add the sugar, salt, lemon juice and rind. Let chill until the mixture begins to set. Fold in the stiffly beaten egg whites. Pour into a square pan 8″ x 8″ which has been brushed with salad oil. Chill until firm. Cut in squares; roll in cookie crumbs; serve with Custard Sauce. Serves 12.

LEMON SNOW

1 tablespoon gelatine
  ¼ cup cold water
½ cup white sugar
  1 cup boiling water
Pinch of salt

1 tablespoon grated lemon
  rind
¼ cup lemon juice
  2 egg whites
¼ cup white sugar

Soak the gelatine in the cold water for 5 minutes. Add ½ cup white sugar and the softened gelatine to the boiling water; stir until dissolved. Add the salt, lemon rind and juice; let chill until the mixture begins to set. Stiffly beat the egg whites; add ¼ cup sugar; beat again until the mixture peaks. Fold into the chilled lemon mixture, using a dover beater. Pour into a clear glass serving dish or into individual dishes. Use the egg yolks to make a thin custard sauce; have it very cold. Serves 6.

NOTE TO BRIDES: *To vary the flavor, substitute ¼ cup orange juice and 1 tablespoon grated orange rind for the lemon rind and juice.*

MAPLE SPONGE

1½ cups milk, scalded
  2 eggs, separated
1 tablespoon gelatine
  ¼ cup cold water

1 cup maple syrup
  ⅛ teaspoon salt
½ teaspoon vanilla

Scald the milk in the top of a double boiler. Beat the egg yolks slightly; combine with a little hot milk; return to the mixture in the double boiler. Blend well; let cook for 3 minutes. In the meantime, soak the gelatine in the cold water. Add to the hot milk mixture; stir until dissolved. Add the maple syrup and salt; blend well. Chill until the mixture begins to set; fold in the stiffly beaten egg whites and the vanilla. Chill before serving. Serve with Fluffy Sauce. Serves 6.

STRAWBERRY SPONGE

1 tablespoon gelatine	2 tablespoons lemon juice
¼ cup cold water	1 teaspoon grated orange rind
½ cup boiling water	Dash of salt
½ cup white sugar	1 pint ripe strawberries
¼ cup orange juice	1 egg white

Soak the gelatine in cold water for 5 minutes; dissolve in the boiling water. Add the sugar; stir till dissolved. Add the orange and lemon juice, the grated rind and the salt. Chill the mixture until it begins to set. Stem the strawberries, saving 8 for garnishing; crush the remainder and fold into the chilled mixture. Fold in the stiffly beaten egg white. Chill in a mould until set. Unmould; serve with chilled Custard Sauce. Serves 6.

STEAMED APPLE DELIGHT

¼ cup shortening	½ teaspoon baking soda
½ cup brown sugar	1 teaspoon baking powder
1 egg	1 teaspoon ginger
½ cup molasses (warm)	1 teaspoon cinnamon
1 tablespoon grated orange rind	½ cup thick sour milk
1½ cups sifted all-purpose flour	1 cup apples, finely chopped

Cream together the shortening and brown sugar. Add the unbeaten egg; beat till light. Add the slightly warm molasses and the orange rind; again beat. Add the sifted dry ingredients alternately with the sour milk; fold in the finely chopped apples. Fill an oiled mould ⅔ full; cover tightly. Steam in a covered steamer for 1½ hours. Serve with Lemon Sauce. Serves 6.

BLUEBERRY ROLY POLY

2 cups sifted all-purpose flour	⅓ cup milk
	1 teaspoon grated lemon rind
3 teaspoons baking powder	3 cups blueberries
½ teaspoon salt	(canned or fresh)
2 tablespoons white sugar	2 tablespoons brown sugar
½ cup shortening	1 tablespoon flour
1 egg, well-beaten	1 teaspoon lemon juice

Sift together the 2 cups flour, the baking powder, salt and white sugar; cut in the shortening. Make a well in the centre; add the well-beaten egg, milk and lemon rind. Mix with a few quick strokes; turn on a floured board and roll into an oblong ½" thick. Sprinkle with a mixture of the blueberries, brown sugar, flour and lemon juice. Roll as for jelly roll; place on an oiled plate. Steam for 1½ hours; serve with Butterscotch Sauce. Serves 6.

CHOCOLATE FEATHER PUDDING

1 egg, well beaten
1 cup white sugar
1 cup milk
1 tablespoon melted fat
1½ ounces unsweetened
chocolate, melted

1½ cups sifted all-purpose
flour
¼ teaspoon salt
2 teaspoons baking powder
½ teaspoon vanilla

Beat the egg till light; gradually beat in the sugar. Blend well; add the milk, melted fat and melted chocolate. Mix with the dover beater till blended. Add the sifted dry ingredients and vanilla; beat well. Pour the batter into an oiled 2-quart mould, filling it ⅔ full. Cover closely and place in a steamer. Cook, covered, for 45 minutes. Serve with Vanilla Sauce. Serves 6.

STEAMED CHRISTMAS PUDDING

1 cup raw carrots, grated
1 cup raw potatoes, grated
1 cup soft bread crumbs
¾ cup suet, finely chopped
2 tablespoons sour milk
½ cup sifted all-purpose
flour
1 teaspoon cinnamon

½ teaspoon allspice
⅛ teaspoon nutmeg
1 cup seedless raisins
1 cup currants
½ cup brown sugar
½ cup corn syrup
½ teaspoon baking soda
1 teaspoon salt

Measure all the ingredients in the order given into a large mixing bowl. Mix lightly with the hands; turn into a 2-quart mould or 8 individual moulds which have been brushed with oil. The moulds should be about ⅔ full. Cover tightly with wax paper. Place in a steamer on a rack; steam until cooked. Small moulds will require about 1½ hours; large moulds about 3 hours. Serve with Fluffy Sauce. Serves 8-10.

DARK SECRET PUDDING

¼ cup shortening
¼ cup brown sugar
¼ cup molasses or corn syrup
1 egg, well beaten
2 cups sifted cake flour
3 teaspoons baking powder

⅔ teaspoon salt
½ teaspoon cinnamon
¼ teaspoon cloves
¼ teaspoon nutmeg
¼ cup milk

Cream together the shortening, sugar and molasses or syrup; beat till fluffy. Add the well-beaten egg; add the sifted dry ingredients alternately with the milk; mix till smooth. The mixture should be thin enough to pour. Fill an oiled 2-quart casserole half full; cover tightly. Steam for 1½ hours; serve hot with Fluffy Sauce. Serves 8.

STEAMED FRUIT PUDDING

½ cup molasses
1 egg, well beaten
1 cup unsweetened applesauce
½ cup raisins, chopped
½ cup uncooked prunes, chopped
1 cup dry bread crumbs

2½ cups sifted all-purpose flour
1 teaspoon salt
½ teaspoon baking soda
1½ teaspoons baking powder
1 teaspoon cinnamon
½ teaspoon ginger
½ cup suet, chopped

Mix together the molasses, well beaten egg and applesauce. Mix the chopped raisins and prunes with the dry bread crumbs; combine with the molasses mixture. Add all the remaining ingredients; mix thoroughly. Turn into one large mould or individual moulds which have been oiled, filling them only half full. Put on oiled lids or tie on wax paper. Place in a steamer and cook for 2½ hours (large mould) or 1½ hours (individual moulds). Serve hot with Orange Sauce. Serves 8-10.

RICH PLUM PUDDING

1 cup stale bread crumbs
½ cup grape juice
3 eggs, lightly beaten
1 cup seeded raisins
½ cup currants
1 cup mixed peel
1 cup suet, chopped

½ cup sifted all-purpose flour
¼ teaspoon nutmeg
1 teaspoon cinnamon
¼ teaspoon mace
½ teaspoon salt
¼ cup brown sugar
2 tablespoons cream

Soak the bread crumbs in the grape juice; beat till smooth. Add the eggs, lightly beaten; add all the remaining ingredients; blend well. Pour into a large oiled mould; cover tightly and steam for 3 hours. Invert on a hot platter; serve with Rich Sauce. Serves 10.

STEAMED PUMPKIN PUDDING

½ cup shortening
¾ cup brown sugar
¼ cup corn syrup
2 eggs, unbeaten
¾ cup canned pumpkin
2 cups sifted pastry flour
1½ teaspoons baking powder

¼ teaspoon baking soda
½ teaspoon nutmeg
½ teaspoon ginger
1 teaspoon cinnamon
1 teaspoon salt
¼ cup thick sour milk
¼ cup nuts, chopped

Cream together the shortening, brown sugar and corn syrup. Add the eggs, one at a time; beat the mixture till light. Add the pumpkin and blend. Add the sifted dry ingredients alternately with the sour milk; add the chopped nuts. Pour into a 1½-quart oiled mould; cover tightly and place in a steamer. Adjust the lid; steam for 2 hours. Serve hot with Fluffy Sauce. Serves 8.

LIGHT STEAMED PUDDING

¼ cup shortening
½ cup white sugar
1 teaspoon vanilla
1 egg, well beaten
1 teaspoon lemon rind, grated
1 teaspoon lemon juice
⅔ cup orange juice

1½ cups sifted all-purpose flour
½ teaspoon salt
3 teaspoons baking powder
1 tablespoon butter
1 tablespoon orange rind, grated
1 tablespoon white sugar

Cream together the shortening, ½ cup white sugar and the vanilla; add the well beaten egg. Combine the grated lemon rind with the fruit juices; add alternately with the sifted dry ingredients; stir lightly. Rub a 1½-quart mould with the butter; sprinkle with the grated orange rind and 1 tablespoon white sugar. Pour the batter into the mould and cover; place in a steamer over boiling water and cover tightly. Steam for 1½ hours. Unmould and serve with Lemon Sauce. Serves 8-10.

STEAMED MARMALADE PUDDING

¼ pound suet or shortening
½ cup white sugar
2 eggs, separated
1 tablespoon vanilla
1 cup orange marmalade

¾ cup soft bread crumbs
½ cup milk
1 teaspoon baking powder
⅛ teaspoon salt

Run the suet through the chopper; blend with the sugar; cream well with a spoon. Beat the egg yolks till light; blend with the first mixture. Add the vanilla and marmalade. Combine the bread crumbs and milk; beat till smooth; add the baking powder and salt. Combine with the suet mixture; fold in the stiffly beaten egg whites. Cover tightly; steam 2½ hours. Serve with a rich Butter Sauce. Serves 8.

NOTE TO BRIDES: *This pudding may be steamed in 2 or 3 containers for extra desserts.*

RASPBERRY ROLY-POLY

1 cup sifted all-purpose flour
2 teaspoons baking powder
¼ teaspoon salt

2 tablespoons shortening
⅓ cup milk
1 cup raspberry jam

Sift together the flour, baking powder and salt. Cut in the shortening; add the milk. Mix lightly; roll in an oblong about ¼″ thick. Spread with the raspberry jam; roll up as a jelly roll. Place on a plate dredged with flour; cover with a square of clean cheese cloth. Place in the steamer; cover tightly; steam for 45 minutes. Serve hot with a fruit sauce. Serves 6.

WHOLE WHEAT STEAMED PUDDING

⅓ cup shortening
  1 cup brown sugar
4 eggs, well beaten
  ¼ cup sifted all-purpose
    flour
  2 teaspoons baking powder

1 teaspoon salt
  ½ teaspoon cinnamon
  ½ cup whole wheat flour
  1 cup mixed peel, chopped
1½ cups raisins, chopped
  ½ cup currants

Cream the shortening; gradually add the sugar; add the well beaten eggs. Sift together the flour, baking powder, salt and cinnamon; add the whole wheat flour, chopped peel and fruit. Combine the two mixtures; mix well. Turn into an oiled 2-quart mould; cover tightly. Steam on a rack in a large kettle or steamer for 3 hours. Serve with Burnt Sugar Sauce. Serves 6.

DO'S AND DONT'S FOR HOME-MADE ICE CREAM

Sugar does not freeze nearly so well as honey or corn syrup, so keep the sugar content low.

A small amount of gelatine makes a smoother ice cream.

Stir after the mixture begins to set, stirring the half-frozen edges in to the centre.

Set the refrigerator at quick freezing half an hour before the mixture is poured into the tray. When the ice cream is well frozen, turn your dial back again to normal.

Don't beat the cream till stiff, but just until it is like thick custard. If it's stiffly beaten, it freezes like cheese.

Don't expect a mixture to freeze in less than 3 hours.

BUTTERSCOTCH ICE CREAM

½ cup white sugar
  ¼ cup corn syrup
1¾ cups milk, scalded
  1 tablespoon corn starch

⅛ teaspoon salt
  1 tablespoon cold milk
2 teaspoons vanilla
1 cup whipping cream

Measure the sugar and corn syrup into an iron frying pan. Stir and cook over low heat until caramelized; the whole mixture should be brown and bubbly. Slowly add the scalded milk; stir till dissolved. Stir in a paste made by combining the corn starch, salt and cold milk; cook and stir until smooth and thick. Continue cooking over low heat for 5 minutes; cool; add the vanilla. Pour into the freezing tray of the refrigerator; freeze till the mixture begins to set. Remove from the tray; fold in the whipped cream. Return to freezing tray; continue freezing for 2 hours. Serves 6-8.

CUSTARD ICE CREAM

1 can condensed sweetened milk (15 oz.)	1 can water
	2½ tablespoons corn starch
1 can water	2 eggs
1 can evaporated milk (15 oz.)	1½ teaspoons vanilla

Combine the condensed milk, the evaporated milk and the 2 cans of water in the top of the double boiler. Mix a little of the milk mixture with the corn starch to make a paste. Scald the milk; stir in the corn starch paste; stir and cook till smooth and thick. Slightly beat the eggs; mix with a little of the hot mixture; stir into the starch mixture. Stir well, cover and cook for 5 minutes. Chill; add the vanilla; freeze in a 2-quart crank freezer, using 8 parts crushed ice to 1 part coarse salt. Serves 8.

FRESH STRAWBERRY ICE

¾ cup white sugar	1 cup fresh strawberries, crushed
2 cups water	(pulp and juice)
¼ cup corn syrup	1 tablespoon lemon juice

Make a syrup by boiling together the sugar, water and corn syrup for 10 minutes. Cool; add the strawberry pulp and juice; add the lemon juice. Pour into the freezing tray of an automatic refrigerator and freeze, stirring every 5 minutes until mixture begins to set. Serves 6 to 8.

NOTE TO BRIDES: *This ice must be served at once as it melts very quickly. The same recipe may be used for raspberries and peaches.*

HOMEMADE ICE CREAM

1 teaspoon gelatine	⅛ teaspoon salt
1 tablespoon cold water	1 egg, slightly beaten
1 cup rich milk	1 teaspoon vanilla
⅜ cup white sugar	1 cup 18% cream
½ tablespoon corn starch	

Soak the gelatine in the cold water for 5 minutes. Scald the milk in the top of the double boiler. Mix together the sugar, corn starch and salt. Add a little hot milk; blend well and stir into the remaining milk. Cook over boiling water till smooth and thick (about 10 minutes). Pour some of the hot mixture into the beaten egg; blend well and stir into the corn starch mixture. Continue cooking for three minutes. Remove from the heat; add the softened gelatine; stir till dissolved. Chill; add the vanilla and cream. Pour into the freezing tray of the refrigerator; freeze, stirring two or three times as the mixture sets. Serves 8-10.

BAKED ALASKA

Temperature: 450°F.   Time: 4-5 minutes

Sponge cake, 1″ thick   5 tablespoons white sugar
   1 quart brick ice cream   1 teaspoon corn starch
3 egg whites

Cover a board or heavy cardboard with paper; place the cake in the centre; unmould the ice cream on the cake. There should be at least 1″ of cake extending beyond the ice cream on all sides. Stiffly beat the egg whites; add the sugar and corn starch. Beat again until the mixture peaks. Cover the ice cream and cake with the meringue; place on a rack in a hot oven to brown. Slip from the board to a serving dish and serve at once. Serves 6.

CANDIED DESSERT

1 cup brown sugar   4 cups cornflakes
   ¼ cup butter

Measure the sugar and butter into a heavy frying pan; let melt and bubble till the mixture is brown but not burned. Have ready on oiled mixing bowl; measure the cornflakes into the bowl. Pour the hot sugar mixture over the cornflakes and mix quickly. Press the mixture into a small oiled ring mould; let cool. When ready to serve, unmould on a plate; fill the centre with vanilla ice cream. It's like a rich candied cookie. Serves 6.

WHIPPED APPLE SAUCE

1 egg white   ½ teaspoon vanilla
   1 apple, grated   *or* 1 teaspoon lemon juice
2 tablespoons white sugar   *or* ½ teaspoon cinnamon

Stiffly beat the egg white. Peel, core and grate the apple; fold in the egg white; fold in the sugar and flavoring. Chill. This sauce should be made at the last minute and served immediately. Serves 4-5.

RICH BUTTER SAUCE

½ cup butter   1 teaspoon vanilla
   1 cup fine white sugar   1 tablespoon grated orange rind
1 egg, well beaten

Cream the butter till creamy but not oily. Sift the sugar; add gradually while creaming the butter. Blend in the well beaten egg, the vanilla and the orange rind. Cook over boiling water, beating constantly, until the sauce is slightly foamy. Serves 8.

BITTERSWEET SAUCE

¾ cup orange juice
1 teaspoon grated lemon rind
1½ teaspoons lemon juice
5 tablespoons white sugar

1 teaspoon corn starch
2 eggs, separated
⅛ teaspoon salt
¼ teaspoon almond flavoring

Measure the orange juice, the lemon rind and lemon juice, sugar and corn starch into the top of a double boiler; blend well; simmer over direct heat for 5 minutes. Beat the egg yolks till light; pour the hot sauce over them; heat again for 3 minutes. This mixture should never actually boil. Remove from the heat; fold in the stiffly beaten egg whites, the salt and the almond flavoring. Keep heated over boiling water. Serve with steamed puddings. Serves 6.

BURNT SUGAR SAUCE

⅓ cup white sugar
⅓ cup corn syrup
1 cup boiling water
⅛ teaspoon salt

⅔ tablespoon corn starch
1 tablespoon cold water
2 tablespoons butter
½ teaspoon vanilla

Measure the sugar and corn syrup into an iron frying pan; cook slowly over low heat till brown and bubbly. Add the boiling water slowly; blend. Mix the salt and corn starch to a paste with the cold water; add to the hot mixture. Simmer gently 5 minutes, stirring occasionally. Remove from the heat; beat in the butter and vanilla. Serves 6.

WHIPPING CREAM SUBSTITUTES

1. *Top Cream:* Syphon off the top 1½" of cream from your quart bottle of Jersey milk. Let that stand for 24 hours; it whips up well.

2. *Evaporated Milk:* Use small 6-ounce cans of evaporated sweetened milk and prepare it this way: The secret of success is to have the milk very cold. Milk merely allowed to stand in the food compartment of the refrigerator will not be cold enough to insure satisfactory results. If you have an automatic refrigerator the best plan is to empty the milk into the freezing tray and keep it there till fine crystals begin to form around the edges. Or you may place an unopened can in one of the freezing compartments until it is thoroughly chilled. If you use ice, pack the unopened can in a bowl with a salt-ice mixture. No matter what method you use, the milk should be chilled to about 40°F. Then pour it into a cold bowl and whip rapidly with a cold beater. If the milk does not whip properly, it should be re-chilled and whipped again. It will

not turn to butter. The addition of 2 tablespoons lemon juice to 1 can results in a stiffer and more lasting "whip", and this is recommended in cases where the tart flavor will be agreeable.

3. *Egg Whites:* Stiffly beat an egg white, add as much finely grated apple as it will absorb, plus 1 tablespoon of sugar for sweetening. A meringue baked in the oven on an oiled sheet and then lifted to the top of the pudding has a better appearance than if baked on the dessert.

4. *The Gelatine Topping:*

1½ teaspoons gelatine	1 tablespoon sugar
2 tablespoons milk	½ teaspoon vanilla
1 cup light cream	

Measure the gelatine and cold milk into a glass. Let stand for 5 minutes; place the glass in a pan of hot water; let stand till dissolved. Have the cream well chilled; pour it into a deep bowl so that the cream covers the beaters. Add the gelatine; beat until the cream whips. If the cream is to be used for topping, add 1 tablespoon of sugar and ½ teaspoon of vanilla; beat till dissolved. 6 servings.

BUTTERSCOTCH SAUCE

3 tablespoons fat	¼ cup thin cream
1 cup brown sugar	2 tablespoons corn starch
¾ cup water	⅛ teaspoon salt

Melt the fat in a heavy saucepan; add the brown sugar; stir and cook over moderate heat until brown and bubbly. Slowly add the water; heat until dissolved. Make a paste with the cream, corn starch and salt. Stir into the hot mixture. Reduce the heat; cook and stir till smooth and thick. This is a rich sauce and may be thinned down with cream if desired. We like it rich and not too much of it. Serves 4-5.

EASY CHOCOLATE SAUCE

½ cup white sugar	2 squares (2 ounces) unsweetened chocolate
½ cup water	¼ teaspoon vanilla

Measure the sugar, water and chocolate into a saucepan. Cook and stir over low heat until dissolved. Let simmer until the sauce is thick. Remove from the heat; add the vanilla. Serve hot with vanilla ice cream. Serves 6.

Peppermint Chocolate Sauce: Add six crushed after-dinner mints to the hot chocolate sauce; serve hot.

CHOCOLATE MILK SAUCE

2 squares (2 ounces)
  unsweetened chocolate
1 cup white sugar
2 tablespoons corn syrup

2 cups milk
2 tablespoons butter
1 teaspoon vanilla

Measure the chocolate, sugar, corn syrup and milk into a heavy saucepan. Stir over a hot burner till the sugar is dissolved; reduce the heat; cook, without stirring, until a little of the mixture dropped in cold water forms a soft ball. Remove from the heat; let stand till the bubbling ceases. Beat in the butter and vanilla; serve warm. Delicious with hot cake puddings or ice cream. Serves 6.

CUSTARD SAUCE

2 cups milk
3 egg yolks
¼ cup white sugar

Dash of salt
1 teaspoon vanilla

Scald the milk. Lightly beat the egg yolks; add the sugar and salt; stir into the hot milk. Cook over hot water (not boiling) till the mixture coats the spoon. Add the vanilla. Chill before serving. Serves 6.

CREAM CUSTARD SAUCE

2 cups milk, scalded
1 tablespoon corn starch
¼ cup white sugar

⅛ teaspoon salt
2 egg yolks
1 teaspoon vanilla

Scald the milk in the top of the double boiler. Combine the corn starch, sugar and salt; mix with a little of the hot milk; stir into the remainder of the milk. Cook and stir till smooth and thick; continue cooking for 10 minutes. Beat the egg yolks slightly; mix them with a little of the hot starch mixture; stir back into the remainder of the mixture. Cook over hot (not boiling) water for three minutes. Remove from the heat and beat in the vanilla. Chill before serving. Serves 6.

FLUFFY SAUCE

2 eggs, separated
  Dash of salt
½ cup white sugar

1 teaspoon vanilla
½ teaspoon almond flavoring

Separate the eggs. Beat the whites till stiff and glossy; add the salt and ¼ cup white sugar; beat again. Beat the yolks until light and lemon colored; add ¼ cup white sugar; beat again until light. Combine the two mixtures; fold in the flavorings. Chill until ready to serve. Serves 6.

FOAMY SAUCE

2 egg whites
Few grains of salt
½ cup brown sugar

Grated rind and
juice of 1 orange
Juice of ½ lemon

Beat the egg whites and salt until very stiff. Gradually add the sugar and beat until mixture peaks. Add the grated orange rind and fruit juices. Serve at once. Serves 4-6.

FRUIT SAUCE

1 cup fruit juice (peach, orange
or any fruit juice)
1 teaspoon lemon juice
¼ teaspoon grated lemon rind

2 tablespoons corn starch
3 tablespoons sugar
3 tablespoons cold water
Dash of salt

Heat the fruit juices to boiling. Make a paste of the lemon rind, corn starch, sugar, cold water and salt. Stir into the hot mixture. Cook and stir over slow heat until smooth and clear (about 5 minutes). Serve hot with hot puddings. Serves 6.

FUDGE MARSHMALLOW SAUCE

⅓ cup white sugar
2 squares (2 ounces)
unsweetened chocolate, grated
1 teaspoon corn starch

½ cup water
¼ teaspoon vanilla
12 marshmallows

Mix together the sugar and grated chocolate in a heavy sauce-pan; heat gently until the chocolate is melted. Make a paste of the corn starch and cold water; stir into the chocolate mixture; cook and stir until smooth and thick. Remove from the heat; add the vanilla. While the sauce is still hot cut in the marshmallows. Serve warm with frozen desserts. Serves 6.

LEMON SAUCE

1 cup scalded milk
1 teaspoon corn starch
2 tablespoons white sugar

Dash of salt
1 egg, separated
½ teaspoon grated lemon rind

Scald the milk in the top of the double boiler; combine the corn starch, sugar, salt and unbeaten egg yolk. Stir till smooth; add to the hot milk. Cook over hot water, stirring occasionally, till the mixture coats the spoon. Cool slightly; fold in stiffly beaten egg white and lemon rind. Chill before serving. Serves 6.

RICH LEMON SAUCE

¾ cup white sugar
  2 tablespoons corn starch
⅛ teaspoon salt
  ½ cup boiling water

1 egg
  ¼ cup lemon juice
  ½ teaspoon grated lemon rind
  2 tablespoons butter

Mix together the sugar, corn starch and salt in the top of the double boiler. Slowly add the boiling water; stir and cook over direct heat until smooth and thick, about 5 minutes; continue cooking over boiling water for 10 minutes. Beat the egg lightly; add a little of the hot starch mixture. Blend well and stir back into the starch mixture; continue cooking for 3 minutes. Remove from the heat; add the lemon juice, rind and the butter. Beat till smooth; serve hot. Serves 6.

MAPLE CUSTARD SAUCE

2 cups milk, scalded
  ⅓ cup maple syrup
2 eggs

1 tablespoon corn starch
  ¼ teaspoon salt
  ½ teaspoon vanilla

Scald the milk in the top of the double boiler; add the maple syrup; heat over boiling water until blended. Beat the eggs lightly; add the corn starch and salt. Stir into the hot mixture; cook and stir until smooth and thick. Cover; continue cooking 8 minutes. Remove from the heat; add vanilla. Chill and serve with hot gingerbread. Serves 6.

RICH MOCHA SAUCE

⅓ cup butter
  1 cup fine white sugar
1 tablespoon strong coffee infusion

2 eggs, separated
  ½ cup cream
2 tablespoons vanilla

Beat the butter till creamy; gradually add the sugar; beat in the coffee. Add the unbeaten egg yolks one at a time; blend well; mix in the cream. Cook over boiling water till slightly thickened. Remove from the heat; add the vanilla; fold in the stiffly beaten egg whites. Serve with plum pudding. Serves 10.

ORANGE SAUCE

2 egg yolks
  3 tablespoons white sugar

⅔ cup orange juice

Beat the egg yolks lightly; add the sugar and orange juice. Blend well. Cook over direct heat until the mixture coats the spoon. Chill; serve with desserts. Serves 6.

FLUFFY ORANGE SAUCE

½ cup orange juice
  1/16 teaspoon salt
1 teaspoon grated lemon rind
  1½ teaspoons lemon juice

4 tablespoons white sugar
1 teaspoon corn starch
1 egg yolk, slightly beaten
1 egg white, stiffly beaten

Combine all the ingredients except the egg white; beat well; cook over low heat till thick and clear. Remove from the heat; fold in the stiffly beaten egg white. Serve with steamed puddings. Serves 6.

PEACH SAUCE

1 cup canned peach juice
  1 tablespoon corn starch
⅛ teaspoon salt
  1 tablespoon lemon juice

1 teaspoon lemon rind
2 tablespoons (or more) sugar
1 tablespoon butter

Heat the peach juice to boiling in a saucepan. Mix together the corn starch, salt, lemon juice, lemon rind and sugar. Stir into the hot liquid; cook and stir until smooth and thick. Remove from the heat; add the butter; beat till light. Serves 6.

VANILLA SAUCE

½ cup brown sugar
  1 tablespoon flour
Dash of salt

1 cup boiling water
1 tablespoon butter
1 teaspoon vanilla

Mix together in a saucepan the brown sugar, flour and salt. Add the boiling water slowly; cook and stir over direct heat till smooth and slightly thickened; simmer for 5 minutes. Remove from the heat; add the butter and vanilla. Stir till dissolved; serve hot. Serves 6.

WHIPPED SAUCE

¼ teaspoon gelatine
  1 teaspoon cold water
½ cup evaporated milk

1 tablespoon white sugar
1 teaspoon vanilla

Soak the gelatine in the water for 5 minutes. In the meantime heat the evaporated milk to scalding. Dissolve the gelatine in it; chill. When it is quite cold, beat with a dover beater till the mixture peaks. Add the sugar and vanilla; beat again. Serve like whipped cream on hot gingerbread. Serves 6.

CHAPTER 10

Fish and Fish Sauces

FISH CHOWDER

¼ pound salt pork, diced
  1½ cups onion, chopped
1½ pounds fresh haddock
  or cod fillet
2 teaspoons salt

½ teaspoon pepper
  4 medium sized potatoes, diced
1 cup carrots, diced
3 cups hot water
3 cups milk

Pan fry the salt pork in a deep kettle or Dutch Oven till golden brown and crisp. Add the onion; cook and stir till tender. Have the fish cut in small pieces; rub it with a mixture of the salt and pepper; add to the kettle together with the potatoes and carrots. Add the hot water; simmer 25 minutes, uncovered. Add the milk, bring to a rapid boil. Serve hot with crisp crackers. Serves 6.

BOILED ATLANTIC COD

Wrap the cod in thin cheesecloth; place on a rack in a deep kettle; cover with boiling water to which has been added a little salt and vinegar. Allow 1 teaspoon salt and 1 tablespoon vinegar to each quart of water. After the fish has been boiling for 5 minutes, add some cold water to reduce the temperature quickly. Simmer till tender.

BAKED FILLETS WITH TOMATO JUICE

Temperature: 350°F.

2 pounds quick frozen fillets
  3 tablespoons fat or salad oil
1 onion, chopped
  2 tablespoons sifted flour
1 cup tomato juice or
  canned tomatoes

Time: 30 minutes

¼ cup celery, chopped
  1 teaspoon salt
Dash of pepper
  1 whole clove
1 teaspoon white sugar

Place the fish fillets in a well oiled, shallow baking dish. Heat the fat in a saucepan; add the chopped onion; cook and stir till the onion is tender. Blend in the flour; add the tomato juice or canned tomatoes; stir and cook till smooth and thick. Add all remaining ingredients; blend well; pour over the fillets. Bake in a moderate oven (350°F.) until the fish will flake. Serve with baked potatoes and green peas; a Baked Lemon Pudding for dessert completes the meal. Serves 6.

COD CASSEROLE

3 tablespoons butter
3 tablespoons flour
2 cups milk
½ teaspoon salt

Dash of pepper
½ cup cheese, grated
3 cups cooked cod, flaked
½ cup buttered cracker crumbs

Melt the butter in a saucepan; blend in the flour; let bubble for 3 minutes, stirring constantly. Add the milk slowly; cook and stir until smooth and thick. Remove from the heat; add the seasonings and cheese. Stir till the cheese is melted. Put a layer of fish in a 1½-quart casserole; cover with the sauce. Continue until the dish is full; cover with the buttered crumbs. Bake in a moderate oven (350°F.) till the crumbs are brown. Serves 6.

BAKED FILLETS

Temperature: 550°F.
2 pounds fillet haddock or cod
½ cup water
½ cup milk
1 tablespoon salt
¾ cup yellow corn meal
or cracker crumbs

Time: 10-15 minutes
Dash of pepper and
paprika
1 teaspoon lemon rind,
grated
1 tablespoon lemon juice
2 tablespoons salad oil

Cut the fillet in serving pieces and dip in a mixture of the water, milk and salt. Mix the corn meal or crumbs, the pepper, paprika and grated lemon rind; roll the liquid-dipped fish in the mixture; place in a shallow oiled pan. Mix the lemon juice and salad oil; sprinkle over the fish. Bake in a very hot oven; do not turn during baking. Lift carefully from the baking pan to a hot platter and serve at once. Serves 6.

FILLETS IN BATTER

2 pounds fresh fillets
1 tablespoon vinegar
1 cup sifted all-purpose flour
½ teaspoon salt

Dash of pepper
1 egg, slightly beaten
1 cup milk
1 tablespoon melted shortening

Cut the fillets in serving pieces; brush lightly with vinegar. Sift together the flour, salt and pepper. Slightly beat the egg; add the milk and melted shortening; mix till light with the dover beater. Pour into the flour mixture all at once; again beat till thick and smooth. Have the fat hot (375°F.); dip the fillet in batter till well covered; deep fry till golden brown. The fillets may also be pan fried, using about 4 tablespoons of fat in the frying pan. Serves 6.

FILLET ROLL-UPS

Temperature: 425°F.   Time: 15-20 minutes

2 fresh fillets of cod or haddock   2 tablespoons fat
  1½ cups soft bread crumbs   ¼ teaspoon salt
½ cup cooked or canned   Dash of pepper
  mushrooms, chopped   1 egg, well beaten

Cut the fillets in half crosswise. Mix together the crumbs, mushrooms, fat, seasoning and egg. Spread each half-fillet with the mixture; roll up and fasten with toothpicks or tie with string. Place in a shallow baking dish and bake in a hot oven till tender and brown. Serve with mashed potatoes and buttered green cabbage. Serves 4.

BAKED HALIBUT STEAK

Temperature: 350°F.   Time: 1 hour

1½-2 pounds halibut steak   ½ cup milk
  cut 1″ thick   1 tablespoon green pickle or
2 teaspoons salt   green pepper, chopped
  6 tablespoons fat   Dash of paprika
½ cup flour

Sprinkle each side of the steak with ½ teaspoon salt. Melt the fat in the saucepan; blend in the flour and the remaining teaspoon of salt; bubble very gently for 3 minutes. Add the milk slowly. Stir and cook till smooth and thick. Add the chopped green pickle or green pepper. Spread half this mixture in a shallow oiled baking dish. Place the halibut steak on top of the mixture; spread the remainder over the fish. Sprinkle lightly with the paprika. Bake uncovered in a moderate oven (350°F.) for one hour. Serve with oven browned potatoes, canned green beans and a Peach Upside-down Cake for dessert. Serves 4-5.

BAKED WHOLE HADDOCK

Temperature: 500°F.   Time: 10 minutes
            400°F.   20 minutes

1 haddock, 3 to 4 pounds   1 teaspoon poultry dressing
  1 cup celery, chopped   4 cups day-old bread crumbs
1 cup boiling water   ¾ teaspoon salt
  3 tablespoons fat   ¼ teaspoon pepper
¼ cup onion, chopped

Cook the celery in the boiling water till tender. Drain; reserve ¼ cup of the liquid. Heat the fat in a saucepan; add the chopped onion; cook slowly till tender, stirring to keep from browning. Add the poultry dressing, crumbs, seasonings, celery and the celery liquid. In the meantime, let the fish stand in salt water for 5 minutes, allowing 1 tablespoon of salt to each cup of water. Drain and dry. Make 3 or 4 incisions in the skin so that it will not crack during baking. Stuff with the prepared filling; close the opening with toothpicks or sew with coarse thread. Brush lightly with oil; bake in a hot oven. Serve with mashed potatoes, Tartar Sauce and a salad. Serves 6.

BAKED FISH LOAF

Temperature: 400°F.   Time: 30 minutes

2 tablespoons fat   ½ teaspoon salt
  2 cups cooked potatoes,   ⅛ teaspoon pepper
    thinly sliced   Dash of mace
1½ pounds fresh or salt   ½ cup milk
  finnan haddie (or any fish   2 tablespoons parsley,
    in season)   chopped
1 egg, well beaten   1 tablespoon sweet green
  ¾ cup soft bread crumbs   pickle, chopped

Melt the fat; pour into the bottom of a loaf pan 9″ x 5″ x 3″. Cover the bottom with over-lapping layers of the thinly sliced potatoes. Dust lightly with salt and pepper. Freshen the fish, if necessary; flake; add the well beaten egg, crumbs, seasonings, milk, parsley and pickle. Pack tightly in the pan on top of the potatoes. Bake in a hot oven for 30 minutes. Loosen with a spatula; invert on a hot platter. Serve with a tossed green salad. Serves 6.

SPECIAL BAKED SALMON

Temperature: 375°F.   Time: 30 minutes

2 cups bread cubes, 1½″ thick   1 teaspoon salt
  1 pound can salmon,   ⅛ teaspoon pepper
    (2 cups)   2 cups milk, scalded
3 tablespoons butter   ¼ cup celery, chopped
  1 small onion, chopped   2 tablespoons green pickle,
3 tablespoons sifted pastry flour   chopped

Use stale bread for cubing. Toast the cubes in moderate oven till golden brown. Place in bottom of an oiled 1½ quart casserole. Remove the skin, bones and oil from the salmon; flake. Place on top of the toasted cubes. Melt the butter in the saucepan; add the chopped onion. Stir gently until cooked; add the sifted flour, salt and pepper; let bubble for 3 minutes. Slowly add the milk; stir and cook until smooth. Add the chopped celery and pickle. Pour over the flaked salmon; bake in a moderate oven for 30 minutes. Serve with hot buttered cabbage. Serves 6.

SALMON ROUND

Temperature: 350°F.   Time: 45 minutes

1 pound can salmon
  ⅓ cup scalded milk
⅔ cup soft bread crumbs
  1 tablespoon corn starch
    dissolved in 1 tablespoon
    cold milk

1 egg
  1 teaspoon salt
  ½ teaspoon dry mustard
  1 tablespoon lemon juice
  1 tablespoon parsley or green
    pickle, chopped

Remove the skin and bones from the salmon; flake. Scald the milk in the top of the double boiler; cook the crumbs and dissolved corn starch in the hot milk for 5 minutes. Remove from the heat; add the slightly beaten egg, seasonings, lemon juice, parsley and fish. Turn into a 2-quart oiled casserole. Bake in a moderate oven in a pan of hot water until firm. Serves 6.

SALMON RING WITH CREAMED EGGS

3 tablespoons butter
  1 tablespoon onion,
    finely chopped
3 tablespoons corn starch
  ½ teaspoon salt
Dash of pepper

1½ cups scalded milk
  1 pound can salmon, flaked
2 tablespoons lemon juice
  1 tablespoon parsley,
    chopped
1 egg, well beaten

Melt the butter in a saucepan; add the onion; cook until golden brown. Add the corn starch and seasonings. Let bubble over low heat for 3 minutes. Add the milk; cook and stir till smooth and thick. Add the salmon, lemon juice, parsley and well beaten egg; stir well. Pour into an oiled 9″ ring mould; set in a pan of hot water; oven bake for 1 hour. Loosen the edge of the mould; let stand a few minutes before unmoulding. Fill the centre with creamed eggs or peas and carrots. Serves 8.

SALMON ROLL

Temperature: 350°F.   Time: 45 minutes

Turn an empty salt bag inside-out; butter it well; dust with fine crumbs. Fill with this mixture:

1 pound can salmon, flaked
  (2 cups)
1 egg
  1 tablespoon sugar
1 teaspoon salt

1 teaspoon mustard
  1 tablespoon vinegar
1 cup milk
  ½ cup cracker crumbs
1 cup cooked macaroni

Drain the fish; remove the skin and bones; flake. Slightly beat the egg; add all the remaining ingredients. Mix well; pack into the bag; place on a trivet in a roasting pan; bake uncovered in a moderate oven for 45 minutes. Slit the bag with scissors;

serve the salmon in slices with tartar sauce, escalloped potatoes and peas. This loaf may be baked in a pan 9″ x 5″ x 3″. Serves 6.

ESCALLOPED FINNAN HADDIE

Temperature: 400°F.   Time: 14 minutes

2 tablespoons fat
  2 cups cooked or canned
    finnan haddie
  1 cup cooked rice
2 hard cooked eggs, chopped
  ½ cup hot milk

½ teaspoon salt
  Dash of pepper
1 tablespoon parsley or green
  pickle, chopped (optional)
½ cup soft bread crumbs
½ cup cheese, grated

Heat the fat in the top of the double boiler. Add the flaked fish, rice, chopped eggs, milk, seasonings and parsley or pickle. Heat thoroughly; pour into a shallow oiled baking dish. Cover with a mixture of the crumbs and cheese. Bake in a fairly hot oven till browned. Serve with a green salad. Serves 6.

OVEN BAKED FISH STEAKS

Temperature: 350°F.   Time: 25-30 minutes

2 pounds fresh fish steaks
  1 teaspoon salt
Dash of pepper and cayenne
  2 tablespoons salad oil

⅛ teaspoon powdered thyme
  2 cups hot milk
½ cup fine cracker crumbs

Lay the steaks singly in a well oiled baking pan. Sprinkle with ½ teaspoon salt, the pepper and cayenne. Heat the salad oil; add the thyme and the reserved ½ teaspoon salt. Brush over the fish steaks; pour the milk carefully around them. Over all, sprinkle the cracker crumbs. Bake in a moderate oven; lift out carefully to a hot platter. Serve with Tartar Sauce. Serves 6.

LEMON BUTTER

¼ cup butter
  1 tablespoon parsley, minced
½ teaspoon salt
  Dash of pepper and paprika

½ teaspoon lemon rind, grated
  4 teaspoons lemon juice
1 green onion, finely chopped

Cream the butter till soft but not oily. Stir constantly while adding all the remaining ingredients. Serve with fish. Serves 6.

EASY TARTAR SAUCE

1 cup mayonnaise (chilled)
  1 teaspoon onion,
    finely chopped
1 teaspoon parsley,
  finely chopped

1 tablespoon green pickle,
  finely chopped
1 teaspoon cider vinegar
1 tablespoon green celery,
  finely chopped

Mix all the ingredients just before serving. Serves 6.

CHAPTER 11

Meat, Meat Sauces and Garnishes

Beef

Beef goes into Canadian homes more often than any other kind of meat. It makes blood and bones, it is rich in body-building proteins, but far too often the last ounce of nourishment isn't squeezed from that meat. The cooking—that's what does the trick.

Here is our guide in using cuts of beef, for the food value of the less tender cuts is high.

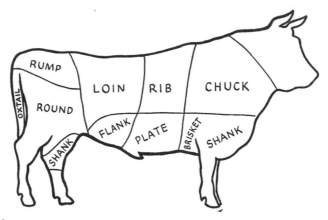

Chuck:

This cut, as you can see, lies between the neck and the rib roast cuts. In Red Brand Beef a chuck roast cut from the 4th and 5th ribs is less expensive than a prime rib roast and yet it's tender and juicy. The rest of the chuck is just right for pot roasts, stewing beef, chopped meat dishes.

Short Ribs:

These are the lower end of the ribs found in the plate. They're rather bony and fat but the meat is tender and flavorsome. Braised short ribs of beef are delicious and thrifty.

Rib Roasts:

The shank and rolled rib roasts are juicy and tender. These roasts are usually cut from the 6th rib through to the 12th, numbering from the neck backward. The tender, mealy portion often called the "rib eye" is largest in the 12th rib; it decreases in size from the 12th forward to the 6th. That's why shank or rolled ribs from the 12th rib are very choice.

Loin:

From the loin come the sirloin steaks, a good buy for 5 to 6 people. The sirloin steaks next the round are larger but not quite so tender as those nearer the short loin. Sirloin roasts come from the large end of the loin. The short loin, that part lying between the loin end and the rib, yields the Porterhouse, T-bone and club steaks. The Porterhouse steaks are cut from the large end, have the greatest amount of tenderloin and weigh approximately 2 lbs. for a 1 inch steak. T-Bone steaks are cut closer to the centre of the short loin and have less tenderloin. Club steaks are cut from close to the rib section and have little or no tenderloin. Filet mignon, the smallest steak of all, is cut from the tenderloin, a long muscle lying inside the rib bones almost the length of the loin.

Rump:

Here's a cut that's superlative in flavor and very reasonable in price. It's a juicy wedge-shaped piece, it's the very best for pot roasts, meat pie, or, if it's Red Brand, it may be roasted.

Round:

Cuts from the round are solid meat, juicy and flavorsome. Again, if it's Red Brand, the top steaks may be broiled or a roast cut from the best. The bottom round is a great favorite for Swiss steak, mock duck, chopped beef and meat loaves.

Oxtail:

You've heard of oxtail soup? The original oxtail comes from the tail, and makes delectable soup.

Shanks, Fore and Aft:

As you can see from the picture, the front shank has a lot more meat than the back. If you're looking for soup bones, the back shank is quite satisfactory, but if you want jellied meat then buy the front shank. It will give you a delicious pot of soup and a loaf 7 inches by 5 inches of jellied meat. Use some flavoring in cooking the meat; chopped celery tops, onions and a clove or two make a nice combination.

Flank:

Here is a practically boneless cut and it's about two-thirds lean. More than that, the price is very moderate. The flank steak which the butcher will peel from the flank makes a delicious steak rolled and stuffed. The steak can also be filleted and baked. The lean part of the flank cut up makes a delectable stew or meat pie. Run it through the coarse knife of the chopper and you have the perfect base for a hamburger meat loaf or individual meat rolls.

The Plate:

This cut, as you can see, lies just below the beef ribs and between the brisket and the flank. It's a thin piece of meat about one-third fat, fairly well flavored but usually tough. It can be used for chopped meat, for stews, for corned beef or for pot roasts. Remember, when buying it, to allow for plenty of shrinkage; the fat cooks away.

The Brisket:

It's a very juicy and well-flavored piece of meat, the brisket. It's a favorite cut for corned beef. It has a large fat content, so if you're using brisket for stews, meat pies or hamburgers, be sure to remove some of the fat before cooking.

BEEF ROASTING POINTS

Beef roasted at a high temperature shrinks about 40%. Roasted at a constant lower temperature, the shrinkage is about 25%. The lower temperature gives a tender, well cooked meat and more of it.

Do not cover, baste or turn the roast. Do not add water to the pan.

Whether the salt is added before or during cooking does not affect the tenderness.

BEEF ROASTING TEMPERATURES

Cut of Beef	Approximate Time		Tempera-ture
	3-5½ lbs. weight	5½-8 lbs. weight	
ROLLED RIB ROAST			
Weight after boning, rolling			
Rare..........	40 min. per lb.	31 min. per lb.	
Medium ...:....	46 min. per lb.	36 min. per lb.	325°F.
Well-Done	52 min. per lb.	41 min. per lb.	
STANDING RIB ROAST			
Rare...........	27 min. per lb.	21 min. per lb.	
Medium	34 min. per lb.	27 min. per lb.	325°F.
Well-Done	41 min. per lb.	33 min. per lb.	

FRENCH CANADIAN BRAISED BEEF

2 pounds stewing beef	1½ cups water
¼ cup corn starch	1 cup carrots diced,
2 teaspoons salt	1 cup green beans (Cut in
Dash of pepper	1″ lengths)
¼ cup fat	12 new potatoes
1 medium onion, finely	1 cup cream of mushroom
chopped	soup, (condensed)

Wipe the meat and cut in serving pieces. With the edge of a saucer, pound in as much corn starch as it will take. Sprinkle with the salt and pepper. Heat the fat in an iron frying pan or Dutch Oven; add the chopped onion; cook until golden brown. Turn in the beef; sear on all sides. Cover with water. Simmer gently till almost tender. Add the carrots, beans and new potatoes; add the mushroom soup. Simmer until the vegetables are tender. Serves 6.

DELICIOUS CORNED BEEF

Temperature: 350°F.	Time: 30 minutes
6 pounds corned beef	1 tablespoon prepared mustard
2 whole cloves	¼ cup brown sugar
1 onion	⅓ cup chili sauce
1 stalk celery	¼ cup cider vinegar
3 tablespoons fat	¼ cup cold water

Have the butcher give you a solid, well shaped piece of corned beef, preferably a brisket cut. Wipe, trim and tie into shape. Put in a large kettle; cover with cold water, add the cloves, onion and celery; bring to a boil. Skim, cover and simmer gently until tender (about 5 hours). Lift from the pan to a shallow baking dish. Melt the fat; add all the remaining ingredients. Cook and stir till well blended. Pour over the meat; bake in a moderate oven for 30 minutes. Baste the meat two or three times during the baking. Serve hot with a savoury sauce. Serves 10.

SPECIAL HAMBURGER CAKES

6 slices stale bread	Dash of pepper
½ cup tomato juice or	¼ teaspoon nutmeg
canned tomatoes	1 onion, finely chopped
1½ pounds chuck steak, ground	3 tablespoons fat
1½ teaspoons salt	

Cut the crusts from the bread; pour the tomato juice over the slices. Let stand till soft; stir till smooth; add the meat, seasonings and onion. Blend well; shape into 12 small flat cakes. Heat the fat; pan fry the hamburgers till brown. Serve with cole slaw. Serves 6.

HAMBURGER SQUARES

Temperature: 425°F.

Time: 25 minutes

2 cups sifted all-purpose flour
  3 teaspoons baking powder
2 teaspoons salt
  ½ cup shortening
1 egg, well beaten
  ⅓ cup milk

1 tablespoon fat
  ¼ cup onion, chopped
1 pound chuck steak, ground
  Dash of pepper and mace
1 tablespoon prepared mustard
  ¼ cup Chili Sauce

Sift together the flour, baking powder and 1 teaspoon salt; cut in the shortening. Make a well in the centre; add the well beaten egg and milk. Stir lightly; turn the batter on a floured board. Knead for 20 counts; divide the batter in half; roll one half into a rectangle 12″ x 6″. Heat the fat in a frying pan; add the onion; cook and stir until tender. Add the meat; cook, stirring with a fork, until almost tender. Add the remaining 1 teaspoon salt, the pepper and mace; spread on the tea biscuit rectangle and press into shape. Spread with a mixture of the mustard and Chili Sauce. Roll out the second half of the batter; place on top of the meat. Cut into squares and place on an oiled cookie sheet. Bake in a hot oven for 25 minutes; serve with a tomato sauce. Serves 6.

BEEF HAMBURGER PIE

Temperature: 450°F.

Time: 20 minutes

2 onions, diced
  6 potatoes, cubed
2 stalks celery, diced
  6 carrots, diced
1 pound chuck steak, ground
  ½ pound fresh pork, ground
½ teaspoon salt
  Dash of pepper
¼ teaspoon dry mustard

3 tablespoons flour
  3 tablespoons fat
2½ cups canned tomatoes
  ½ cup vegetable water
1 teaspoon sugar
  ½ teaspoon salt
Plain pastry
  2 tablespoons cream

Dice the vegetables; combine and cook till tender, using as little water as possible. When tender, drain and save the vegetable water (you should have ½ cup). Mix together the meats, ½ teaspoon salt, the pepper and mustard; shape into 12 small balls; roll in the flour. Heat the fat; sear the small patties in it till crisp and brown; place in a deep casserole. Heat the tomatoes; add the vegetable water, sugar and ½ teaspoon salt; add the cooked vegetables. Pour over the meat balls. Cover with a rich pastry top and glaze with cream; bake in a hot oven till golden brown. Serves 8.

HAMBURGER LOAF

Temperature: 350°F.   Time: 55 minutes

1 pound chuck steak, ground   ¾ teaspoon salt
  ¼ pound fresh pork, ground   Dash of pepper and paprika
  ¼ pound smoked ham, ground   1 loaf bread
  1 onion, finely chopped   2 tablespoons melted fat

Blend the meats, onion and seasonings. Remove the crusts from the bread; cut a square from the centre, leaving the walls of the loaf about 1" thick. Brush them inside and out with melted fat (bacon fat is ideal); bake in a moderate oven for 10 minutes. Remove from the oven and fill with the meat mixture; bake again for 45 minutes. Serve with tomato sauce. Serves 6.

BROILED HAMBURGERS

Temperature: 450°F.   Time: 20 minutes

3 cups mashed potatoes   ⅓ cup chili sauce
  ¼ cup hot milk   ¼ teaspoon dry mustard
½ teaspoon salt   1 onion, finely chopped
  Dash of pepper and paprika   1 teaspoon salt
1½ pounds chuck steak, ground   Dash of pepper and paprika

Beat up the mashed potatoes, hot milk, ½ teaspoon salt, a dash of pepper and paprika. Divide into 6 portions; shape into 6 flat cakes; place on an oiled cookie sheet. Bake in a hot oven (450°F.) for 10 minutes; remove from the oven. Mix together the ground meat, chili sauce, mustard, onion, 1 teaspoon salt, pepper and paprika. Shape into 6 cakes; place on top of the potato patties. Broil or bake in the hot oven for 10 minutes; turn once during baking. Serve hot with buttered green cabbage. Serves 6.

BAKED BEEF HEART

Temperature: 350°F.   Time: 3 hours

1 beef heart—3½-4½ pounds   ¾ teaspoon salt
  3 tablespoons melted fat   Dash of pepper
2 tablespoons celery,   Dash of paprika
  chopped   ¾ cup syrup from pickled
1 medium onion, chopped   peaches, pears or green
  2 cups soft bread crumbs   pickles

Wash the heart under running water. Cut out centre veins and tough cords; dry. Heat the fat in a heavy saucepan; cook the celery and onions until golden brown. Add the crumbs and seasonings; fill the heart cavity; sew or skewer together. Dredge the heart with flour; place in a roasting pan. Pour round it the spiced syrup. Bake in moderate oven till tender, basting frequently. Serves 6.

MARY'S HAMBURGER CAKES

1½ pounds chuck beef, ground
  1 teaspoon salt
Dash of pepper and paprika
  1 onion, finely chopped

½ cup cornflakes, rolled
  2 tablespoons milk
  2 tablespoons fat

Mix together the meat, seasonings, onion, cornflakes and milk; measure the cornflakes after rolling. Shape the meat into small flat cakes. Heat the fat; pan fry the cakes until crisp and brown. Cover with the barbecue sauce and let simmer 20 minutes. Serve hot with the sauce; serves 6.

Barbecue Sauce

¼ cup fat
  ⅓ cup onion, chopped
1 teaspoon salt
  1 teaspoon white sugar

2 tablespoons lemon juice
  1 teaspoon Worcester Sauce
½ cup hot water

Heat the fat in a heavy saucepan; add the onion; cook and stir till tender. Add all the remaining ingredients; simmer for 5 minutes. Serve with hamburgers or meat loaves.

ROLLED MEAT LOAF

Temperature: 350°F.

Time: 1 hour

1½ pounds chuck steak, ground
  ½ pound fresh pork, ground
1 egg, unbeaten
  ¼ cup vegetable water
    from carrots
1 cup bread crumbs
  1 onion, chopped

2 teaspoons salt
  ¼ teaspoon pepper
Dash of mace
  1 cup canned peas
1 cup cooked carrots, diced
  ½ cup buttered crumbs

Mix together the ground steak, pork, unbeaten egg, carrot water, bread crumbs, onion, salt, pepper and mace. Spoon the mixture on a piece of waxed paper. Cover with a second piece of the paper. Press with the rolling pin into a rectangle 14″ x 8″, keeping the sides even. Take off the top paper; spread the roll with a mixture of peas and carrots. Roll as for a jelly roll; it's tricky but it can be done. Spread the paper with the buttered crumbs and roll the finished roll back through them. If you have a long, narrow loaf pan you can turn it on its side and roll the meat right into it. Bake in a moderate oven till done. Slice and serve with creamed potatoes. Serves 6.

BAKED MEAT CAKES

Temperature: 350°F.   Time: 1 hour

1 pound shoulder of veal, ground	½ cup tomato juice
½ pound fresh pork, ground	1 egg, well beaten
¾ pound chuck steak, ground	1 tablespoon corn starch
½ teaspoon poultry dressing	1 cup cooked carrots, sliced
1½ teaspoons salt	1 tablespoon cider vinegar
¼ teaspoon pepper	2 large tomatoes
¼ teaspoon dry mustard	2 tablespoons flour
½ cup soft bread crumbs	2 tablespoons fat

Combine all the ingredients except the tomatoes, flour and fat; blend well. Take out 6 spoonfuls of the mixture, each one large enough for an individual serving. Shape each into a flat cake and roll in flour. Heat the fat in a heavy frying pan; sear the meat cakes on both sides. Cut 1″ slices of firm tomatoes; place a meat cake on top of each slice; bake in a moderate oven for 15 minutes. Serve with new potatoes and buttered cabbage. Serves 6.

ROAST BEEF

Choose a Sirloin Roast, wipe it and rub with seasoned flour. It saves time to have this flour ready mixed and in a shaker. Add 1½ teaspoons of salt and ¼ teaspoon of pepper to each cup of flour. Put in shaker and shake well before using. When the roast is floured, put it on a rack in the roasting pan. If you want to get the most eating from your roast, keep an even temperature of 325°F. throughout. For a 5 pound Roast (weighed after boning and rolling) allow from 40 to 45 minutes to the pound. Don't cover the meat, don't add water and don't turn the roast; if you can keep from opening the oven door, so much the better. Lay the roast fat side up, so that as the fat melts it bastes the roast. The meat will be tender and by carefully browning the flour you get just as luscious a gravy as if the meat had been seared. Serve with brown gravy and Yorkshire Pudding.

GRAVY

When the roast is cooked, lift it to a warm platter and keep in the oven until the gravy is made. Pour off the fat in the roasting pan but keep all the meat juices. For each cup of gravy needed use 2 tablespoons of fat; for the average roast, allow sufficient fat for 2 cups of gravy. Put the 4 tablespoons of fat back in the roasting pan; blend in 4 tablespoons of flour; cook over low heat. Stir constantly until the flour is a rich brown and bubbly. Add 2 cups of cold water, vegetable water, or if you want something quite different, tomato juice. Cook and stir till smooth and thick. A teaspoon of Worcester Sauce gives a nice flavor. Serves 6.

YORKSHIRE PUDDING

Temperature: 450°F.   Time: 10-15 minutes

1 egg, well beaten   ½ cup sifted all-purpose flour
  ½ cup milk   ¼ teaspoon salt

Pour off ¼ cup hot dripping and divide it between 6 muffin tins. Combine the well beaten egg and milk; beat till light. Gradually beat in the sifted flour and salt; beat with a dover beater till smooth. Pour into the muffin pans and let stand 30 minutes; bake in a hot oven till done. Serves 6.

BRAISED FILLET OF FLANK

2 pounds flank steak   2 teaspoons salt
  ¼ pound suet   ¼ teaspoon pepper
2 tablespoons fat   1 teaspoon sugar
  1 green pepper, chopped   2 tablespoons flour
2 cups tomato juice   4 tablespoons water
  1 onion, chopped

Have the butcher flatten the steak. Criss-cross it with a sharp knife; brush lightly with vinegar. Cut the suet in 1″ strips; place lengthwise down the centre of the steak, having the strips touching one another. Roll up as for jelly roll; fasten with tooth picks. Now cut crosswise in 2″ slices. Heat the fat in a deep frying pan; sear the fillets on both sides. Add the green pepper, tomato juice, onion, salt, pepper and sugar. Cover tightly; simmer for 1½ hours or till tender. Lift the fillets to a hot platter; thicken the gravy with a paste of the flour and water. Pour over the fillets and serve. Serves 6.

SOUR CREAM POT ROAST

5 pound pot roast, rolled   2 bay leaves
  1 teaspoon salt   1 tablespoon mixed pickling spice
½ teaspoon dry mustard   ¼ cup brown sugar
  Dash of pepper   Flour for dredging
1½ cups cider vinegar   3 tablepooons fat
  1½ cups water   1 cup sour cream
½ cup onion, sliced

Wipe the pot roast; rub it with a mixture of the salt, mustard and pepper; fit it into a close-fitting deep pan. Measure the vinegar, water, onion, bay leaves, spices and brown sugar into a saucepan. Heat almost to boiling and pour over the roast. Marinate for 24 hours or longer, turning occasionally. Drain and dredge the roast with flour; strain the liquid. Heat the fat in a heavy pan; sear the meat on all sides; place it on a trivet and add the liquid a little at a time. Simmer till tender; just before serving, add the sour cream; heat the gravy to boiling. Serve with parsley potatoes and glazed carrots. Serves 10.

CRUSTY MEAT PIE

Temperature: 375°F.

Time: 45 minutes

2 tablespoons salad oil
  3 cups cooked roast beef,
    diced
  ½ cup onion, diced
2 teaspoons salt
  1 cup tomatoes, chopped
1 cup raw carrots, diced

1 cup raw potatoes,
    diced
⅛ teaspoon hot red pepper
  2½ cups boiling water
½ cup yellow corn meal
  2 eggs, well beaten
2 tablespoons butter

Heat the salad oil; cook the meat and onion till golden brown. Add 1 teaspoon of the salt, the tomatoes, carrots, potatoes and pepper; cover closely and simmer for 15 minutes. Turn into a 2-quart casserole. Have the water rapidly boiling; add the remaining 1 teaspoon of salt; stir in the corn meal. Cook, stirring all the time, till smooth and thick. Remove from the heat; beat in the eggs, one at a time; add the butter. Spread over the meat; bake till brown. Serves 6.

MOCK FILET MIGNON

1 pound chuck steak, ground
  ½ pound fresh veal or pork,
    ground
⅓ cup chili sauce
  ¼ teaspoon dry mustard
1 teaspoon salt
  Dash of pepper and paprika

1 onion, finely chopped
  6 strips breakfast bacon
4 cups hot mashed
    potatoes
¼ cup hot milk
  ½ teaspoon salt

Combine the ground meats, chili sauce, seasonings and onion. Mix well; shape into 6 round cakes. Bind each one with a strip of bacon; fasten with a tooth pick. In the meantime, beat together the hot mashed potatoes, the milk and ½ teaspoon salt. Shape into 6 flat cakes and place on a cookie sheet. Place a filet mignon on each potato cake. Bake in a hot oven for 10 minutes; reduce the heat and continue baking for half an hour or until the meat is crisp and tender. Turn the meat once during the baking. Serve with a green salad. Serves 6.

SPICED POT ROAST

4 to 5 pound pot roast (round or chuck)
2½ cups tomato juice
1 tablespoon brown sugar
¼ teaspoon cinnamon
¼ teaspoon ginger
2 whole cloves

¼ cup cider vinegar
¼ cup flour
1 teaspoon salt
Dash of pepper
4 tablespoons fat
1 onion

Fit the roast into a rather close-fitting dish. Mix together the tomato juice, sugar, spices and vinegar. Pour the mixture over the meat; let it stand for 24 hours, turning occasionally. Lift the meat from the liquid; wipe it and dust with the flour, salt and pepper. Heat the fat in a heavy saucepan or Dutch Oven; sear the meat on all sides. Slip a rack under the meat (or use a jar ring). Slice in the onion; add a cup of the spiced liquid and simmer gently. Add more liquid as needed; simmer till tender. The roast should be beautifully tender in 3 to 4 hours. Slice and serve with the gravy and new potatoes. Serves 10.

BRAISED SHORT RIBS OF BEEF

3 pounds short ribs,
   cut in 3″ pieces
1 tablespoon vinegar
2 teaspoons salt
½ teaspoon pepper
3 tablespoons flour
2 tablespoons fat

2 cups boiling water
8 medium sized potatoes, diced
2 onions, quartered
6 carrots, diced
1 cup canned peas
2 tablespoons flour
4 tablespoons sour cream

Brush the ribs with the vinegar; roll in a mixture of the salt, pepper and flour. Heat the fat in a heavy iron frying pan or heavy saucepan; sear the meat; add the water. Simmer slowly over low heat for an hour. Add the vegetables; continue cooking for another hour. Place the short ribs and vegetables on a hot platter; thicken the gravy with 2 tablespoons of flour mixed to a paste with 4 tablespoons of sour cream. Serves 6.

BARBECUED SHORT RIBS OF BEEF

Temperature: 325°F.   Time: 2 hours

3 pounds short ribs
3 tablespoons flour
1 teaspoon salt
Dash of pepper and paprika
2 tablespoons fat
1 onion, chopped
¼ cup cider vinegar

2 tablespoons brown sugar
1 cup chili sauce
½ cup water
½ teaspoon dry mustard
½ cup celery, diced
1 teaspoon salt

Have the butcher cut the ribs in 3″ pieces. Combine the flour, 1 teaspoon salt, the pepper and paprika; rub the seasoned flour on the meat. Heat the fat; sear the floured short ribs; lift into the casserole. Add the chopped onion to the fat; cook and stir till golden brown. Add all the remaining ingredients and heat to near boiling. Pour over the short ribs. Cover closely and oven bake till tender. Serve with baked potatoes. Serves 6.

OVEN BAKED SPICED ROAST

Temperature: 320°F.   Time: 2½ hours

5 pounds chuck roast   1½ teaspoons salt
  ½ cup cider vinegar   Dash of pepper
1 cup tomato juice   2 onions, finely chopped
  2 onions, sliced   4 carrots
1 teaspoon cinnamon   1 stalk celery
  1 teaspoon cloves   6 radishes
¼ teaspoon mace   2 tablespoons fat

Let the roast marinate overnight in a mixture of vinegar, tomato juice, onions, cinnamon, cloves, mace, salt and pepper. In the morning drain and save the liquid. Place the roast on a rack in the roasting pan and pour the spiced liquid over it. Cover and bake in a moderate oven till tender. Finely chop the onions, carrots, celery and radishes. Pan fry the mixture in the hot fat until golden brown; add to the roast for the last 30 minutes of baking. Thicken the gravy with a little flour. Serves 10.

TENDER BEEFSTEAK CASSEROLE

1½ pounds chuck steak, cubed   1 cup tomato juice
  3 tablespoons pastry flour   1 teaspoon salt
¼ teaspoon dry mustard   Dash of pepper and mace
  2 tablespoons fat   1 cup raw potatoes, diced
1 medium onion, chopped   ½ cup raw carrots, diced
  ¼ cup celery, finely chopped   1 cup buttered crumbs

Have the butcher cut your steak in cubes or do it yourself with a sharp knife. Measure the flour and mustard into a paper bag; add the meat cubes; twist the top and shake it; the meat cubes will be perfectly floured. Heat the fat in a frying pan; add the onions and celery. Cook and stir till golden brown. Add the meat cubes; cook and stir till seared. Add the tomato juice; simmer, tightly covered, till the meat is tender. Stir occasionally and add water if necessary. Half an hour before serving, add the seasonings, potatoes and carrots. For serving, pour into a round serving casserole. Cut a round of paper about ½″ smaller than the top of dish; fold it over in eighths; cut a pattern and unfold. Place the paper on the meat dish; into the cut pattern and around the edges dust the finely rolled buttered crumbs. Serves 6.

BROILED MEAT LOAF

Temperature: 350°F.   Time: 1 hour, 15 minutes

1 cup cracker crumbs
  ½ cup milk
1¼ pounds chuck steak, ground
  ¼ pound smoked ham, ground
½ pound fresh pork or veal,
  ground
1 cup loaf cheese, cubed

1 egg yolk
1 onion, chopped
6 young green onions,
  chopped
2 teaspoons salt
  ¼ teaspoon pepper
Dash of cayenne

Measure the cracker crumbs and milk into a bowl; let stand 10 minutes. Add all the remaining ingredients and blend well. Spoon into a pan 9″ x 5″ x 3″; bake in a moderate oven till done, about 1 hour, 15 minutes. Pour off the liquid two or three times during baking; when done invert the meat loaf on a heat-proof platter and cover with this frosting.

Frosting

2 cups mashed potatoes
  ¼ cup cheese, grated
½ teaspoon salt

Dash of pepper
  ¼ teaspoon dry mustard
1 egg white

Combine the mashed potatoes, the grated cheese, the salt, pepper and mustard. Fold in the stiffly beaten egg white. Cover the top and sides of the meat loaf with this mixture. Return to the oven and broil till the cheese melts. Serve hot with buttered asparagus. Serves 6.

CHICKEN CUBED STEAK

2 pounds chuck steak, cubed
2 eggs, slightly beaten
2 tablespoons water
  1 cup fine dry crumbs
½ teaspoon salt
  ¼ teaspoon dry mustard

Dash of pepper
4 tablespoons fat
2 cups boiling water
  1 teaspoon Worcester Sauce
2 tablespoons flour
4 tablespoons tomato juice

Have the steak cut in 1″ cubes. Slightly beat the egg; add the 2 tablespoons water. Mix together the dry crumbs, salt, mustard and pepper. Heat the fat in a heavy frying pan or Dutch oven. Roll the steak cubes in the crumb mixture, the egg mixture, then again in the crumbs. Sear in the hot fat till brown on all sides. Add the boiling water; cover closely and simmer till tender, about 1½ hours. Lift the small steaks to a hot platter. Add the Worcester Sauce to the gravy; thicken with a paste made by combining the flour and tomato juice. Pour the gravy over the steak cubes. Serve with oven browned potatoes and green beans. Serves 6.

FLANK STEAK, STUFFED

Temperature: 325°F. Time: 1 hour, 15 minutes

Flank steak, about 2 pounds
  1 teaspoon salt
Dash of pepper and paprika
  ¼ cup fat
1 onion, chopped
  1½ cups soft bread crumbs
¼ teaspoon salt
  1 tablespoon parsley, chopped

3 tablespoons celery,
  chopped
1 egg, slightly beaten
  2 tablespoons salad oil
2 tablespoons flour
  1 cup water
1 cup tomato juice
  1 teaspoon white sugar

Wipe the steak; season with 1 teaspoon salt, the pepper and paprika. Heat the fat in a heavy pan; add the onions; cook and stir till tender. Add to the bread crumbs. Add ¼ teaspoon salt, the parsley, celery and beaten egg. Spread the dressing on the steak; roll up and tie securely. Heat the salad oil in the pan; sear the steak on all sides; lift into a casserole. Blend the flour in the hot fat; add the water, tomato juice and white sugar. Pour over the steak; cover closely and oven bake till tender. Serve with the baked potatoes and buttered cauliflower. Serves 6.

BEEFSTEAK PIE

Temperature: 450°F. Time: 15 minutes

1½ pounds round steak,
  1½" thick
½ cup flour
  1 teaspoon salt
¼ teaspoon pepper
  ¼ teaspoon dry mustard
¼ teaspoon celery salt
  4 tablespoons fat
2 cubes Bovril
  2 cups boiling water

3 carrots, diced
  2 onions, sliced
2 potatoes, diced
  1½ cups sifted all-purpose
  flour
¼ teaspoon salt
  3 teaspoons baking powder
¼ cup shortening
  ¾ cup milk
¼ cup grated cheese

Cut the steak in 1½" cubes. Mix together the ½ cup flour, 1 teaspoon salt, the pepper, mustard and celery salt. Dredge the meat cubes. Heat the fat; sear the meat cubes. Add the Bovril cubes and the boiling water. Cover and simmer 1½ hours. Add the diced vegetables and simmer for another hour, adding water as necessary. Pour into a 1½-quart baking dish. Sift together the 1½ cups flour, the ¼ teaspoon salt and the baking powder. Cut in the shortening. Add the milk and stir lightly. Turn on a floured board and knead to a ball. Roll to ½" thickness and sprinkle with the grated cheese. Roll up as a jelly roll and cut in ¾" pieces. Place on top of the meat pie. Bake in a hot oven till brown. Serve with red cabbage relish. Serves 6.

STEAK DINNER

1½ pounds steak, round or rump
¾ teaspoon salt
⅛ teaspoon pepper
4 tablespoons flour
⅛ teaspoon dry mustard
2 tablespoons fat
1 medium onion, chopped

1 tablespoon green pickle, chopped
1 can tomatoes (28 oz.)
1 teaspoon sugar
½ pound macaroni
3 quarts boiling salted water

Have the steak cut 3″ thick. Mix the salt, pepper, flour and mustard; pound into the steak on both sides, using the edge of a saucer; cut in serving pieces. Heat the fat in a heavy iron frying pan; sear the meat on all sides. Add the chopped onion; cook and stir till lightly browned. Add the green pickle, tomatoes and sugar. In the meantime, cook the macaroni in the boiling salted water until tender. Drain and add to the meat mixture. Cover tightly; simmer gently until tender, about 2 hours. This makes an all-in-one dinner dish with 6 servings.

BEEFSTEAK AND KIDNEY PIE

Temperature: 450°F.

1 pound chuck steak, cubed
1 pound pork kidneys
2 tablespoons flour
1 teaspoon salt
½ teaspoon ginger
⅛ teaspoon cinnamon

Time: 40 minutes

2 tablespoons fat
½ teaspoon dry mustard
2 onions, chopped
2 cups water
Plain pastry

Have the steak cubed. Clean, wash and slice the kidneys. The small pork kidneys are much cheaper and just as good as beef kidneys. Mix together the flour, salt, ginger, cinnamon, steak and kidneys. Stir until the meat is well coated. Heat the fat; sear the meat. Add the mustard, onions and water. Cover and simmer till tender (about an hour). Pour into an oiled 1½-quart casserole. Make half the recipe for plain pastry. Moisten the edge of the baking dish; cover the meat with the pastry, fluting on the outside edge. Bake in a hot oven for 40 minutes. Serves 6.

BROILED PORTERHOUSE STEAK

Have the butcher cut you a steak about 2″ thick. One hour before you broil it, brush with salad oil mixed with ½ teaspoon prepared mustard. Preheat the broiler and grease it. Place the steak in the middle of the broiler rack so that the top of the steak is about 3″ from the top element. Broil for approximately 15 minutes on each side, cooking only till well browned. Turn once during the broiling; leave the door open to prevent smoking. Remove to a hot platter; dress with butter. Allow ½ pound of steak per serving.

Pan fry enough onions to cover the steak, stirring and cooking constantly so that the onions will be tender but not too brown. Serve with Creole sauce.

ROUND STEAK WITH TOMATOES

Temperature: 300°F.   Time: 2 hours

1½ pounds round steak, 2″ thick   1½ cups canned tomatoes
4 tablespoons flour   3 large onions, peeled
1 teaspoon salt   and sliced
⅛ teaspoon pepper   1 stalk celery, diced
⅛ teaspoon dry mustard   ½ cup carrots, diced
3 tablespoons fat   1 tablespoon catsup

Wipe the steak; nick the outside edges. Mix together the flour, salt, pepper and mustard. Sprinkle half the mixture on one side of the meat, pound with the edge of a saucer until it is all absorbed. Turn over, add the remainder of the flour mixture and pound well. Heat the fat in an iron frying pan; sear the steak well on both sides. Add all the remaining ingredients and cover closely. Bake in a slow oven (300°F.) until tender. Uncover the dish for the last half hour and turn the meat, spooning the liquid over it. Serve with oven browned potatoes and baked squash. Serves 6.

BROILED SIRLOIN STEAK

2½ pounds sirloin steak, 2″ thick   ½ teaspoon paprika
4 tablespoons fat   3 tablespoons Worcester
1 tablespoon prepared   Sauce
mustard   6 tablespoons salad oil
2 teaspoons salt   3 tablespoons catsup
1 teaspoon white sugar   2 teaspoons brown sugar
½ teaspoon pepper   3 teaspoons salt

Wipe the steak; mix together the fat, mustard, salt, white sugar, pepper and paprika. Rub this mixture well into the steak on both sides. Heat a heavy frying pan and oil lightly. Sear the steak quickly on both sides, then lift to the broiler. Prepare a sauce of the Worcester Sauce, salad oil, catsup, brown sugar and salt. Brush this over the meat. Broil for 45 minutes, turning the steak only once. Have the steak 3″ from the heating element; reduce the heat slightly for the last half-hour of cooking. Brush the steak frequently with the sauce. Serve hot. Serves 4-5.

PANBROILED SIRLOIN STEAK

2 pounds sirloin steak,
  cut 2″ thick
4 tablespoons fat
  2 tablespoons dry mustard

3 teaspoons salt
  2 teaspoons white sugar
½ teaspoon pepper
½ teaspoon paprika

Wipe the steak; cream together all the remaining ingredients. Rub this mixture well into the meat on both sides; sear the steak on both sides in a lightly oiled frying pan. Reduce the heat and continue cooking until the steak is done (about 12 minutes). Pour off the fat as the steak cooks; it makes the steak more tender. Serve hot with small new potatoes. Serves 4.

SWISS STEAK

2 pounds round steak, 1″ thick
  ¼ cup flour
4 slices side bacon, diced
  1 teaspoon salt
Dash of pepper and paprika
  1½ cups tomato juice

1 teaspoon white sugar
  ¼ teaspoon dry mustard
1 onion, sliced
  2 tablespoons flour
4 tablespoons water

Wipe the steak; pound in as much flour as possible on both sides of the meat. Pan fry the bacon till crisp. Cut the steak in serving pieces and sear on both sides. Sprinkle with the salt, pepper and paprika. Combine the tomato juice, sugar and mustard; pour over the meat. Add the sliced onion; simmer till the meat is tender. Remove to a hot platter; thicken the gravy with a mixture of the flour and water. Pour over the meat; serve with potato cakes and Golden Bantam corn.

OVEN BAKED TENDERLOIN STEAKS

Temperature: 350°F.
8 small pieces beef tenderloin,
  flattened
1 teaspoon salt
  Dash of pepper and cayenne

Time: 40 minutes
1 tablespoon flour
  2 tablespoons fat
1 onion, chopped
1 cup sour cream

Rub the slices of tenderloin on both sides with a slice of onion; toss in a mixture of salt, pepper, cayenne and flour until well coated. Heat the fat in an iron frying pan; add the chopped onion, cook and stir for two or three minutes. Lift out the onions, sear the tenderloin on both sides till crisp and brown. Add the onions and the sour cream. Oven bake for 40 minutes. Turn occasionally and spoon the gravy over the slices. Serve hot with the gravy and mashed potatoes. Serves 4.

NO-DISH MEAT LOAF

Temperature: 350°F.   Time: 1 hour

3 pepper squashes   1 medium onion, finely chopped
1 tablespoon butter   1 green pepper, diced
½ tablespoon brown sugar   1 egg, unbeaten
1 pound chuck steak, ground   ½ cup soft bread crumbs
¼ pound salt pork, ground   2 teaspoons salt

Cut the squashes in half; brush with a mixture of butter and brown sugar; bake in the oven for 15 minutes. Mix all the remaining ingredients; shape into 6 meat balls. Press one ball into each half squash; return to the oven; continue baking for 40-45 minutes. Serve with sliced tomatoes. Serves 6.

IRISH STEW WITH DUMPLINGS

2 cups cooked meat, diced   ½ cup cabbage, chopped
   Meat gravy and 2 cups water   ¾ teaspoon salt
4 onions, sliced   Dash of pepper
1 carrot, diced (½ cup)   Dash of mace
4 potatoes, diced

Cut up the meat from a pot roast; heat with the gravy and water. Add the vegetables and seasonings; simmer gently one-half hour. Fifteen minutes before serving, make dumplings; drop by spoonfuls on top of the stew. Cover tightly and continue cooking for 15 minutes. Serve immediately. Serves 6.

RICH BROWN STEW

2 pounds chuck beef   1 tablespoon celery leaves, chopped
1 teaspoon salt   1 onion, chopped
⅛ teaspoon pepper   2 whole cloves
   Dash of paprika   1 cup celery, chopped
6 tablespoons flour   1 cup potatoes, diced
2 tablespoons fat   1 cup carrots, diced
3 cups boiling water

Cut the meat in serving pieces; toss in a mixture of the salt, pepper, paprika and flour. Heat the fat in a Dutch Oven or heavy frying pan; sear the meat on all sides. Now is the time for browning; after the water is added the color won't deepen. When the meat is seared all over, add the boiling water, celery leaves, onions and whole cloves. Cover tightly and simmer gently until almost tender (about 2½ hours). Add the vegetables, more water if necessary, and continue cooking for half an hour. Serve on a hot platter with a border of mashed potatoes, boiled rice or noodles. Serves 6.

Liver

Nutrition experts recommend liver in the diet at least once a week. Calf's liver, because of its flavor and tenderness, is the most popular—but also the most expensive. Beef liver, lamb liver and pork liver are much less expensive and just as valuable in the diet.

PAN FRIED LIVER

1½ pounds liver, thinly sliced
 ½ teaspoon salt
⅛ teaspoon pepper
 2 tablespoons flour
1 teaspoon dry mustard

2 tablespoons hot fat
2 onions, sliced
1 cup water
 ½ cup sour cream

Have the liver thinly sliced. Mix together the salt, pepper, flour and mustard; roll each piece of liver in the mixture till coated. Heat the fat and brown the liver slices. Add the onion; cook and stir until tender. Add the water; cover tightly and simmer till the liver is tender. Just before serving, add the sour cream and heat well. Serves 6.

DINNER LIVER LOAF

Temperature: 350°F.

Time: 50-60 minutes

1½ pounds liver
 4 tablespoons fat
6 tablespoons flour
 1 teaspoon salt
Dash of pepper
 1½ cups milk

3 tablespoons mashed potatoes
 2 eggs, slightly beaten
1 onion, finely chopped
1 teaspoon vinegar
1 cup cooked carrots, sliced

Simmer the liver in salted water till tender; drain; chop finely or run through the food chopper. Melt the fat; blend in the flour, salt and pepper; let bubble 3 minutes. Slowly add the milk; cook and stir till smooth and thick. Combine the liver, the sauce and all remaining ingredients except the carrots. Cover the bottom of an oiled loaf pan 9″ x 5″ x 3″ with the sliced carrots; add the liver mixture. Bake in a moderate oven till firm. Yield: Serves 8.

LIVER LOAF

Temperature: 250°F.

Time: 1¼ hours

1½ lbs. young beef liver
 3 slices breakfast bacon
½ cup onion, finely chopped
 2 cups soft bread crumbs

1 egg, unbeaten
 1 teaspoon salt
¼ cup chili sauce

Cover the liver with boiling water; let stand, closely covered, for five minutes; drain and put through the food chopper. Dice the bacon (try scissors for this job); cook till crisp in the frying pan. Remove the crisp bacon and pan fry the finely chopped onion till golden brown. Add onions, bacon and bacon fat to the liver. Add the bread crumbs, unbeaten egg, salt and chili sauce; mix lightly. Pack into an oiled pan 9″ x 5″ x 3″; bake in a moderate oven till firm. At the end of the first ½ hour drain all liquid from the pan so that the meat will brown on the bottom. When cold, slice and serve with salad. Yield: 14 slices.

BARNSTON LIVER LOAF

Temperature: 350°F.

Time: 1 hour, 10 minutes

¾ pound liver
  1 onion, chopped
6 carrots, grated
  1 cup warm, cooked cereal
    (oatmeal or cream of wheat)
2 eggs, slightly beaten

¼ cup milk
  ¾ cup soft bread crumbs
3 tablespoons dripping
  1 teaspoon salt
⅛ teaspoon pepper
  Dash of mace

Cover the liver with boiling water and let stand until cool; drain; finely chop or run through the coarse knife of the grinder. Add all remaining ingredients and mix lightly. Spoon into an oiled pan 9″ x 5″; bake in a moderate oven till done. This loaf will serve 2 meals. If you want the second helping hot, slice the loaf, place each slice on an equal sized piece of bread which has been brushed with butter. Heat in a hot oven and serve with vegetables. Yield: 12 servings.

Veal

Veal is the meat from young calves, very much relished by some meat eaters, not so well liked by others. It is a lean meat with very little fat and not much waste in cooking. Its color is pinkish gray, its flavor delicate. Here are the most popular cuts and their uses.

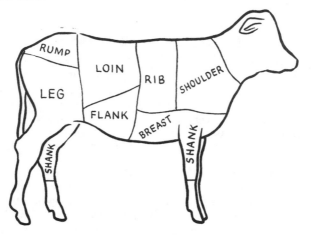

Shoulder of Veal:

Here is an economical cut with a small proportion of bone. A favorite way to prepare it is this: Have it boned and rolled for a roast. Another favorite: Have the butcher bone it for you, and stuff it with a highly seasoned dressing.

Ribs of Veal:

The ribs are usually cut into rib chops or into a Rib or Crown Roast. The chops are pan-fried or braised.

Loin of Veal:

Here is one of the expensive veal cuts; from this section come the Sirloin Veal Steaks and the Loin Chops. The chop cut with the kidney is an especial delicacy. The roasts cut from the loin run from 2½-4½ lbs. and take long, slow cooking. We like a 325°F. oven and allow at least 45 minutes to the pound for a 4-lb. roast.

Leg of Veal:

In this cut we get the largest percentage of lean meat to bone; hence it is the highest priced veal cut. The round roasts and the

Veal Rump roasts come from here. The roasts may be boned and rolled or roasted with the bone in. If the roast is boned and stuffed it's a very succulent dish; again the low temperature and thorough cooking are necessary. Cutlets and steaks are also sliced from the leg. They are pan-fried slowly till crisp on the outside and golden brown, or breaded and pan-fried.

Veal Shank:

Here is an excellent source for the jelly in jellied meats. A veal shank added to a beef shank and some veal stewing meat makes a rich, clear jellied meat. Veal shank is inexpensive and jellies easily.

Flank and Breast of Veal:

Here are two low cost cuts of veal. Both may be stuffed and baked or may be braised. Either cut ground makes a flavorsome addition to meat loaves and patties. The veal for the famous Veal and Ham Pies also comes from these cuts.

Cooking Pointers for Veal

Cook at a uniformly low temperature (325 degrees F.). Roast on a rack in an uncovered roaster; do not add water or baste. Because all veal is deficient in fat, top all veal roasts with breakfast bacon or fat pork. Always cook veal thoroughly.

VEAL BIRDS

Temperature: 325°F.   Time: 1 hour

1½ lbs. veal steak   ½ teaspoon poultry dressing
2 slices breakfast bacon, diced   ¾ teaspoon salt
½ cup stale bread crumbs   Dash of pepper, paprika and
2 tablespoons onion, finely   celery salt
  chopped   2 tablespoons fat
1 tablespoon green pepper,   ¾ cup hot water
  parsley or pickle, chopped   1 cup sour cream

Have the butcher cut the steak ½″ thick; cut into 4″ squares. Pound with a mallet to flatten. Dice the bacon and pan-fry till crisp; add the crumbs, onion, green ingredients and poultry dressing. Cook and stir till tender. Place 1 tablespoon of dressing on each veal square and roll cornerwise; fasten with a toothpick. Roll each bird in a mixture of salt, pepper, paprika, celery salt and flour. Heat the fat in a heavy pan; sear the birds on all sides. Add the hot water; cover closely and let simmer for half an hour. Place in a casserole; add the sour cream. Cover closely and oven bake for 1 hour. Serve with sweet potatoes and apples. Yield: 6 servings.

CURRIED VEAL

3 cups cooked, plumped rice
3 tablespoons fat
1 cup onions, sliced
1 cup tart apples, diced
2 cups cooked veal, diced
1 teaspoon curry powder
2 teaspoons flour

½ teaspoon salt
dash of pepper
1 tablespoon concentrated meat essence
1 cup boiling water
1 tablespoon lemon juice

Cook ⅔ cup rice in boiling salted water till tender; drain and rinse with boiling water to separate the kernels. Cover the rice and let stand in the warming closet till each grain is fluffy. Pack into an oiled ring mould, then unmould on a hot platter. Keep warm till the veal is ready to serve. Heat the fat in a heavy saucepan; add the onions and apple. Stir and cook till tender (about 15 minutes); remove from the pan. Place the meat in the same pan; brown it lightly; add to the onions and apples. Blend into the pan the curry powder, flour and seasonings; add the concentrated meat essence dissolved in the hot water. Cook and stir until smooth. Add the veal, onions, apples and lemon juice. Blend over the heat; serve with the rice. Yield: 4 or 5 servings.

VEAL CUTLET SUPREME

Temperature: 400°F.

Time: 1 hour, 15 minutes

4 tablespoons salad oil
1 tablespoon cider vinegar
½ teaspoon salt
½ teaspoon paprika
½ teaspoon sugar
2 whole cloves
1½ lbs. veal cutlet, in one piece
4 tablespoons fat

4 tablespoons flour
1 cup water
1 cup tomato juice or canned tomatoes
1 cup raw potatoes, thinly sliced
1 large onion, thinly sliced
½ cup dry crumbs

Combine the salad oil, vinegar, seasonings, sugar and whole cloves; pour over the veal cutlet; let stand for 4 hours, turning occasionally; drain. Reserve this liquid for salad dressing. Heat the 4 tablespoons fat in a heavy iron frying pan; sear the cutlet on both sides. Remove from the pan; blend in the flour with the fat. Let bubble 3 minutes; add the water and tomato juice; stir till smooth. Return the cutlet to the pan and cover with the sliced potatoes and onions. Cover tightly and simmer till tender (about 1 hour, 15 minutes). Lift to a serving dish; top with the crumbs which have been mixed with bacon fat or dripping. Brown in a hot oven; serve at once. Yield: 4 or 5 servings.

ROLLED FRONT OF VEAL

Temperature: 400°F.

Time: 1½ to 2 hours

5 lbs. front of veal, boned
1½ lbs. sausage meat
½ cup green pickle, chopped
2 hard cooked eggs

1½ teaspoons salt
¼ teaspoon pepper
½ teaspoon dry mustard
3 tablespoons fat

Lay the veal flat; spread it with half the sausage meat. Over the sausage meat sprinkle the chopped green pickle and slices of hard cooked eggs. Spread with the remainder of the sausage meat; roll up like a jelly roll. Tie and roll in a mixture of salt, pepper and mustard. Heat the fat; sear the meat on all sides. Add a little water and oven bake uncovered till tender, allowing 20 minutes to the pound. Roast the meat on a trivet and baste it occasionally with the fat in the pan. Serve it sliced cold with salad, and with the tag ends make shepherd's pie. This roast will make one hot dinner, one cold dinner.

STUFFED SHOULDER OF VEAL

Temperature: 325°F.

Time: 2 hours

1 cup apple, finely chopped
1 tablespoon lemon juice
1 shoulder of veal, 5 to 6 lbs.
1½ teaspoons salt
¼ teaspoon pepper
¼ teaspoon dry mustard

5 tablespoons fat
1 cup celery, chopped
1 tablespoon parsley or green
pickle, chopped
1 tablespoon onion, chopped
4 cups soft bread crumbs

Peel, core and chop a large, tart apple; there should be 1 cup; sprinkle it with the lemon juice. Have the butcher remove the bone from the veal shoulder; this gives you a large pocket for stuffing. Combine the salt, pepper and mustard; rub the meat inside and out. Melt the fat in a heavy pan; add the celery, parsley and onion. Cook and stir over low heat till tender but not browned; add the crumbs and apples. Stuff the pocket and sew the opening. Wrap the roast in a piece of heavy brown paper which has been oiled on the inside; place on a rack in an uncovered roasting pan. Do not add any water. Bake in a moderate oven till tender, about 2 hours. The roast will come out of its paper wrapping beautifully browned and moist. Don't cover at any time; don't add any water. Yield: 6 servings for 2 meals.

Lamb

In Canada there is very little demand for mutton and a big and constant demand for lamb, the flesh of young sheep. There is a continuous supply of lamb the year round but during the winter we get frozen lamb. The fresh spring lamb begins to come on the market in late February or early March, and really gets into full production about May. The average spring lamb weighs from 40 to 42 pounds dressed, and is divided into the following cuts:

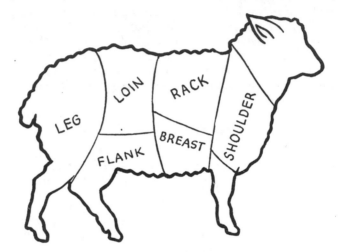

Leg of Lamb:

This is the favorite cut for roasting. The average leg of lamb weighs from five to six pounds. Allow about half a pound of meat and bone for one serving. If your family is small, have the butcher cut off a few chops from the end of the leg. Broil the chops and use for one dinner or lunch. For easy carving and serving have the butcher bone and roll the leg. The thin, papery covering of the lamb is called the fell and supplies the necessary fat.

Loin of Lamb:

The loin makes a delicious roast. The loin also gives you loin chops; they cook with less waste and are less expensive than rib chops. For Kidney Chops have the butcher cut in the kidney with the chop. Loin Chops, English Style, are cut across the undivided loin; the backbone is then removed.

The Rack:

The Rack lies between the loin and shoulder and is usually cut into rib chops, one of the most expensive of lamb cuts. When the rib chops have the meat and fat scraped down from the end of the bones so that only the "eye" of the meat is left, we call them French chops.

The very special crown roast of lamb comes from the rack. Ribs are cut from both sides of the lamb; the chop ends are trimmed of meat and the backbone trimmed off. The two sections are bent to half circle with the ribs outside. They are fastened together and the crown is formed. Allow two ribs per person; to prevent excessive browning, fill the crown with cubes of raw potatoes and remove before serving. The butcher will put the meat trimmings in the crown; take them out, run through the food chopper and use for a meat loaf.

Shoulder of Lamb:

The shoulder is one of the less expensive cuts of lamb. Shoulder chops may be cut from this piece, and while they are not quite so tender as the loin or rib chop, they are delicious braised or baked. The best meal from the shoulder is the rolled, stuffed shoulder.

Breast of Lamb:

The breast of lamb is a long, narrow strip of meat, inexpensive and lean. It is delicious when boned, stuffed and braised or roasted.

Shank:

Here is a bony cut that makes excellent stews or jellied meat.

Flank:

The Flank is a low-cost cut that's ideal for lamb stews and meat pies.

Baking Guide for Lamb:

Roast a leg of lamb in a 325 degrees F. oven and allow about 35 minutes to the pound. To vary the flavor, mix together $\frac{1}{3}$ cup salad oil, 1 tablespoon chopped onion, 2 teaspoons poultry spice, $\frac{1}{2}$ teaspoon dry mustard, 1 teaspoon salt, $\frac{1}{2}$ teaspoon paprika. Spread over the lamb four hours before roasting. Let stand, turning occasionally; roast in a 325 degrees F. oven.

LAMB ROASTING TEMPERATURES

Cut of Lamb	Approximate Time	Oven Temperatures
LEG OF LAMB		
4¼-6 lbs.	35 min. per lb.	325°F.
6-8 lbs.	32 min. per lb.	325°F.
BONED ROLLED LEG LAMB		
3¾-5 lbs.	45 min. per lb.	325°F.
5-6¾ lbs.	42 min. per lb.	325°F.
(Wgt. after boning)		
ROLLED LAMB SHOULDER		
3¾-5 lbs.	45 min. per lb.	325°F.
(Wgt. after boning and rolling)		
STUFFED LAMB SHOULDER		
3-5¼ lbs.	45 min. per lb.	325°F.
(Wgt. after boning and before stuffing)		
CROWN OF LAMB		
3-4 lbs. (18-20 chops)	45 min. per lb.	350°F.
(No filling in center)		

STUFFED BREAST OF LAMB

Temperature: 350°F.　　　　Time: 2½ hours

2 pounds breast of lamb, boned
1 teaspoon salt
Dash of pepper and paprika
1 tablespoon flour
¼ cup fat
1 small onion, diced
½ cup celery, diced
6 cups soft bread crumbs
¼ teaspoon poultry dressing
1 egg, slightly beaten
2 tablespoons fat
½ cup boiling water
½ cup jelly or jam
¼ cup lemon juice
1 teaspoon grated lemon rind

Have the butcher bone the lamb and flatten it. Rub it with a mixture of the seasonings and flour. Heat ¼ cup of fat in a saucepan; add the diced onion and celery. Stir and cook till tender. Remove from the heat; add the crumbs and poultry dressing; add the egg. Spread the lamb with the dressing; roll up and tie tightly. Heat the 2 tablespoons of fat in a roasting pan; sear the roll on all sides; place on a rack; add the boiling water.

Cover; bake for 2 hours. Uncover; spread the lamb with a mixture of the jelly or jam, the lemon juice and rind. Continue baking for another half hour, basting frequently. Serve with pan gravy, oven browned potatoes and new green peas. Serves 8.

BAKED LAMB CHOPS

Temperature: 350°F.   Time: 35 minutes

4 lamb chops, 1½" thick   ½ teaspoon poultry dressing
  2 tablespoons jelly   3 tablespoons hot fat
2 cups soft bread crumbs   1 small onion, finely chopped
  ¼ teaspoon salt   2 tablespoons flour
Dash of pepper   ¼ teaspoon dry mustard

Have the butcher cut a pocket in the chop running right to the bone. Beat up the jelly; add the bread crumbs and the seasonings. Heat 2 tablespoons of fat in a frying pan; add the onions; cook and stir till tender. Add the stuffing and mix well. Fill the pockets with the mixture and fasten together. Heat the remaining tablespoon of fat in the pan. Rub the chops with a mixture of the flour and mustard. Sear on both sides in the fat. Place in a casserole. Add a little water; bake in a moderate oven till tender. Serves 4.

CURRY OF LAMB WITH RICE

1½ pounds shoulder of lamb   ½ cup celery, chopped
  3 tablespoons fat   2 tablespoons green pickle,
1½ cups boiling water   chopped
  ¾ teaspoon salt   2 tablespoons flour
¼ teaspoon pepper   1 teaspoon vinegar
  1 teaspoon curry powder   ¼ cup cold water
2 tablespoons onion, chopped

Cut the shoulder of lamb in serving pieces. Heat the fat and sear the meat on all sides. Add the boiling water, the seasonings, the chopped onion, celery and pickle. Cover and simmer till tender. Make a paste with the flour, vinegar and water. Stir into the curry; cook and stir till smooth and thickened. While the curry is cooking, prepare the steamed rice. Measure 3 cups of boiling water and 1 teaspoon of salt into the top of a double boiler. Have the water rapidly boiling; stir in 1 cup of washed rice. Cook over direct heat for 5 minutes. Place over boiling water; cover and cook till tender (about 45 minutes). Stir the rice frequently; when tender add 1 tablespoon of butter. Uncover and continue cooking over boiling water till dry. Pour in a mound in the centre of a hot platter. Surround with the Lamb Curry. Serve with diced turnips and carrots. Serves 4-5.

SPECIAL ROAST LAMB

Temperature: 325°F.　　　　Time: 3 hours

1 leg of lamb, 5 to 6 pounds
　1 teaspoon salt
1 teaspoon grated onion
　¼ teaspoon pepper
¼ bay leaf, crushed

¼ teaspoon ginger
　¼ teaspoon thyme
¼ teaspoon sage
1 tablespoon salad oil

Wipe the lamb; with a sharp knife cut small gashes ¼″ long on the top surface. Combine all the ingredients except the salad oil; rub the mixture well into the meat so that all the gashes are completely filled. Brush with the salad oil. Place on a rack in a roasting pan. Bake in a moderate oven until tender. Do not baste, cover or add water to the pan. Serves 8.

STUFFED SHOULDER OF LAMB

Temperature: 325°F.　　　　Time: 2½-3 hours

3 to 4 pounds shoulder of lamb,
　boned
1 teaspoon salt
　Dash of pepper
4 tablespoons fat
　1 medium onion, diced
1 tablespoon green pickle,
　chopped

6 cups bread crumbs
　½ cup celery, chopped
1 cup apples, finely chopped
　½ cup fruit juice (any kind)
1 teaspoon salt
　1 teaspoon poultry dressing
¼ teaspoon dry mustard

Have the butcher bone the shoulder so that it has a good pocket. Mix 1 teaspoon salt and a dash of pepper; rub the mixture into the meat, both inside and out. Heat the fat; add the onion; cook and stir till tender and golden brown. Add all the remaining ingredients and blend well. Fill the pocket and sew up. Shape the filling that is left into 6 flat patties; pan fry before serving. Place the meat on a rack in the roasting pan and roast until tender, allowing about 45 minutes to the pound. Do not cover, add water or baste. Serves 6-8.

ROAST SHOULDER OF LAMB

Temperature: 325°F.　　　　Time: 3 hours

1 shoulder of lamb, boned
　(4-4½ pounds)
4 tablespoons fat
　¼ cup onion, chopped
2½ cups soft bread crumbs

2 tablespoons chili sauce
　1 tablespoon chopped
　parsley
½ teaspoon salt
　Dash of pepper and paprika

Have the shoulder boned. Heat the fat in a saucepan; add the onion; cook and stir till the onion is tender but not brown;

add the crumbs, chili sauce, parsley and seasonings. Toss lightly; fill the shoulder pocket; sew or tie the edges together. Place on a rack in an uncovered roasting pan. Bake in a moderate oven till tender. Serves 8.

LAMB STEW

4 tablespoons fat
4 onions, sliced
2 tablespoons flour
1 teaspoon salt
¼ teaspoon pepper
Dash of paprika

2 pounds shoulder of lamb, cut in serving pieces
2 cups tomatoes
1 tablespoon celery, chopped
1 tablespoon apple, chopped
1 cup thick sour cream
1 tablespoon parsley, chopped

Heat the fat in an iron frying pan or Dutch Oven; pan fry the onions till delicately brown; mix together the flour and seasonings; roll each piece of lamb in the mixture till coated; sear in the pan with the onions. Add the tomatoes, the celery and the apple. Cover tightly and simmer for 2 hours. It may be necessary to add some water during this cooking. Ten minutes before serving, add the sour cream and the parsley. Serves 6.

STUFFED LAMB CHOPS

Temperature: 350°F.
4 lamb chops, ¾″ thick
¾ cup soft bread crumbs
2 tablespoons celery, chopped
¼ cup onion, chopped
1 tablespoon parsley, chopped

Time: 50-60 minutes
¼ teaspoon salt
Dash of pepper and paprika
Milk to moisten
2 tablespoons fat
¼ cup cream

Cut a pocket in each chop right in to the bone. Mix together the bread crumbs, celery, onion, parsley and seasonings. Add just enough milk to moisten. Fill the chops and sew together again. Heat the fat in a baking dish; sear the chops well; add the cream and cover closely. Bake in a moderate oven till tender. Remove the chops to a hot platter and take out the bastings. Slightly thicken the gravy and pour around the chops. Serve with parsley potatoes. Serves 4.

Pork

Next in popularity to beef comes Canadian pork. Pork has a great diversity of flavors; we can have it smoked or fresh, salt or pickled. Pork needs long, moderate cooking and we need to know the cuts. Here is the chart showing just where the various cuts come from. If you check this chart it will help you with your ordering.

Ham:

Here is what most of us figure is the choice piece of pork. The hams are bought either fresh or smoked. Fresh pork shrinks a great deal in the roasting or boiling; allow for that in calculating your servings.

Smoked Ham:

The new smoked hams do not require par-boiling, so look to your label for directions. A whole smoked ham may be baked or boiled. If you have a whole ham, it pays to break it up into several meals. Have the ham cut in half; use the centre slices for baking, broiling or pan frying. Bake the butt end for one hot meal; you'll have enough left for cold slices and for sandwiches. Simmer the shank end with vegetables and have what our Old Country friends call Ham Chowder.

The Loin:

The loin in fresh pork is divided into three parts. The end next the ham provides very tender loin roasts; the centre cuts also provide loin roasts with very little fat; the shoulder end Loin Roasts are a little fatter, not quite so tender. The ham and centre cuts have the tenderloin in them which makes them nicer; the shoulder and end roast has no tenderloin. The tenderloin is a long, tapering, meaty length which lies just beneath the back bone. Some butchers cut it out and sell it separately. It is very tender, juicy and bakes with very little shrinkage. One tenderloin weighs from one-half to three-quarters pound and is delicious stuffed and baked.

Chops:

The loin and rib pork chops also come from the loin. The loin chops have both the "eye" muscle and the tenderloin; the rib chops have only the "eye" muscle. If the rib chops are cut thick, there will be a rib in each chop. If they're cut thin, then every other chop will be minus a rib.

Crown Roast of Pork:

Crown Roast of Pork comes from the loin too. To make the crown, the butcher uses the rib section of two loins, each with the same number of chops. The chop bones are trimmed, the back bone is trimmed. Then the two sections are bent to half circles with the ribs outside. Fastened together, you get your circular crown with the rib bones projecting upward.

Pea Meal Back Bacon:

Here you have the loin of pork cured, smoked and finished with the pea meal. It can be roasted in the piece, pan fried by the slice or slit, stuffed and baked. This last method makes a very attractive cold dish.

Spare Ribs:

Here is what some people call the most delectable part of any porker. The spare ribs are the end of the ribs. They have about 50 percent bone, 50 percent meat, but the meat is sweet and juicy. Bake them, boil them, stuff them, they're all good.

PICNIC SHOULDER

Fresh Pork:

This lower part of the shoulder looks like a small fresh ham, oval at one end and squared off at the other. The fresh shoulder may be roasted or braised whole; it may be boned and rolled or boned and stuffed; roast or braise to finish.

Smoked Pork:

The smoked pork picnic shoulder should be parboiled, then cooked like a fresh shoulder.

The Boston Butt:

The Boston Butt lies next the head; in the fresh pork this cut may be roasted or braised with the bone removed.

The smoked butt is cured, smoked and wrapped as a Cottage Roll or Smoked Boneless Shoulder. It weighs from 2 to 4 pounds; it may be simmered or baked.

The Bacon:

The breakfast bacon comes from the underside, which in beef we call the plate. This strip is trimmed, squared, sugar cured and smoked. Start all bacon in a cold pan—there is less wastage.

PORK ROASTING POINTERS

The loin, shoulder and ham of fresh pork make the best roasts.

Pork should always be thoroughly cooked; there should be no trace of pink in it when cut.

Serve roast pork with some complimentary flavor such as spiced applesauce, spiced peaches or bittersweet relish.

PORK ROASTING TEMPERATURES

Cut of Pork	Approximate Time	Temperature
CROWN OF PORK (no filling in the centre)		
6 lbs. (about 21 chops)	45 min. per lb.	350°F.
7 lbs. (about 24 chops)	40 min. per lb.	350°F.
FRESH HAM		
8-10 lbs.	33 min. per lb.	350°F.
10-12 lbs.	31 min. per lb.	350°F.
LOIN		
2½-3½ lbs. (about 9 chops)	38 min. per lb.	350°F.
3½-4½ lbs. (about 12 chops)	34 min. per lb.	350°F.
4½-6 lbs. (about 15 chops)	32 min. per lb.	350°F.
SHOULDER, ROLLED		
4½-5½ lbs. (after boning and rolling)	45 min. per lb.	350°F.
SHOULDER, STUFFED		
6-8 lbs. (after boning and before stuffing)	40 min. per lb.	350°F.

BAKED PORK CHOPS

Temperature: 350°F.

6 rib pork chops, 1″ thick
2 tablespoons fat
¼ cup celery, chopped
¼ cup onion, chopped
1 cup soft bread crumbs
1 tablespoon parsley

Time: 1 hour

¼ cup milk
¼ teaspoon salt
Dash of pepper and mace
2 tablespoons fat
¼ cup cream

Have the butcher cut a pocket in each chop. Heat 2 table-spoons of fat in a saucepan; add the celery and onions; cook till tender. Add the bread crumbs, parsley, milk and seasonings. Mix well; fill the pockets and sew together. Heat 2 tablespoons fat in the pan; sear the chops on both sides. Add the cream and cover. Bake in a moderate oven till the chops are tender. Serve with spiced apple sauce. Serves 6.

BAKED STUFFED PORK CHOPS

Temperature: 325°F.

4 large pork chops
¾ cup raisins
½ cup celery, diced
½ cup apples, diced
2 eggs, well beaten
¼ cup milk

Time: 1½ hours

5 tablespoons flour
¾ teaspoon salt
Dash of pepper and mace
2 tablespoons fat
½ cup fruit juice (peach or
   pear is the best)

Buy loin chops and have them cut 2″-3″ thick. Have the butcher slit them to the bone to form a pocket. Plump and dry the raisins; combine with the celery and apples; add the eggs, milk and flour. Stuff the chops and fasten the pocket. Sprinkle them with a mixture of the salt, pepper and mace. Heat the fat; sear the chops on both sides. Place singly in a shallow baking dish; add the fruit juice to the fat; heat well; pour over the chops. Cover and bake for 1½ hours; turn once during the baking. Serve with the pan gravy and spiced sweet apples. Serves 4.

BAKED HAM WITH CHEESE

Temperature: 350°F.

1 ham slice 1″ thick (1¼ lbs.)
½ cup rich milk
1 cup cheese, cubed

Time: 1 hour, 15 minutes

2 tablespoons lemon juice
½ teaspoon dry mustard
Dash of cayenne and paprika

Nick the edges of the ham slice to prevent it curling. Heat the milk, cheese, lemon juice, dry mustard, cayenne and paprika; pour this mixture over the ham. Bake in a moderate oven till tender. Serves 4.

BAKED HAM WITH ORANGE

Temperature: 350°F.   Time: 1 hour, 15 minutes
2 tablespoons fat   2 tablespoons brown sugar
  1 slice smoked ham, 1½" thick   ½ teaspoon cinnamon
2 oranges, thinly sliced

Heat the fat in a heavy iron frying pan; sear the ham well on
both sides. Remove from the heat; cover the ham slice with the
thinly sliced oranges. Sprinkle with a mixture of the sugar and
cinnamon. Cover closely; bake till the ham is tender. Uncover
for the last 10 minutes of baking. Serves 5.

BAKED HAM CASSEROLE

Temperature: 400°F.   Time: 30 minutes
1 cup broken macaroni   ¾ cup water
  1½ cups boiling water   2 tablespoons green onions,
1½ teaspoons salt   chopped
  2 cups cooked ham, diced   ¾ cup grated or cubed
1 can condensed tomato soup   cheese
  (10 oz.)

Cook the macaroni in boiling salted water until tender
(about 20 minutes); drain and rinse with boiling water. To the
macaroni add the ham, tomato soup, ¾ cup water and the chopped
onions. Put in an oiled 1½ quart casserole. Bake in a hot oven
for 20 minutes. Ten minutes before the baking is complete, take
out the casserole, sprinkle with the cheese and return to the oven.
Serve the ham casserole with fresh buttered asparagus and brown
rolls. Serves 6.

ESCALLOPED HAM

Temperature: 325°F.   Time: 1 hour, 15 minutes
1 slice smoked ham, 1" thick   1 onion, chopped
  (1¼ lbs.)   6 tablespoons brown sugar
1 tablespoon flour   2 cups canned tomatoes
  1 tablespoon peanut butter   1 bay leaf
2 tablespoons fat

Nick the edges of the ham; rub both sides with a mixture of
flour and peanut butter. Place in an oiled baking dish. Heat the
fat in a saucepan; add the chopped onion; cook and stir till golden
brown. Sprinkle over the ham; add the brown sugar, the tomatoes
and the bay leaf. Cover and bake in a moderate oven till the ham
is tender. Take out the bay leaf; serve with broiled mushrooms.
Serves 4.

GLAZED HAM

Temperature: 325°F.

Time: 2½-3 hours

1 ham, 8 to 10 pounds
5 tablespoons fat
1 medium sized onion, chopped
1 cup celery, chopped
½ cup raisins
4 cups soft bread crumbs
1 teaspoon salt

¼ teaspoon poultry dressing
¼ cup sour cream
¼ teaspoon mace
½ cup brown sugar
1 tablespoon flour
Whole cloves
8 maraschino cherries

Select a ham that doesn't require par-boiling; have the butcher bone it. Heat the fat in a roasting pan; cook the onion till golden brown; add the celery, raisins, bread crumbs, salt, poultry dressing, sour cream and mace. Stuff and tie the ham; bake in a moderate oven (350°F.) for 2½-3 hours. Remove from the oven and take off the skin. Score the fat surface into squares or diamonds. Mix together the brown sugar and flour; press into the fat; stick with whole cloves; decorate the squares with half cherries cut in petals. Return to a hot oven (400°F.); glaze for 15 minutes. Serves 20.

CRISP HAM LOAF

Temperature: 350°F.

Time: 1 hour, 10 minutes

2 cups cooked potatoes,
  thinly sliced
1 pound flank steak, chopped
1 pound fresh pork, chopped
¼ pound smoked ham, chopped
1 tablespoon dry mustard

1 tablespoon corn starch
1 teaspoon salt
¼ teaspoon pepper
1 egg, unbeaten
1½ cups bread crumbs
1 onion, finely chopped

Place a layer of potatoes in the bottom of a loaf pan 9″ x 5″ x 3″. Combine the remaining ingredients in the order given; mix thoroughly. Press into a loaf pan on top of the potatoes; bake in a moderate oven. At the end of half an hour's baking, drain off all liquid; return to the oven for half an hour. Draining off the liquid gives a well-browned, crisp crust. When done, invert on a platter and serve. Serves 6.

ROAST FRESH HAM

Temperature: 350°F.

Time: 5 hours

10-pound fresh ham
  2 tablespoons brown sugar

½ cup dry crumbs
18 whole cloves

Place the ham on a rack in a roasting pan. Bake, uncovered, till tender, allowing 30 minutes to the pound. When done, remove the rind. Mix the brown sugar and crumbs; press into the soft fat. Stick with the whole cloves. Glaze in a hot oven (400°F.) for 10 minutes. Serve with sweet potatoes and relish.

BAKED HAM LOAF

Temperature: 375°F.   Time: 2 hours

1 pound smoked ham,   ½ tablespoon green pickle,
  ground   chopped
1¾ pounds fresh lean pork,   ½ teaspoon salt
  ground   Dash of pepper and mace
¼ pound sausage meat   1 cup brown sugar
  2 eggs, well beaten   3 teaspoons dry mustard
1 cup milk   ½ cup cider vinegar
  1 cup dry crumbs   ½ cup water

Have the two meats ground; mash the sausage meat and leave
it separate. Combine the beaten eggs, milk, crumbs, pickle and
seasonings; add to the mixture of ham and pork. Mix well; press
half the mixture into an oiled loaf pan 9″ x 5″ x 3″. Use the sausage
meat as a filling; add the second half of the ham mixture. Press
firmly in the pan; loosen, then invert the meat on a small trivet or
rack. Place the rack and meat in a roasting pan. Combine the
sugar, mustard, vinegar and water in a saucepan; simmer for
5 minutes. Baste the meat loaf with this mixture several times
during the baking. When the loaf is done, thicken the liquid
slightly; serve with the slices of the loaf. This quantity will
serve 2 meals, one hot, one cold for 6 persons.

BAKED SPARERIBS

Temperature: 325°F.-350°F.   Time: 2 hours

2 strips spareribs, about 3 pounds   1 cup boiling water
  3½ teaspoons salt   6 sausages
½ teaspoon pepper   1 onion, chopped
  1 tablespoon flour   6 cups stale bread, cubed
2 cups celery, diced   1 teaspoon poultry dressing

Wipe the spareribs; mix together 2 teaspoons of salt, ¼ teaspoon pepper and the flour; rub the ribs inside and out. Dice the
celery; cook in the boiling water till tender; drain. Dice the
sausages; pan fry till crisp; add the chopped onion; cook and stir
till golden brown. Remove from the heat; add the celery, the
bread cubes, the poultry dressing and the remainder of the seasonings. Lay the first strip of spareribs on a sheet of heavy brown
paper which has been oiled. Cover the ribs with the dressing,
then the second strip of ribs. Wrap around with the brown paper,
leaving both ends open. Place on a rack; bake in a moderate oven
till tender. The paper conserves all the moisture in the meat and
still allows it to be beautifully browned. Serves 6.

BAKED PORK TENDERLOIN

Temperature: 350°F.

Time: 1-1¼ hours

2 pork tenderloins (approximately 1¾ pounds)
4 tablespoons fat
¼ cup onion, chopped
2 cups soft bread crumbs

3 tablespoons milk
½ teaspoon salt
⅛ teaspoon pepper
¼ teaspoon poultry dressing

Open each tenderloin lengthwise, using a sharp knife and being careful not to cut through to the bottom of the meat; flatten out. Heat 2 tablespoons fat; cook the onion until golden brown. Add remaining ingredients and mix well. Spread the dressing on one tenderloin and cover with the other tenderloin. Tie in place. Heat the remaining fat in a pan 14″ x 5″ x 3″. Sear the meat on both sides. Cook, uncovered, in a moderate oven till done. Serve hot with escalloped potatoes or cold with cole slaw. Serves 6.

HAM AND VEAL PIE

Temperature: 325°F.

Time: 1½ hours

¾ pound stewing veal
½ pound smoked ham
3 tablespoons fat
6 small onions, chopped
2 tablespoons brown sugar
1 cup canned tomatoes
1 tablespoon concentrated essence of beef

1 cup boiling water
1 teaspoon salt
Dash of pepper and paprika
2 cups raw potatoes, diced
½ cup carrots, diced
¼ cup celery, diced
3 tablespoons flour
½ cup water

Cut the veal and smoked ham in serving pieces. Heat 1 tablespoon fat in a saucepan; sear the meat in it; lift the meat to a large casserole. Add the remaining 2 tablespoons fat to the pan; add the chopped onions; cook and stir till tender; add the sugar, tomatoes, beef essence dissolved in the boiling water, and the seasoning. Cover and oven bake for 45 minutes. Add the chopped vegetables and continue baking till tender. Thicken the pie with a paste of flour and water. Bake uncovered the last 15 minutes. Serves 6.

SAUSAGES DE LUXE

Place the sausages in a heavy pan with very little water; cover and oven bake for 10 minutes. Move the sausages to the top of the stove; cook, uncovered, until brown and crisp. The fat should be poured off 2 or 3 times in the cooking, strained into an open jar and set away for pan frying. Serve with broiled tomatoes.

SAUSAGE ROLLS

In making sausage rolls, steam the sausages for 5 minutes; let cool enough to handle; cut in half. Roll out plain pastry; brush lightly with prepared mustard. Roll each sausage half in the pastry; seal the edges; chill until ready to use. Bake in a hot oven (425°F.) for 10 minutes and serve hot. If you haven't time to make pastry, try a thin slice of fresh bread for the top.

HAM SOUFFLE

Temperature: 375°F.
3 tablespoons fat
4 tablespoons flour
1 teaspoon salt
Dash of pepper
¼ teaspoon dry mustard

Time: 1½ hours
2 cups milk
3 eggs, separated
2 tablespoons green onion, chopped
2 cups cooked ham, ground

Melt the fat in the top of the double boiler; blend in the flour and seasonings. Let bubble over low heat for three minutes. Gradually add the milk; stir and cook until smooth and thick. Place over boiling water; continue cooking for ten minutes, stirring occasionally. Separate the eggs; beat the yolks slightly. Pour the hot sauce over the egg yolks, stirring all the time. Add the chopped onions and cool. Add the ground ham; fold in the stiffly beaten egg whites. Turn into a 2-quart oiled baking dish. Place in a pan of hot water; oven bake until a silver knife inserted in the centre of the souffle comes out clean. Serve with escalloped potatoes and hot muffins. Serves 6.

CROWN ROAST OF SPARERIBS

Temperature: 325°F.
2 strips pork spareribs, 4½″-5″ high (approximately 2 pounds)
2 tablespoons fat
1 onion, chopped
2 cups soft bread crumbs
1½ pounds, chuck steak, ground

Time: 2 hours
½ pound lean pork, ground
½ cup celery, chopped
⅛ teaspoon pepper
1 teaspoon salt
¼ teaspoon poultry spice

Sew the small end of one strip of spareribs to the large end of the other strip; overlap slightly and have the curved surface out. Complete the circle by sewing the other end similarly. Place the circle in a Dutch Oven or small round roasting pan. Heat the fat in a heavy saucepan; add the chopped onion; cook and stir till the onion is tender. Add the bread crumbs, chopped meats, celery and seasonings. Mix well; press into the circle of the spareribs.

Bake till the meats are tender. Cook small potato balls till tender; drain and toss with melted butter and parsley. Fill the crown with potatoes; serve with green beans and a salad. Serves 6.

Cold Meats

SUGAR-GLAZED TONGUE

Temperature: 350°F.   Time: 30 minutes

One 4-pound beef tongue   8 whole cloves
  ⅓ cup cider vinegar   3 tablespoons brown sugar
1½ teaspoons salt   1 tablespoon lemon juice

Use a fresh smoked tongue; cover with cold water; bring to the boil and drain. Again cover with water; add the vinegar and salt; simmer until tender; let cool in the liquid. Remove the skin, small bones and cartilage; stud with cloves and place in a shallow baking dish. Mix together the brown sugar and lemon juice; brush over the tongue. Bake for half an hour in a moderate oven (350°F.), basting frequently. Slice and serve hot. Don't discard the liquid in which the tongue was cooked; save it for making split pea soup. Serves 6.

FROSTED CHICKEN LOAF

1 boiling fowl, 4½-5 pounds   ¼ cup celery, chopped
  1 onion   ½ cup mayonnaise
2 whole cloves   ¼ cup green pickle, chopped
  1 tablespoon salt   One 4-ounce package plain
1 tablespoon gelatine   cream cheese
  ¼ cup cold water   ¼ cup mayonnaise
½ teaspoon salt   Sliced, stuffed olives
  Dash of pepper and paprika

Singe, disjoint and wash the bird; place in a heavy kettle; cover with hot water. Add the onion, which has been stuffed with 2 whole cloves, and 1 tablespoon salt; simmer gently till tender. Strain the stock and remove the fat; dice the chicken. The loaf requires 1½ cups of hot stock and 2 cups diced chicken. Soak the gelatine for 5 minutes in ¼ cup cold water. Heat the stock to boiling; add ½ teaspoon salt, the pepper and paprika. Add the soaked gelatine; stir till dissolved; let chill until the mixture begins to set. Add the diced chicken, the celery, ½ cup mayonnaise and the chopped green pickle. Pour into a loaf pan; chill till firm. Mash the cream cheese with ¼ cup mayonnaise; beat till smooth. Just before serving frost the chicken loaf with the mixture; garnish with slices of stuffed olives. This loaf serves 10.

JELLIED MEAT

5 pounds beef shank,
front quarter
2 pounds boiling pork
1 onion, stuck with 2 whole
cloves
1 carrot, diced

1 tablespoon salt
1 stalk celery or dry celery
leaves, chopped
1 teaspoon pepper
1 teaspoon dry mustard
1 tablespoon sugar

Wipe the meat; place in a large kettle and cover with cold water. Heat to the boiling point, boil for 5 minutes and remove the scum. Reduce the heat; add the vegetables, seasonings and sugar; simmer gently until tender. Remove the meat from the bones and pull apart with forks. Strain the stock; add the clear stock to the meat. Pour a little stock into a loaf pan 9″ x 5″ x 3″; when it begins to set, make a pattern with slices of hard cooked eggs and carrot strips. When that is set, pour in the jellied meat; chill until firm. Unmould on a flat platter; garnish with Apple Butter in lettuce cups. Serves 10-12.

NOTE TO BRIDES: *For variation, pour half the meat mixture into an oiled loaf pan 9″ x 5″; chill until set. Spread with a mixture of 1 cup finely chopped cabbage and ¼ cup chopped mustard pickle; cover with the remainder of the meat mixture. Chill until firm.*

JELLIED TONGUE

1 fresh beef tongue, 5 pounds
1 onion, sliced
½ cup celery and celery leaves,
chopped

2 bay leaves
1 teaspoon pickling spice
1 teaspoon salt

Wash the tongue; cover with cold water; bring to the boil and drain. Add sufficient cold water to almost cover the tongue; add the vegetables, spices and seasonings; simmer till tender (about 3 hours). Leave the tongue in the liquid till cool enough to handle; skin and chill while the jelly is being prepared:

3 tablespoons gelatine
½ cup cold tongue stock
1½ cups boiling tongue stock
¼ cup cider vinegar
1 tablespoon white sugar

¼ teaspoon salt
1 teaspoon Worcester Sauce
½ cup green pickle, chopped
½ cup celery, chopped
2 hard cooked eggs

Soak the gelatine in the cold stock for 5 minutes; dissolve in the boiling stock. Add the vinegar, sugar, salt and Worcester Sauce. Pour a little of this mixture on the bottom of an oiled loaf pan and decorate with hard-cooked eggs; arrange the tongue in the pan. Let the rest of the jelly thicken slightly; add the chopped pickle and celery. Pour over the tongue; let the whole mould chill till firm. Unmould and slice with a very sharp knife. Serves 6-8.

JELLIED CHICKEN WITH HAM
(*White Meat*)

1 tablespoon gelatine	Dash of mace
2 tablespoons cold water	Dash of paprika
3 tablespoons butter	2 cups rich milk
1½ tablespoons corn starch	2 cups cooked chicken,
½ teaspoon salt	diced
⅛ teaspoon pepper	4 slices cooked ham

Soak the gelatine in the cold water for 5 minutes. Melt the butter in a heavy saucepan; blend in the corn starch and seasonings; let bubble for 3 minutes. Add the milk slowly; cook and stir till smooth and thick, about 5 minutes. Add the gelatine; stir till dissolved; add the diced chicken. Line an oiled ring mould or a loaf pan with the ham; pour in the chicken mixture. Let stand till firm; unmould on a bed of lettuce and serve with Cole Slaw. Serves 6-8.

COLD HAM LOAF

Temperature: 350°F.	Time: 1 hour
1 cup milk	½ cup carrots, grated
1 cup soft bread crumbs	1 tablespoon parsley or green
1 egg, unbeaten	pickle, chopped
2 cups cooked smoked ham,	1 small onion, chopped
ground	¼ teaspoon dry mustard
1 can condensed tomato	¼ teaspoon mayonnaise
soup (10 oz.)	1 tablespoon chili sauce

Soak the milk and bread crumbs together for 10 minutes; add the unbeaten egg; beat till smooth. Add the chopped ham, tomato soup, carrots, parsley, onion and mustard. Mix well; spoon into an oiled loaf pan 7″ x 5″ x 3″. Bake in a moderate oven till done; drain off the liquid twice during baking. Remove from the pan and cool; mix together the mayonnaise and chili sauce; frost the loaf. Slice thinly; serve with the cole slaw. Serves 6.

GALANTINE OF VEAL

1 small breast of veal (5 lbs.)	½ cup pecans or walnuts,
1½ pounds sausage meat	chopped
½ pound cooked tongue, diced	½ cup green pickle, chopped

Have the butcher bone and flatten the veal. Unroll it on the table; cover it with half the sausage meat. Over the sausage meat shake the diced tongue, chopped nuts and pickle; cover with another layer of sausage meat. Roll the meat in a cloth, just as you would a steamed pudding; boil very gently for 3 hours. When cool, fasten with a strip of cotton around the outside; chill under a heavy weight. When sliced, this meat shows the various layers and colors. It is delicious in flavor and the colors are attractive. Serves 12.

VEAL AND HAM PIE

Temperature: 450°F.   Time: 20-25 minutes

3½ pounds shoulder of veal   ⅛ teaspoon mace
  1 cup celery, chopped   2 tablespoons gelatine
½ cup carrots, diced   ¼ cup cold water
  1 medium onion, chopped   ½ pound cooked ham, cut in
2 teaspoons parsley, chopped   2″ strips
  1 teaspoon salt   2 hard cooked eggs
⅛ teaspoon pepper   Plain pastry

Wipe the veal and place in a kettle; cover with cold water; simmer gently until the meat is tender. Pull the meat from the bones and dice. Strain the stock; there should be 3 cups. Add to it the diced vegetables and seasonings; cook until the vegetables are tender. Soak the gelatine in the cold water for 5 minutes; add to the hot vegetable stock; stir till dissolved. Fill an oiled 2-quart casserole with alternate layers of veal, ham and slices of hard cooked eggs; pour over all the vegetable stock. Cover with plain pastry; bake in a hot oven (450°F.), until the pastry is golden brown. Let stand till cold and jellied; remove carefully to a silver serving platter; serve in slices. Serves 8-10.

Meat Sauces

SPICED APPLE SAUCE

6 tart apples   1½ tablespoons cider vinegar
  1 cup boiling water   ⅓ cup white sugar
3 whole cloves   1 tablespoon butter

Core and quarter the apples; do not peel. Put in a saucepan with the water and cloves. Simmer, tightly covered, till the apples are tender; press through a sieve. Return to the heat; add the vinegar and sugar; simmer 10 minutes. Remove from the heat; beat in the butter. Serve either hot or cold with roast fowl or roast pork. Yield: 1½ cups.

BARBECUE SAUCE

2 tablespoons fat   1 tablespoon onion, finely chopped
  1¼ cups water   1½ teaspoons salt
¼ cup cider vinegar   ⅛ teaspoon cayenne pepper
  1 teaspoon dry mustard   1 tablespoon Worcester Sauce
1 tablespoon sugar

Combine all the ingredients; simmer gently for 20 minutes. Pour over the meat; continue simmering another 20 minutes. This is a grand sauce for any meat. Serves 6.

CRANBERRY RELISH

4 cups cranberries
1 cup water
¼ cup cider vinegar

1 orange
½ cup seedless raisins, chopped
½ cup brown sugar

Wash and pick over the cranberries. Add the water and vinegar; cook gently till the cranberries are tender and the skin unbroken. Add the orange, run through the chopper, the chopped raisins and the sugar; simmer for 20 minutes. This relish will keep in the refrigerator or in sealed sterile jars. Yield: 3 cups.

CREOLE SAUCE

4 slices breakfast bacon, diced
2½ tablespoons sifted flour
½ teaspoon salt

Dash of pepper and paprika
2 cups tomato juice
1 tablespoon Worcester Sauce

Pan fry the diced bacon until crisp; blend in the flour and seasonings; let bubble 3 minutes. Slowly add the tomato juice and Worcester Sauce. Cook and stir till smooth and thick. Serve with steak and onions. Serves 6.

MUSTARD SAUCE

2 tablespoons dry mustard
¼ teaspoon salt
Dash of pepper and paprika
2 tablespoons white sugar

½ tablespoon sifted flour
⅓ cup cider vinegar
½ cup water
1 egg, slightly beaten

Mix together the mustard, salt, pepper, paprika, sugar and flour in the top of a double boiler; add the vinegar and water; blend well with the dover beater. Cook over boiling water for 10 minutes, stirring constantly. Pour over the lightly beaten egg; return to the double boiler; continue cooking for 3 minutes. Serve either hot or cold with roast ham or cold meats. Serves 6.

ONION SAUCE

4 tablespoons fat
1 cup onions, thinly sliced
2 tablespoons raw carrot, grated
4 tablespoons sifted flour

2 condensed meat cubes
2 cups boiling water
¾ teaspoon salt
Dash of pepper

Heat the fat in a heavy saucepan; add the onions and carrots; stir and cook till tender. The onions should be so thin as to disappear in the sauce. Blend in the flour; let bubble 2 or 3 minutes; add the meat cubes which have been dissolved in the hot water. Add the seasonings; stir till smooth. Serve hot with sliced meat loaf. Serves 6.

RAISIN SAUCE

¾ cup raisins
  4 whole cloves
1 cup water
  ¼ cup brown sugar

1 teaspoon corn starch
1 tablespoon cider vinegar
1 tablespoon butter
Dash of pepper

Cover the raisins and cloves with the water; simmer till tender; remove the cloves. Add the sugar and corn starch which have been mixed to a paste with the vinegar; simmer for 5 minutes; add the butter and pepper. Serve hot with glazed ham. Serves 6.

TOMATO SAUCE

2 tablespoons fat
  2 tablespoons sifted flour
¾ teaspoon salt
  Dash of pepper and paprika

1 teaspoon white sugar
  1 cup tomato juice
Pinch of mace

Melt the fat in a saucepan; blend in the flour; let bubble for three minutes. Add the seasonings and sugar; slowly stir in the tomato juice. Cook and stir till smooth and thick; add the pinch of mace. Serve hot with omelettes, meat loaves or meat pies. Serves 4.

TOMATO-CHEESE SAUCE

4 tablespoons butter
  4 tablespoons sifted flour
1 cup condensed tomato soup
  1 cup hot water
½ teaspoon salt

Dash of pepper
  ⅛ teaspoon dry mustard
1 teaspoon sugar
  ½ cup grated cheese

Melt the butter in a saucepan and stir in the flour, mixing carefully; let bubble over low heat for 3 minutes. Add a mixture of the soup and hot water; add the seasonings and sugar; cook and stir till smooth and thick. Remove from heat; add the grated cheese; stir till dissolved. Pour over buttered strips of bread or use as a meat sauce. Serves 6.

THREE-MINUTE TOMATO SAUCE

1½ cups canned tomatoes
  ½ teaspoon salt
½ teaspoon white sugar

Dash of pepper
  1 tablespoon cream cheese
¼ cup cracker crumbs

Measure the canned tomatoes into a saucepan; add the salt, sugar, pepper and cream cheese. Heat; add the cracker crumbs; stir again until piping hot. Serve with hamburgers. Serves 6.

Meat Garnishes

SPICED APPLES

4 pounds sweet apples (12)
Whole cloves
1 cup cider vinegar
¼ cup water
1½ cups brown sugar

1 tablespoon ginger root
2 tablespoons mixed pickling
spice
1 tablespoon lemon juice
1 teaspoon grated lemon rind

Wipe the apples; stick each apple with four whole cloves. Make a syrup of the vinegar, water and brown sugar. Add the spices, tied in a bag, the lemon juice and the rind. Simmer 5 minutes. Add the apples; cook slowly till tender, spooning the liquid over them occasionally. Lift out on a platter and chill. Serve round the meat. Yield: 12 apples.

BEET RELISH

1 tablespoon gelatine
¼ cup cold water
1 cup boiling water
½ cup beet liquid
¼ cup cider vinegar
½ teaspoon salt

1 tablespoon brown sugar
1 teaspoon onion, finely
chopped
¼ cup horseradish
1 cup cooked beets,
finely chopped

Soak the gelatine in the cold water for 5 minutes; dissolve in the boiling water. Add ½ cup water in which the beets were cooked, the vinegar, salt, sugar and onion. Chill until the mixture begins to set; fold in the horseradish and beets. Pour into an oiled pan 8″ x 12″; chill. Cut in diamonds, circles or squares; serve with chicken or turkey. Yield: 16 squares.

CARROT GARNISHES

Scrape the carrots; cut in shoe-string lengths about 2½″ long. Chill in cold water; just before serving, drain and dry.

Scrape a large carrot; score with a fork and cut in slices ⅛″ thick. Cut a grapefruit in half; make regular incisions in the skin so that the carrot slices will slip half-way in. They look like ten dollar gold pieces ready to be picked up.

Scrape and grate crisp, fresh carrots; serve in a mound on a long plate with a pile of crisp crackers at one end and cottage or cream cheese at the other end.

STUFFED CELERY

Scrub the celery; dry and chill. Fill the stalks with a mixture of cream cheese, salt, a dash of paprika and mayonnaise. Select two even round stalks of celery, fill them and press together to form a circle. Chill the celery; just before serving, cut in rounds, using a very sharp knife.

GRAPEFRUIT GARNISH

Try this unusual garnish with your turkey. Drain grapefruit sections and season with salt and sugar; wrap in half a strip of bacon and broil under a medium flame. The bacon should be crisp, the grapefruit heated through. Fasten the bacon around the grapefruit with a wooden toothpick.

MUSHROOM TEASERS

The large brown mushrooms are a meal in themselves. Peel them; place them individually, upside down, on small squares of buttered bread.

Chop the stems; mix with 2 tablespoons chopped blanched almonds. Spread this mixture over the inverted caps; top with a little butter. Dust with salt and pepper and broil for five minutes. Serve hot as a "come on" for a chicken dinner. They look smart too, ranged round a platter of baked chicken.

BROILED ORANGE SLICES

Temperature: 400°F.   Time: 4 minutes
12 slices orange, ¼" thick   ½ teaspoon cinnamon
  2 tablespoons brown sugar   6 maraschino cherries

Slice the oranges; nick the edges into eighths. Spread the slices with a mixture of the brown sugar and cinnamon. Put a half cherry in the centre. Broil till hot and bubbly. Serve with meat. Serves 6.

SUGARED ORANGE GARNISH

3 large oranges   1 teaspoon grated lemon rind
  1 cup white sugar   3 tablespoons lemon juice
1 cup water   1 small bottle maraschino cherries

Wipe the oranges; cut in ½" slices. Place in a saucepan; cover with boiling water. Simmer for an hour; drain well; save the orange water. Make a syrup of the white sugar, the orange water, the lemon rind and juice. Drain the cherries; add that liquid to the syrup. Add the orange slices; simmer for 5 minutes. Place in a pan to cool; when ready to serve, cut the cherries in petal-like pieces and lay on orange slices. Serve with cold meats.

RHUBARB RELISHES

Use tender, pink rhubarb and cut it in 2" lengths. Slit each length down ½" as you would in preparing celery. Drop into ice-cold water; chill until it curls. Serve with salads and hot dishes. It's especially good with hot macaroni and cheese.

CHAPTER 12

Pastry

The most popular dessert in Canada, winter and summer, is pie; that's why every woman wants to place on her table the perfect pie with a flaky, golden brown crust, a well-cooked filling and a perfect undercrust.

Pie Success Rules: Sift the flour carefully before measuring. You'll notice in the pastry recipes there is a choice of flours and of ingredients. Many women feel that rich pastry can be made only with pastry flour; others prefer all-purpose flour for all pastry both flaky and plain. Try them all; select the one your family likes best.

Cut the shortening in coarsely. Use lard, vegetable shortening, or any other shortening you like. An all butter shortening is harder, tougher, and not so short in the grain as the vegetable and animal fats. To cut in the shortening use a dough blender, a cookie cutter, a couple of knives or the tips of your fingers.

Be stingy with the water and have it cold.

Start with a hot oven, finish with a moderate oven.

The Soggy Undercrust: This is the despair of many young cooks but it can be overcome. In fruit pies a pinch of white sugar added to the dry ingredients will help seal the undercrust. In pumpkin and custard pies if the bottom crust is pre-cooked 5 minutes before the filling is added, the undercrust will stay dry and will cut well.

Temperature for Pies: Baked Shells: Prick the crust well; bake in a hot oven (450°F.) for 15-18 minutes.

Two-Crust Pies: Place these pies in a hot oven (450°F.) for 15 minutes; reduce the heat to 350°F. for the remainder of the baking period.

HOT WATER PASTRY

½ cup shortening
¼ cup boiling water
1½ cups sifted pastry flour
½ teaspoon baking powder
½ teaspoon salt

Measure the shortening into a bowl; add the boiling water. Beat until cold and creamy. Chill the mixture. Sift together the flour, baking powder and salt. Add the liquid shortening; stir until it forms a smooth ball. Cover and chill until firm. Roll on a floured board. This quantity will make a 2-crust 8″ pie or two small 7″ open faced pies, ideal for a small family.

PLAIN PASTRY

3¼ cups sifted pastry flour   1 cup shortening
  1 teaspoon salt   Cold water (⅓ to scant ½ cup)

Sift the flour before measuring, then re-sift with the salt. Cut in the shortening with a dough blender, a cookie cutter or a case knife; it should be about as large as a pea. Sprinkle with just enough cold water to hold together. Mix lightly with a knife. Turn on a floured board and shape in a roll. Wrap in wax paper; chill slightly before rolling. This quantity will make a 2-crust pie, a 9″ baked shell, and ½ dozen tarts. The pastry need not all be baked at one time if the roll is kept chilled and tightly wrapped.

NOTE TO BRIDES: *It saves time and kitchen muss if enough pastry is made up for more than one pie. However, if you wish to make one single or double crust pie, here are the quantities:*

Quantities for One-Crust 9″ Pie

1 cup sifted pastry flour   ⅓ cup shortening
  ⅓ teaspoon salt   2-2 ½ tablespoons cold water

Quantities for Two-Crust 9″ Pie

1¾ cups sifted pastry flour   ½ cup plus 1 tablespoon
  ½ teaspoon salt   shortening
                              4 tablespoons cold water

CHEESE PASTRY

3¼ cups sifted pastry flour   ¾ cup cheese, grated
  1 teaspoon salt   Cold water (⅓ to ½ cup)
⅔ cup shortening

Sift the flour before measuring; sift again with the salt. Cut in the shortening, having the pieces fairly coarse; add the grated cheese; blend. Sprinkle with just enough cold water to bind the mixture. Mix lightly; wrap in waxed paper and chill before rolling. Yield: 2 covered 8″ pies.

NOTE TO BRIDES: *This pastry is especially good for apple pie, for meat pies and meat roll-ups.*

CORNFLAKES PIE CRUST

4 cups cornflakes, unrolled   ¼ cup fine white sugar
  ⅓ cup melted butter

Roll the cornflakes till very fine; measure; there should be 1 cup. Mix with the melted butter, slightly warm, and the sugar. Brush a 9″ pie pan lightly with melted shortening. Line the bottom and sides with the cornflakes mixture; chill at least one hour before filling. Yield: One 9″ pie shell.

GINGERSNAP PIE CRUST

¼ cup brown sugar 1½ cups gingersnap crumbs
⅓ cup softened butter

Blend the brown sugar and softened butter until creamy. Add the crumbs and blend well. Rub a 9″ pie pan with oil; pat the crumb mixture firmly on the bottom and sides of the pan, crimping the edge with the tines of a fork; chill well before filling. This pie shell requires no baking and may be made the night before using. Yield: One 9″ pie shell.

APPLESAUCE PIE

Temperature: 425°F. Time: 5 minutes
350°F. 40 minutes

Plain pastry
1 cup strained, thick, unsweetened applesauce
¾ cup white sugar
½ cup 18% cream
2 tablepoons melted shortening

2 eggs, beaten lightly
½ teaspoon grated nutmeg
2 teaspoons grated lemon
rind
3 tablespoons lemon juice

Line a 9″ pie pan with pastry. Flute on an edge; bake in a hot oven (425°F.) for 5 minutes. Remove from the oven and fill with the following mixture:

Mix together the applesauce, sugar, cream, melted shortening, eggs, nutmeg, lemon rind and juice. Beat till well blended. Pour into the partially baked shell. Return to the oven (now 350°F.); continue baking until set. Serve slightly warm. Serves 6.

FRESH BLUEBERRY PIE

Temperature: 450°F. Time: 15 minutes
350°F. 25 minutes

Plain pastry
4 cups fresh blueberries
2 tablespoons flour
½ cup white sugar

⅛ teaspoon salt
1 teaspoon lemon juice
1 tablespoon butter

Line a 9″ pie pan with plain pastry. Mix together the flour, sugar and salt. Sprinkle ¼ of this mixture on the uncooked bottom crust; add the blueberries; add the remainder of the sugar mixture; sprinkle with lemon juice; dot with butter. Flute on the top crust. Bake in a hot oven, 450°F. for 15 minutes; reduce the heat to 350°F.; continue baking until the berries are tender. Serves 6.

APPLE PIE

Temperature: 450°F.	Time: 15 minutes
350°F.	25-30 minutes

Plain pastry
  2 tablespoons flour
1 cup white sugar
  4½ cups apples, peeled, cored and sliced

1 teaspoon lemon juice
  ¼ teaspoon nutmeg
1 tablespoon butter

Line a 9″ pie pan with pastry. Mix together the flour and sugar. Sprinkle half the mixture on the bottom crust. Add the apples, which have been peeled, cored and sliced ¼″ thick. Sprinkle with lemon juice, the remaining sugar mixture and the nutmeg; dot with butter. Cover with the top crust; bake in a hot oven for 15 minutes; reduce the heat to 350°F. and continue baking until the apples are cooked. Serve slightly warm with cheese. Serves 6.

NOTE TO BRIDES: *When the green apples are available, core and slice but do not peel them; the green skin gives a typical flavor nothing else can touch.*

DUTCH APPLE PIE

Temperature: 450°F.	Time: 20 minutes
325°F.	20 minutes

Plain pastry
  2 cups apples, cut in eighths
¾ cup brown sugar
  ¼ cup hot water
1 egg, well beaten
  ¾ cup cake or cookie crumbs

¼ cup sifted pastry flour
  1 teaspoon cinnamon
¼ teaspoon nutmeg
  ⅛ teaspoon ginger
4 tablespoons softened fat

Line a 9″ pie pan with plain pastry. Pare and core the apples; cut in lengths; arrange on the unbaked pastry in a regular pattern. Mix together the brown sugar and hot water; add the well beaten egg; pour the whole mixture over the apples. Mix together the crumbs, flour, spices and softened fat; sprinkle over the pie filling. Bake in a hot oven (450°F.) until the mixture begins to brown, about 20 minutes; reduce the heat to 325°F. and continue baking another 20 minutes. Serve slightly warm with cheese. Serves 6.

BUTTERSCOTCH CHIFFON PIE

Baked pie shell—9″
  1 tablespoon gelatine
¼ cup cold water
  3 eggs, separated
¾ cup brown sugar

1 cup hot milk
  ⅛ teaspoon salt
1 teaspoon butter
  ½ teaspoon vanilla
2 tablespoons white sugar

Soften the gelatine in the cold water for 5 minutes. Beat the egg yolks slightly; add the sugar, milk and salt. Blend well with the dover beater; cook over boiling water till the mixture coats the back of a spoon, stirring occasionally. When thick, remove from the heat; stir in the softened gelatine, butter and vanilla. Beat with a dover beater till creamy; fold in the stiffly beaten egg whites to which has been added the white sugar. Pour into the baked shell. Chill 1½ hours before serving. Serves 6.

BUTTERSCOTCH PIE

Baked pastry shell—9″
  2 tablespoons fat
¾ cup brown sugar
  1¾ cups hot milk
4 tablespoons corn starch
  4 tablespoons cold milk

⅛ teaspoon salt
  2 eggs, separated
1 teaspoon vanilla
  3 tablespoons white sugar
1 teaspoon corn starch

Melt the fat in the top of the double boiler; blend in the brown sugar; let cook over direct heat till bubbly but not burned. Add the hot milk slowly; stir and cook till blended. Make a paste of the 4 tablespoons of corn starch, cold milk and salt; stir into the milk mixture; stir and cook till thick and smooth. Place over rapidly boiling water; cover and cook for 10 minutes stirring occasionally. Separate the eggs; beat the yolks slightly. Combine them with a little of the hot mixture; stir back into the filling. Blend well; continue cooking for 3 minutes. Remove from the heat; add the vanilla. Beat till smooth; pour into the baked shell. Beat the egg whites till stiff and glossy; add 3 tablespoons white sugar and 1 teaspoon corn starch; beat again till the mixture peaks. Pile lightly on the pie filling; brown in a 350°F. oven. Serves 6.

CANNED CHERRY PIE

Temperature: 425°F.
Plain pastry
  ½ cup white sugar
2 tablespoons flour
  Dash of salt

Time: 40 minutes
¾ cup juice drained from cherries
  2 cups canned cherries, drained
1 tablespoon butter
  ¼ teaspoon cinnamon

Line a 9″ pie pan with plain pastry. Mix together the sugar, flour and salt; sprinkle ¼ of the mixture on the bottom crust. Add the remainder to the cherry juice. Stir till smooth; cook over low heat until smooth and clear, about 5 minutes. Add the cherries, butter and cinnamon; pour into the lined pie plate. Cover with a top crust; bake in a hot oven till the crust is golden. Serves 6.

FRESH CHERRY PIE

Temperature: 425°F.   Time: 15 minutes
          350°F.   25 minutes

Plain pastry   4 tablespoons flour
  3½ cups red cherries, pitted   1 teaspoon lemon juice
  ⅛ teaspoon salt   ⅛ teaspoon nutmeg
  ⅔ cup sugar   2 drops almond flavoring

Line a 9″ pie pan with plain pastry. Trim, and from the trimmings cut a strip 1½″ wide. Moisten the edges of the pie with water; lay the strips half under and half over the edges. Flute on the edge with floured fingers. Mix together the salt, sugar and flour. Sprinkle ¼ of the mixture on the unbaked pie; mix the remainder with the pitted cherries. Fill the pie with the cherries; add the lemon juice, nutmeg and almond flavoring. Cut out a top crust to fit the pie and lay it on top of the cherries. Do not fasten it—it will rise and fall with the cooking cherries but no hot juice boils over. Bake in a hot oven till golden brown, reducing the heat to 350°F. after the first 15 minutes. Serves 6.

CREAM PIE

Baked pastry shell, 9″   ½ cup white sugar
  1¾ cups scalded milk   2 egg yolks, slightly beaten
3 tablespoons corn starch   1 teaspoon vanilla
  ¼ teaspoon salt   ½ teaspoon almond flavoring
¼ cup cold milk   1 tablespoon butter

Scald the milk in the top of the double boiler. Make a paste of the corn starch, salt, cold milk and sugar. Stir slowly into the hot milk; cook and stir until smooth and thick. Cover and continue cooking for 10 minutes, stirring occasionally. Slightly beat the egg yolks; mix with some of the hot mixture, stir back into the filling. Blend and cook for 3 minutes. Remove from heat; add the vanilla, almond flavoring and butter. Beat till light with the dover beater. Pour into the baked shell; cover with meringue. Bake in a moderate oven till the meringue is firm and golden brown. Serves 6.

Meringue

2 egg whites   1 teaspoon corn starch
  3 tablespoons white sugar

Stiffly beat the egg white; add the sugar and corn starch, again beat until the mixture peaks.

COCONUT CREAM PIE

Make the pie as above; sprinkle the meringue with grated coconut before browning.

CHOCOLATE CREAM PIE—GINGERSNAP CRUST

Gingersnap crust
2 cups milk, scalded
2 ounces unsweetened chocolate
1 cup white sugar
4 tablespoons corn starch
¼ teaspoon salt

¼ cup cold milk
2 eggs, separated
1 teaspoon butter
1 teaspoon vanilla
3 tablespoons white sugar
1 teaspoon corn starch

Line a 9″ pie pan with the gingersnap crust. Scald the milk in the top of the double boiler; add the chocolate. When melted, add the sugar and blend well. Make a paste of the corn starch, salt and cold milk. Add to the hot mixture; stir and cook till smooth and thick. Cover and continue cooking for 12 minutes, stirring occasionally. Mix the well-beaten egg yolks with some of the chocolate mixture; stir back into the hot mixture; continue cooking 3 minutes. Remove from the heat; add the butter and vanilla. Beat with the dover beater till creamy. Pour into the gingersnap crust. Stiffly beat the 2 egg whites; add 3 tablespoons white sugar and 1 teaspoon corn starch. Beat again till stiff and glossy. Mound on top of chocolate filling. Brown in a moderate oven. Serves 6.

NOTE TO BRIDES: *This chocolate filling is equally delicious in a baked plain pastry shell.*

BANANA CREAM PIE

Baked pastry shell—9″
1¾ cups scalded milk
½ cup white sugar
3 tablespoons corn starch
¼ cup cold milk
⅛ teaspoon salt

2 eggs, separated
1 teaspoon vanilla
1 tablespoon butter
2 ripe bananas, peeled and sliced
3 tablespoons white sugar
1 teaspoon corn starch

Scald the milk in the top of the double boiler. Mix together the sugar, corn starch, cold milk and salt; stir into the hot milk. Cook and stir over boiling water till thick and smooth. Cover; continue cooking for 10 minutes. Beat the egg yolks slightly; add a little of the hot starch mixture to them; blend, then stir into the filling. Continue cooking 3 minutes. Remove from the heat; add the vanilla and butter. Slice the bananas into the baked shell; cover with the cream filling. Stiffly beat the egg whites; add 3 tablespoons white sugar and 1 teaspoon corn starch; beat again till glossy. Top the filling with this meringue; bake in a 350°F. oven till delicately browned. Serves 6.

CREAM CHIFFON PIE

Pastry

¼ cup brown sugar
  ¼ cup softened butter

1½ cups graham cracker
  crumbs, rolled very fine

Cream together the brown sugar and butter; blend in the finely rolled crumbs. Oil a 9″ pie pan; pat the mixture firmly on the sides and bottom. Bake in a 350°F. oven for a minute; watch it carefully, as it's apt to scorch. Cool; fill with the cream chiffon mixture.

Filling

2 teaspoons gelatine
  2 tablespoons cold water
1½ cups scalded milk
  ½ cup white sugar

¼ teaspoon salt
  2 eggs, separated
2 teaspoons vanilla

Soak the gelatine in the cold water for 5 minutes. Scald the milk in the top of the double boiler. Mix together ¼ cup of the sugar, the salt and the egg yolks; combine with a little hot milk; stir into the remainder of the hot milk. Cook, stirring constantly, until the mixture coats the spoon. Remove from the heat; add the softened gelatine; stir until dissolved. Chill until the mixture begins to thicken; fold in the stiffly beaten egg whites to which has been added the reserved ¼ cup of sugar; add the vanilla. Pile lightly into the crumb crust; chill until set. Serve plain, or top with this mixture:

1 teaspoon butter
  1 teaspoon brown sugar
⅛ teaspoon cinnamon

1 tablespoon graham cracker crumbs,
  rolled very fine

Cream together the butter, sugar and cinnamon; add the crumbs. Spread on a cookie sheet and brown in a 350°F. oven, shaking as the crumbs brown. This is also a delicious topping for plain ice cream. Serves 6.

SOUR CREAM PIE

Temperature: 450°F.
          325°F.

Time: 15 minutes
          35-40 minutes

Plain pastry
  2 eggs, slightly beaten
¼ cup brown sugar
  1½ cups thick sour cream
¾ cup white sugar

1 tablespoon corn starch
  1 teaspoon cinnamon
¼ teaspoon nutmeg
  ¼ teaspoon cloves
1 cup seedless raisins

Line a 9″ pie pan with pastry and flute on an edge; bake in a hot oven (450°F.) for 5 minutes; remove from the oven. Slightly beat the eggs; add the brown sugar and sour cream. Blend; add the white sugar, which has been mixed with the corn starch and spices. Blend with the dover beater; add the raisins. Pour into the partially baked shell; return to the hot oven for 10 minutes. Reduce the heat to 325°F. and continue baking until the custard is set or until a silver knife inserted in the centre comes out clean. Serves 6.

CRUMB PIE

Temperature: 450°F.
           350°F.

Time: 20 minutes
       25 minutes

Plain pastry
  ½ cup raisins, plumped
¾ cup molasses or corn syrup
  ¼ cup hot water
1 egg, well beaten
  ¾ cup dry crumbs

4 tablespoons sifted pastry
  flour
1 teaspoon cinnamon
  ¼ teaspoon nutmeg
⅛ teaspoon ginger
  3 tablespoons fat

Line an 8″ pie pan with plain pastry; bake for 5 minutes in a hot oven. Take out the partially cooked shell; sprinkle the bottom with ½ cup raisins. Mix the molasses or corn syrup with the hot water; blend in the well beaten egg; pour the mixture over the raisins. Crumble together the dry crumbs with the flour, cinnamon, nutmeg, ginger and fat; sprinkle on top of the pie. Bake in a hot oven (450°F.) for 15 minutes; reduce the heat to 350°F. and finish baking. Serve slightly warm. Serves 6.

LEMON PIE

Baked pie shell—9″
3 tablespoons corn starch
  3 tablespoons all-purpose
  flour
1 cup white sugar
  ¼ teaspoon salt

1½ cups boiling water
  2 eggs, separated
6 tablespoons lemon juice
  2 teaspoons grated lemon
  rind
2 teaspoons butter

Mix the corn starch, flour, sugar and salt in the top of a double boiler; add the boiling water, stirring all the time. Cook over direct heat till thick and smooth, stirring constantly. Cover and cook over boiling water for another 10 minutes. Mix together the egg yolks, the lemon juice and rind; stir into the hot starch mixture. Blend well; continue cooking 3 minutes. Remove from heat; add the butter; beat with a dover beater until creamy. Pour into baked shell. Cool; cover with meringue made with 2 egg-whites stiffly beaten, 3 tablespoons white sugar and 1 teaspoon corn starch. Bake till delicately brown in a 350°F. oven. Serves 6.

TWO-EGG CUSTARD PIE

Temperature: 450°F.   Time: 15 minutes
           325°F.   20-25 minutes

Plain pastry   2 eggs, slightly beaten
  ⅓ cup white sugar   2 cups hot milk
  ¼ teaspoon salt   Nutmeg
  1 tablespoon corn starch

Line a 9″ pie pan with pastry; flute on an edge; bake in a hot oven (450°F.) for 5 minutes. In the meantime, prepare the filling so that the shell need not stay out of the oven long. Mix together the sugar, salt and corn starch; add the slightly beaten eggs and the hot milk. Blend well with the dover beater; pour into the pre-cooked shell; sprinkle with grated nutmeg; return to the oven. Continue baking in the hot oven until the crust is set (about 10 minutes); reduce the oven heat and continue baking until the custard is firm. The silver knife test is still the best. Serves 6.

NOTE TO BRIDES: *In a perfect custard pie the filling and crust are baked separately. Bake the crust in a 450°F. oven for 12-15 minutes. Bake the filling in an oiled 9″ pan in a 325°F. oven; loosen the baked custard gently from the plate and slide it quickly and carefully into the baked shell. That gives you the perfect custard pie—well cooked and with no soggy undercrust.*

LEMON CUSTARD PIE

Temperature: 425°F.   Time: 12-15 minutes
           375°F.   10 minutes

1½ cups sifted pastry flour   1 teaspoon white sugar
  ½ teaspoon salt   6 tablespoons white sugar
½ teaspoon baking powder   2 tablespoons water
  ½ cup shortening   3 eggs, separated
2 tablespoons boiling water   3 tablespoons lemon juice
  2 tablespoons lemon juice   1 teaspoon grated lemon rind
1 teaspoon lemon rind, grated   ⅛ teaspoon salt

Sift together the flour, salt and baking powder. Combine the shortening, hot water and 2 tablespoons lemon juice; beat till cold and creamy. Add 1 teaspoon lemon rind, 1 teaspoon of white sugar and the sifted dry ingredients. Chill; roll the dough and line a 9″ pie shell. Moisten the edges and flute on a rim. Prick; bake in a hot oven, 425°F. till golden brown. In the meantime measure into the top of a double boiler 4 tablespoons of white sugar, 2 table-spoons of water, 3 egg yolks, 3 tablespoons lemon juice, 1 teaspoon lemon rind and ⅛ teaspoon salt. Beat well; cook over boiling water till thick and smooth; cool slightly. Beat the egg whites till stiff and glossy; add the reserved 2 tablespoons of sugar; beat again until stiff. Fold into the lemon mixture. Pile in the baked

shell; brown in a 375°F. oven for 10 minutes. Cool and serve.
Serves 6.

CUSTARD PIE

Temperature: 450°F.   Time: 15 minutes
           350°F.   25 minutes

Plain pastry   ½ teaspoon salt
  4 eggs, slightly beaten   ⅓ cup hot milk
⅔ cup white sugar   1 teaspoon vanilla

Line a 9″ pie pan with pastry; flute on the edge; bake in a hot
oven for 5 minutes. In the meantime, combine the slightly beaten
eggs with the sugar, salt, hot milk and vanilla. Pour into the
partially baked shell; continue baking in the 450°F. oven for 10
minutes. Reduce the heat to 350°F.; finish baking until the
custard is set. Serves 6.

NOTE TO BRIDES: *Do not chill custard pie as the filling
separates from the crust.*

MINCEMEAT

6 green tomatoes   ¼ teaspoon ground nutmeg
  6 tart apples, chopped   1 teaspoon salt
1½ cups seedless raisins   ¼ cup cider vinegar
  3 teaspoons ground cinnamon   ¼ cup fruit juice (any kind)
1 teaspoon cloves   ½ cup citron peel, chopped
  ½ teaspoon allspice   1 tablespoon grated orange
½ teaspoon ginger   rind

Chop the tomatoes and apples; cut the raisins with the scissors. Measure all the ingredients into a preserving kettle; simmer
gently until thick. Pour into sterile jars and seal. Yield: 3 quarts
—sufficient to fill three 9″ pies.

NOTE TO BRIDES: *Try using Cheese Pastry for your Mincemeat Pie; the flavor combination is wonderful!*

LEMON CHIFFON PIE

Baked pie shell—9″   1 cup white sugar
  1 tablespoon gelatine   ½ cup lemon juice
¼ cup cold water   1 teaspoon grated lemon rind
  4 eggs, separated   ½ teaspoon salt

Soak the gelatine in the cold water for 5 minutes. Place in the
top of a double boiler the egg yolks, ½ cup white sugar, the lemon
juice, the grated rind and the salt. Cook over boiling water till
smooth and thick, stirring constantly. Add the gelatine; stir until
dissolved. Chill until the mixture begins to set. Beat the egg
whites till stiff and glossy; gradually beat in the remaining ½ cup
sugar. Fold into the gelatine mixture. Pour into the baked shell;
chill until set. Serves 6.

ORANGE CHIFFON PIE

Temperature: 450°F.   Time: 5 minutes

Baked pastry shell—9″
3 eggs, separated
⅛ teaspoon salt
4 tablespoons white sugar
1½ tablespoons corn starch

2 tablespoons water
2 tablespoons lemon juice
¾ cup orange juice
1 teaspoon grated orange rind
1 tablespoon butter

Separate the eggs; beat the egg whites till stiff and glossy; add the salt and 1 tablespoon white sugar; beat again till stiff. Beat the egg yolks till light; add the remaining 3 tablespoons of sugar. Make a paste of the corn starch and water; add to the egg yolk mixture. Add the lemon juice, orange juice and grated orange rind. Cook in the top of a double boiler over boiling water till thick, stirring frequently. Remove from the heat; add the butter and beat till light. Fold in the egg white mixture; pour into the baked shell. Brown in a hot oven for five minutes; cool before cutting.

FRESH PEACH PIE

Temperature: 450°F.   Time: 15 minutes
350°F.   25-30 minutes

Plain pastry
½ cup white sugar
⅛ teaspoon salt
2 tablespoons flour
4 cups peaches, sliced

Skim milk to cover
1 teaspoon lemon juice
½ teaspoon grated lemon rind
1 tablespoon butter

Line a 9″ pie pan with the plain pastry. Mix together the sugar, salt and flour; sprinkle ¼ of the mixture on the raw crust. Scald, skin and slice the peaches. If they are dropped into skim milk they will not discolor. When ready to use them, drain and combine with the lemon juice and rind, the remainder of the sugar mixture. Fill the pie with this mixture; dot with butter; cover with a top crust. If the bottom crust edge is moistened with milk before the top crust is fluted on, no juice will boil out. Bake in a hot oven (450°F.) for 15 minutes; then reduce the heat (350°F.) and continue baking till done. Serves 6.

CANNED PEACH PIE

Temperature: 425°F.   Time: 40 minutes

Plain pastry
2½ cups canned peaches, chopped
¼ cup white sugar
2 tablespoons flour

⅛ teaspoon salt
¾ cup peach juice
1 tablespoon butter
1 tablespoon lemon juice

Line a 9″ pie pan with plain pastry; flute on the edge. Drain the peaches; slice the halves. Mix together the sugar, flour and salt. Sprinkle 1 tablespoon of this mixture on the unbaked pastry. Add the remainder to the peach juice; cook over low heat until clear and smooth (about 5 minutes). Put the chopped peaches in the pie shell. Dot with the butter; sprinkle with the lemon juice. Pour the peach juice mixture over them. Cover with lattice strips of pastry; bake in a hot oven till done. Serves 6.

PEACH CUSTARD PIE

Temperature: 450°F.   Time: 15 minutes
          350°F.   20 minutes

Rich pastry   1 teaspoon corn starch
   6 ripe peaches   3 eggs
6 tablespoons white sugar   1 peach kernel (optional)

Line a 9″ pie pan with rich pastry; moisten the edges and flute on a rim; chill. Save the clippings of the pastry; roll and cut in small circles. Scald, skin and slice the peaches. Mix together the sugar and corn starch. Sprinkle one quarter of this mixture on the uncooked pie shell. Add the peaches, filling the pan well. Slightly beat the eggs; add the remainder of the sugar mixture and again beat. Pour over the peaches; add the peach kernel if you like the almond flavor; dot with the pastry cut-outs. Bake in a hot oven (450°F.) for 15 minutes, reduce the heat (350°F.) and continue cooking for 20 minutes. Serves 6.

RAISIN PIE

Temperature: 450°F.   Time: 15 minutes
          350°F.   20-25 minutes

Plain pastry   ⅓ cup orange juice
   2 cups seedless raisins   1 tablespoon lemon juice
½ cup boiling water   1 tablespoon grated orange
   1 cup white sugar   rind
½ teaspoon salt   1 tablespoon butter
   2 tablespoons corn starch

Line a 9″ pie pan with plain pastry; moisten the edges; cut a long strip of pastry 1½″ wide and flute on an edge. Wash and drain the raisins; place them in a saucepan with the boiling water, sugar and salt; heat to boiling. Mix to a paste the corn starch and 2 tablespoons orange juice; stir into the raisin mixture; cook and stir over low heat until thick and smooth. Remove from the heat; add the remaining orange juice, the lemon juice, orange rind and butter. Stir well; pour into the unbaked shell. Cover with lattice strips of pastry. Bake in a hot oven (450°F.) for 15 minutes; reduce the heat to 350°F.; continue baking until the pastry is golden brown (20-25 minutes). Serve slightly warm. Serves 6.

PUMPKIN PIE

Temperature: 450°F.   Time: 15 minutes
            350°F.   25 minutes

Plain pastry   1 teaspoon cinnamon
  2 eggs, lightly beaten   ¼ teaspoon cloves
  ⅔ cup brown sugar, tightly   ¼ teaspoon ginger
    packed   ½ teaspoon salt
  1½ cups canned or cooked   1 cup milk
    pumpkin   ½ cup cereal cream

Line a 9″ pie pan with plain pastry; flute on an edge; bake in
a hot oven (450°F.) for 5 minutes. Combine the slightly beaten
eggs with sugar, pumpkin, spices, salt and milk. Pour into the
partially baked shell. Bake in a hot oven for 10 minutes. Reduce
the heat to 350°F; pour on the cream. Continue baking until the
filling is set. Serves 6.

CHIFFON PUMPKIN PIE

Baked 9″ pastry shell   1½ cups canned pumpkin
  1 tablespoon gelatine   2 teaspoons cinnamon
  ¼ cup cold water   ½ teaspoon ginger
  ¾ cup brown sugar   ¼ teaspoon allspice
3 eggs, separated   ½ teaspoon salt
  ½ cup milk

Make the baked shell with a high, fluted-on crust as the pie
filling is deep. Soak the gelatine for 5 minutes in the cold water.
Combine the brown sugar, egg yolks, milk, pumpkin, spices and
salt in the top of a double boiler. Beat till smooth; cook and
stir over boiling water until smooth and thick (about 10 minutes).
Remove from the heat; stir in the softened gelatine; chill until
the mixture begins to set. Fold in the stiffly beaten egg whites;
pour into the baked pie shell; let stand till set. Serves 6.

FRESH RASPBERRY PIE

Temperature: 450°F.   Time: 15 minutes
            350°F.   30-35 minutes

Plain pastry   ⅛ teaspoon salt
  2 tablespoons corn starch   4 cups raspberries
  ¾ cup white sugar   1 tablespoon butter

Line a 9″ pie pan with pastry. Mix together the corn starch,
sugar and salt; sift ¼ of this mixture on the raw shell; fill with
raspberries. Sprinkle the remainder of the corn starch mixture
over the fruit; dot with butter; cover with an upper crust. Bake in
a hot oven (450°F.) for 15 minutes, reduce the heat to 350°F. and

continue baking for 30 minutes or until the crust is delicately brown. Serves 6.

APPLE PASTRIES

Temperature: 450°- 350°F. Time: 40 minutes

3 cups apples, finely chopped
  ½ cup white sugar
¼ teaspoon cinnamon
  1 tablespoon corn starch
2 cups sifted cake flour
  2 tablespoons brown sugar

½ teaspoon salt
½ cup shortening
1 egg
¼ cup sour cream
¼ cup dry crumbs
1 tablespoon rich milk

Pare 4 or 5 tart apples; core and finely chop; there should be 3 cups. Mix with the white sugar, the cinnamon and corn starch. Sift together the flour, brown sugar and salt; cut in the shortening until the mixture is like coarse corn meal. Beat the egg slightly; mix with the sour cream. Add to the flour mixture; mix lightly and chill. Divide the batter in 2 parts; roll the first half into a rectangle about ⅛″ thick; lay on an oiled cookie sheet. Sprinkle with the crumbs; cover with the apple mixture. Moisten the edges; roll out the second half and place it on the apples. Pinch the edges together; prick the top with a fork. Brush with the milk; bake in a hot oven (450°F.) for 15 minutes. Reduce the heat to 350°F. and continue baking for 25 minutes. Cut in squares while still warm and serve slightly warm.

NOTE TO BRIDES: *This is one of the most delicious pastries we make. It looks complicated but is worth all the work and time. Yield: 24 squares.*

BUTTERSCOTCH TARTLETS

Plain pastry
  1¾ cups scalded milk
4 tablespoons corn starch
  ¼ teaspoon salt
¾ cup brown sugar

¼ cup cold milk
2 egg yolks
2 tablespoons butter
1 teaspoon vanilla

Line 18 tart shells with plain pastry; prick and bake in a hot oven. Scald the milk in the top of the double boiler over boiling water. Make a paste of the corn starch, salt, brown sugar and cold milk; add to the hot milk; cook and stir until smooth and thick. Cover; continue cooking for 10 minutes, stirring occasionally. Pour a little of the hot mixture over the slightly beaten egg yolks; stir into the starch mixture; continue cooking 3 minutes. Remove from the heat; add the butter and vanilla; beat with the dover beater till creamy. Pour into the baked tart shells; cover with meringue made with the whites of the eggs. Bake in a moderate oven (350°F.) till delicately browned. Yield: 18 tartlets.

BUTTER TARTS

Temperature: 450°F. Time: 10 minutes
        350°F.   15-20 minutes

Pastry for 18 medium sized   ¼ cup butter
   tart tins   ¼ teaspoon salt
1 cup corn syrup   ⅔ cup nuts, chopped
   ⅔ cup brown sugar   (optional)
2 eggs, slightly beaten   ½ teaspoon vanilla

Line 18 medium sized tart tins with pastry. Mix the corn syrup with the brown sugar in a saucepan; cook gently over direct heat for 5 minutes; cool slightly. Pour over the slightly beaten eggs, beating continuously; add the remaining ingredients. Fill the unbaked shells two-thirds full; bake in a hot oven (450°F.) for 10 minutes. Reduce the heat to 350°F.; continue cooking for 15 to 20 minutes or until set. Yield: 18 tarts.

PECAN BUTTER TARTLETS

Temperature: 350°F. Time: 10 minutes
¼ cup butter   1 cup fine dry bread crumbs
   ¼ cup brown sugar   1 teaspoon cinnamon
1 tablespoon water

Measure the butter, sugar and water into a saucepan; heat to boiling. Reduce the heat; stir in the bread crumbs and cinnamon. Mix well; turn into an 8″ x 8″ shallow pan; press against the sides and bottom of the pan. Bake in a moderate oven for 10 minutes. Chill; fill with the nut filling:

FILLING

1 cup brown sugar, firmly   ½ teaspoon vanilla
   packed   ½ cup nuts, chopped
2 tablespoons corn starch   (pecans, walnuts or
   2 tablespoons sifted   almonds)
     all-purpose flour   2 tablespoons butter
2 cups milk, scalded   4 tablespoons white sugar
   2 eggs, separated   ⅛ teaspoon salt
¼ teaspoon salt   1 teaspoon corn starch

Blend the brown sugar, 2 tablespoons corn starch and the flour in the top of a double boiler; stir in the hot milk. Cook over boiling water till thick and smooth; cover and continue cooking 10 minutes. Beat together the egg yolks and ¼ teaspoon salt. Stir into the starch mixture; continue cooking 3 minutes. Add the vanilla, nuts and butter. Cool; pour into the baked shell. Stiffly beat the egg whites, add the white sugar, ⅛ teaspoon salt and 1 teaspoon corn starch. Beat again till stiff and glossy. Pile on the filling; brown delicately in a 350°F. oven. Cool; cut in squares and serve.

RAISIN SQUARES

Temperature: 450°F. Time: 15 minutes
· 350°F.   10-12 minutes

2 cups sifted pastry flour
2 tablespoons white sugar
½ teaspoon salt
½ cup shortening
2 eggs, separated
¼ cup sour cream
1 cup raisins, chopped
½ cup hot water

½ cup brown sugar
2 tablespoons lemon rind, grated
2 tablespoons lemon juice
2 tablespoons corn starch
¼ cup dry crumbs
1 tablespoon white sugar

Sift together the pastry flour, 2 tablespoons white sugar and the salt; cut in the shortening until the mixture is crumbly; make a well in the centre. Beat the egg yolks slightly; add the sour cream. Add to the flour mixture; mix lightly. Turn on a floured board and knead to form a ball; cut in half and chill while the raisins are being prepared. Measure the raisins, hot water, sugar, lemon rind, juice and corn starch into a saucepan. Cook and stir till smooth and thick; cool slightly. Roll out the bottom half of the pastry to a rectangle 10″ x 8″ and place on a cookie sheet; sprinkle with the dry crumbs; spread with the raisin filling. Roll the second half of the pastry; place on top of the raisins, rolling the edges together. Brush the top with the unbeaten egg whites and sprinkle with the white sugar. Bake in a hot oven (450°F.) for 15 minutes. Reduce the heat; continue cooking until done. Yield: 24 squares.

GLAZED STRAWBERRY TARTS

Plain pastry
1½ quarts fresh strawberries
½ cup water
½ cup white sugar

2½ tablespoons corn starch
Red coloring
1 teaspoon butter

Line 18 tart shells with plain pastry; prick and bake in a hot oven. Hull the berries; reserve 1 quart of the choicest. Crush the remaining pint of berries in a saucepan; add the water, sugar and corn starch; mix well. Bring to a boil; simmer gently till clear, about 3 minutes. Remove from the heat; run through the strainer; add enough coloring to make the glaze a strawberry red. Add the butter; spoon the glaze over the choice berries until each one is coated. Fill the tart shells; serve without chilling. Yield: 18 tarts.

BANBURY TARTS

Temperature: 450°F.

Plain Pastry
  2 tablespoons lemon juice
  ¼ cup raisins, chopped
  ¾ cups apples, finely chopped
2 tablespoons nuts, chopped
  1 tablespoon orange
    marmalade

Time: 20 minutes

⅛ cup white sugar
  Dash of salt
  ¼ teaspoon cloves
  ¼ teaspoon mace
  ½ teaspoon cinnamon
  2 tablespoons melted
    butter

Roll the pastry in a thin sheet; cut in 4″ squares; place on an oiled cookie sheet. Mix all the remaining ingredients; place 1 tablespoon of the mixture on each square. Fold over like a handkerchief; press edges together. Prick with a fork; if you want to give each tart the personal touch prick the initial on it—A for Anne, B for Bill and so on. Brush with rich milk; bake in a hot oven for 20 minutes. This quantity makes 12 tarts.

DELICIOUS CHEESE TARTS

Rich pastry
  ¼ cup shortening
⅜ cup white sugar
  1 egg, separated
1 tablespoon old cheese,
  finely grated

Dash of nutmeg
  ⅞ cup sifted all-purpose flour
  ⅛ teaspoon salt
  1 teaspoon baking powder
  ¼ cup milk
  Strawberry or raspberry jam

Line 18 tart tins with rich pastry. Cream together the shortening and sugar; beat till fluffy. Add the unbeaten egg yolks and beat well; add the grated cheese and nutmeg. Sift together the flour, salt and baking powder; add, alternately with the milk, to the egg batter; fold in the stiffly beaten egg whites. Place a half teaspoonful of jam in the bottom of each unbaked tart shell. Fill ¾ full with the batter; cut tiny rounds of pastry with a thimble; place on top like a coin. Bake in a moderate oven. Serve slightly warm. Yield: 18 tarts.

CHOCOLATE CREAM TARTS

Line 18 tart shells with plain pastry; prick and bake in a hot oven. Fill with Chocolate Cream Pie filling (page 193); top with meringue and brown in a moderate oven.

LEMON TARTS

Line 18 tart shells with plain pastry; prick and bake in a hot oven. Fill with Lemon Filling (page 195); top with meringue and brown in a moderate oven.

CHAPTER 13

Fowl

ROASTING CHART FOR CHICKEN

Drawn Weight	Temperature	Approximate Time
2-3 pounds	325°F.	45 minutes per pound
3-4 pounds	325°F.	43 minutes per pound
4-4½ pounds	325°F.	40 minutes per pound
4½ pounds	325°F.	36 minutes per pound

ROASTING CHART FOR TURKEY

Drawn Weight	Temperature	Approximate Time
7-10 pounds	325°F.	30 minutes per pound
10-15 pounds	325°F.	20 minutes per pound
15-20 pounds	325°F.	18 minutes per pound

CHICKEN A LA KING

1 boiling fowl, 5 pounds
1 onion
2 whole cloves
1½ tablespoons salt
3 tablespoons butter
1½ cups fresh or
  canned mushrooms,
  sliced

2 tablespoons green pepper or green
  pickle, chopped
5 tablespoons flour
¾ teaspoon salt
1½ cups chicken stock
¾ cup cream
1½ tablespoons pimento, chopped
1 egg, well beaten

Singe, wash and cut up a boiling fowl. Put in a heavy saucepan; almost cover with boiling water; add the onion, peeled and stuck with the cloves. Cover and bring to a rapid boil. Reduce the heat; add the salt and simmer till tender. Cool slightly; dice the chicken (you will need 3 cups). If the hot stock is strained through a flannel wrung from hot water, all the fat is eliminated. Heat the butter; add the mushrooms and green pepper or pickle. Cook and stir till tender (about 5 minutes). Blend in the flour and salt; let bubble for 3 minutes. Add the stock slowly; cook and stir till smooth and thick. Add the cream, the diced chicken and the pimento; heat to boiling. Pour over the well-beaten egg and serve at once. Serves 8.

To Serve: Here is the neatest way to serve the chicken a la king. Cut thin slices of bread; remove the crusts and brush with the chicken fat. Line oiled muffin pans with the bread and bake in a fairly hot oven. The bread cases lift out easily after baking, are crisp and brown and will hold a good liberal serving.

CHICKEN POT PIE

Temperature: 375°F.

Time: 25 minutes

1 boiling fowl	1½ tablespoons chicken fat
1 onion	1½ tablespoons flour
1 whole clove	Dash of paprika
2 teaspoons salt	½ teaspoon salt
Dash of pepper and mace	2 cups milk
Cold water	1 cup chicken stock

Cut the chicken in pieces; place in a kettle with the onion stuck with the clove. Add the seasonings; add cold water to cover. Simmer gently until tender; strain the stock. Remove the meat from the bones. Blend the chicken fat and flour together; add the paprika and salt. Let bubble for 3 minutes; add the milk; cook and stir till smooth; add 1 cup chicken stock. Combine with the chicken; place in a 2-quart oiled casserole. Pour the following batter over the chicken.

BATTER

2 cups sifted pastry flour	⅞ cup milk
1½ teaspoons salt	2 tablespoons melted chicken fat
2 teaspoons baking powder	2 eggs, well beaten

Sift together the flour, salt and baking powder. Combine the milk, melted chicken fat and eggs. Beat till light; pour into the flour mixture. Stir as little as possible. Pour over the chicken. Bake till the crust is golden brown and light. Serves 6.

ROAST CHICKEN—SAUSAGE STUFFING

Temperature: 325°F.

Time: 2-2½ hours

Roasting chicken, 5-5½ pounds	1 teaspoon onion, grated
3 cups bread crumbs (soft)	1 teaspoon salt
1 cup sausage meat	½ teaspoon pepper
1 tablespoon parsley, finely chopped	Few grains nutmeg
	2 tablespoons melted fat

Dress and clean the chicken. Combine all other ingredients; stuff both the crop and body cavity. Sew or skewer together. Turn the tips of the wings under the back; skewer the legs tight to the body; pass a cord around the end of the skewers and under the back. Brush the breast with salad oil; dust it very lightly with flour (this keeps the breast meat moist, particularly in a tender bird). Wrap the bird in heavy brown paper oiled on the inside. Place breast up on a rack in a roasting pan. Bake uncovered, in a moderate oven until done. Do not turn or baste. Serves 5-6.

ROAST CHICKEN—POTATO STUFFING

Temperature: 325°F.

Time: 2 hours

1 roasting chicken, 5 pounds
  7 large raw potatoes, grated
3 stalks celery, finely chopped
  2 onions, chopped

4 tablespoons melted fat
  ¼ cup celery leaves, chopped
1 teaspoon salt
  ½ teaspoon paprika

Singe the chicken and get it ready for stuffing. Grate the potatoes; add to them the finely chopped celery and diced onions; blend well; add the fat. Add the chopped celery leaves and the seasonings; stuff the chicken. Sew or skewer together. Oil a sheet of heavy brown paper; wrap the chicken in it. Place on a rack and cook, uncovered, in a 325°F. oven till tender. Allow 25 to 30 minutes to the pound. Remove the paper wrapping for the last 15 minutes. Serves 6.

DRESSING FOR ROAST CHICKEN

2½ cups soft bread crumbs
  2½ tablespoons melted butter
    or shortening
1 teaspoon poultry dressing

1 teaspoon salt
  ⅛ teaspoon pepper
1 medium sized onion, chopped

Combine all the ingredients. Use as stuffing for chicken.

SMOTHERED CHICKEN

Temperature: 325°F.

Time: 2 hours

1 boiling fowl, 4 to 5 pounds
  1 teaspoon salt
½ teaspoon paprika
  4 tablespoons flour
4 tablespoons fat
  1 onion, chopped

3 stalks celery, chopped
  ½ cup carrots, diced
1½ cups rich milk
  ½ cup mushrooms, sliced
2 tablespoons flour
  ¼ cup milk

Clean and disjoint the chicken; cut in serving pieces. Measure the salt, paprika and flour into a bag. Add the chicken; shake well till each piece is coated. Heat the fat; sear the chicken till brown all over. Place the chicken in a 2-quart casserole. Add the vegetables to the hot fat; cook and stir till golden brown. Add them to the casserole; over all pour the milk. Cover tightly; cook slowly till tender. Add the mushrooms 15 minutes before the dish comes from the oven. Thicken the gravy by adding a paste made with the flour and milk. The chicken is good but the gravy poured over hot biscuits is the belle of the ball. Serves 6.

CANADIAN BAKED CHICKEN

Temperature: 400°F.   Time: 1 hour

1 roasting chicken   1 teaspoon salt
  (5-5½ lbs.)   Dash of pepper
10 strips breakfast bacon   1 tablespoon corn starch
  Whole cloves   2 tablespoons fat
¼ cup brown sugar   ½ cup hot water

Have the chicken cut in serving pieces. Roll each piece in a slice of bacon and fasten with toothpicks. Stick 3 whole cloves in each section; place in a roasting pan. Sprinkle with a mixture of the sugar, salt, pepper and corn starch; add the fat and hot water. Cover tightly; bake in hot oven till tender. Serve with creamy mashed potatoes. Serves 6.

ROAST GOOSE

Temperature: 325°F.   Time: 3½-4 hours

1 goose, 10 pounds   ½ cup seeded raisins
  (drawn weight)   1 tablespoon parsley, chopped
¾ cup melted fat   1½ teaspoons salt
  1 cup onion, finely chopped   Dash of pepper
3 cups apple, pared and chopped   ¼ teaspoon poultry dressing
  7 cups soft bread crumbs   4 tablespoons sugar

Singe, clean, wash and wipe the goose. Heat the fat in the bottom of the roasting pan, add the onions; stir and cook over low heat till the onions are tender. Add the apple, the crumbs, the raisins, parsley, seasonings and sugar. Stuff the goose (both crop and body cavity); sew and tie; the legs and wings are often too short to truss. Prick the skin in several places and DO NOT brush with fat or oil. Place on a trivet. Roast breast side up and uncovered. Do not use any water, do not baste, do not turn. If the goose is very fat, pour off some of the surplus fat during roasting. The flavor of the stuffing is delicious and unusual. Serves 10.

ROAST DUCKLING—ORANGE SAUCE

Temperature: 325°F.   Time: 1 hour, 25 minutes

1 duckling, 4 pounds   1 teaspoon salt
  6 green apples   Dash of pepper
½ cup raisins   ¼ teaspoon poultry dressing
  2 cups stale bread crumbs   2 tablespoons hot fat

Wipe, singe and clean the duckling. Pare, core and dice the apples. Cover the raisins with boiling water; drain, chop and add to the apples. Add all remaining ingredients and blend well. Stuff the duckling; sew up. Wrap the bird in heavy brown paper, oiled on the inside; leave the ends open so that the fat will flow into the pan.   Place on a rack in a roasting pan; roast uncovered and without water till tender.   In the meantime, peel an orange; scrape off and discard the white membrane; cut the yellow peel in thin strips; cook in 1 cup of boiling water for 15 minutes.   Drain and discard the water.   Remove all the membrane from the orange sections and break them into a pan.   When the duck is tender, add the drippings to the orange; add the cooked peel, ½ teaspoon salt, ½ teaspoon lemon juice and 2 tablespoons red jam or jelly. Simmer for 10 minutes; pour over the duck and serve.   Young peas and small new potatoes are always good with duck.   Don't forget the salad, for dressed duck seems to need the sharp salad flavor to cut the poultry richness. Serves 4-5.

SAUSAGE DRESSING FOR TURKEY

8 cups soft bread crumbs	1 teaspoon salt
2 cups sausage meat	½ teaspoon pepper
1 tablespoon parsley, finely chopped	Few grains nutmeg
	2 tablespoons melted fat
1 teaspoon onion, grated	1 egg, well beaten

Mix the bread crumbs, sausage meat and seasonings; add melted fat and beaten egg. Use as stuffing for turkey.

ROAST TURKEY—SWEET POTATO STUFFING

Temperature: 325°F.   Time: 4 hours

1 turkey, 10 pounds (drawn)	½ cup celery, chopped
1 teaspoon baking soda	1½ teaspoons salt
1 lemon	¼ teaspoon paprika
4 cups sweet potatoes, mashed	⅛ teaspoon black pepper
4 slices breakfast bacon, diced	¼ cup cream
2 cups soft bread crumbs	2 eggs, slightly beaten
½ cup onion, chopped	1 tablespoon parsley, chopped

Singe, clean and wipe the turkey; rinse the inside with water to which 1 teaspoon of baking soda has been added.   Cut the lemon in half; rub the turkey on the outside with the cut lemon. Cook the sweet potatoes till soft; drain; beat till smooth.   Dice the bacon; pan-fry till crisp; pour the bacon and fat over the soft bread crumbs.   Add the mashed sweet potatoes and all other ingredients; stir till blended. Stuff the turkey; fasten with skewers; roll the bird in heavy brown paper which has been oiled on the inside; leave the ends open.   Cook in uncovered roasting pan until golden brown. Serves 10-12.

NOTE: Do not baste, cover or add water.

ROAST TURKEY—CELERY STUFFING

Temperature: 325°F.   Time: 4 hours

1 turkey, 10 pounds   1 onion, chopped
  (drawn weight)   4 quarts day-old bread crumbs
4 cups celery, finely chopped   2 tablespoons poultry dressing
  4 cups boiling water   1 tablespoon salt
½ cup fat   1 teaspoon pepper

Weigh the turkey after it has been drawn and the head and feet have been removed. Simmer the celery in the boiling water till tender. Drain, reserving 1 cup celery liquid. Heat the fat, add the onion. Cook and stir till tender. Add the crumbs; seasonings, cooked celery and liquid. Mix thoroughly. Stuff the turkey lightly, filling both body and crop. Sew or skewer together and cover with heavy brown paper oiled on the inside. Place, breast up, on a rack in a roasting pan; roast uncovered, without basting or turning, until tender. Serves 10-12.

TURKEY SQUARES

Temperature: 350°F.   Time: 40 minutes

2 tablespoons fat   ¾ cup gravy
  2 tablespoons onion,   2 eggs, well beaten
    chopped   1 teaspoon salt
3 cups cooked rice   Dash of pepper, mace and
  1½ cups left-over chicken   cayenne
    or turkey, diced   ¼ cup grated cheese

Heat the fat in a saucepan; add the chopped onion; cook and stir till tender and golden brown. Add all the remaining ingredients and blend well. Bake in an oblong pan 8″ x 12″. Five minutes before taking from the oven, sprinkle with the grated cheese. When firm cut in squares and serve with a tossed salad. Serves 12.

CHAPTER 14

Luncheon and Supper Dishes

STUFFED CABBAGE LEAVES

Temperature: 350°F.

Time: 1 hour

12 cabbage leaves
  1 cup cooked rice
½ pound fresh pork, ground
  ½ pound chuck beef, ground
  ¼ pound smoked ham, ground
  1 egg, well beaten
1 small onion, chopped

1 tablespoon parsley, chopped
  1 teaspoon salt
Dash of pepper and paprika
  1 cup boiling water
1 beef cube
  4 slices breakfast bacon

Take the large, tender leaves from the cabbage, cook them in boiling salted water for 10 minutes; drain. Mix together the cooked rice, the ground meats, the egg, onion, parsley and seasonings; place a spoonful of the mixture on each cabbage leaf. Roll up and fasten with a tooth pick. Place the rolls in an oiled casserole. Dissolve the beef cube in the boiling water; pour over the cabbage leaves. Cover with the bacon slices, cut in thirds. Bake in a moderate oven; serves 6. Serve hot with green beans.

ESCALLOPED CORN WITH SAUSAGES

Temperature: 350°F.

Time: 20 minutes

1 pound pork sausages
  3 tablespoons flour
1½ cups milk
  ½ teaspoon salt
Dash of pepper

1 tablespoon red or green pepper, chopped.
2½ cups cooked corn
  ½ cup cracker crumbs

Put the sausages in a cold pan; add a little water; cover and pan fry till lightly brown (about 8 minutes); remove to a hot platter. Reserve 3 tablespoons of the sausage fat in the pan; blend in the flour. Let bubble for two or three minutes; slowly add the milk; cook and stir till smooth and thick. Add the seasonings and the chopped pepper. Arrange half the sausages in the bottom of a casserole; cover with the freshly cooked corn which has been cut from the cobs, then with the sauce. Top with the crumbs, which have been stirred in the sausage pan with some of the fat. Arrange the remainder of the sausages on top; bake in a moderate oven for 20 minutes. Serves 6. Serve with a tossed salad made by combining chopped lettuce, tomatoes, radishes and young onions.

CHEESE PUDDING

Temperature: 425°F.   Time: 30 minutes

12 slices stale bread
  Butter or cream cheese for
    spreading
½ pound nippy cheese, cubed
  3½ cups milk

4 eggs
1 teaspoon salt
Dash of pepper
¼ cup onion, chopped

Spread the bread lightly with butter if you can spare it or with cream cheese moistened with milk. Arrange alternate layers of bread and nippy cheese in an oiled 2-quart casserole; pour 2 cups milk over the mixture; let stand 10 minutes. Beat the eggs till light; add the remaining milk, seasonings and onion. Pour over the bread; bake in a hot oven until firm. Serve with a tossed salad and thick slices of beefsteak tomatoes. Serves 6.

CHEESE SAVOURY

Temperature: 325°F.   Time: 1 hour, 15 minutes

1 cup soft bread crumbs
  1½ cups hot milk
2 tablespoons melted fat
  ½ cup tomato juice
1 tablespoon greens, chopped
  (Parsley, pepper or pickles)
1 onion, chopped

1½ cups grated cheese
1 teaspoon salt
Dash of pepper and paprika
3 eggs, well beaten
1 cup cooked vegetables (potatoes, carrots, peas, beans or
  any other mixture)

Measure the crumbs into a bowl; cover with the hot milk; beat till smooth. Add the melted fat, the tomato juice, chopped greens, onion, cheese and seasonings; lastly, add the well beaten eggs. Put the vegetables in an oiled 1½-quart casserole; pour the milk and cheese mixture over them. Set in a pan of hot water; bake until the custard is firm. Serve hot with escalloped tomatoes. Serves 6.

EGGS BAKED IN CHEESE

Temperature: 350°F.   Time: 15 minutes

¼ pound Canadian cheese, grated
  ½ teaspoon salt
⅛ teaspoon pepper
  1 teaspoon fat

6 eggs
  ½ teaspoon dry mustard
¼ cup thin cream

Oil a shallow baking dish and sprinkle the grated cheese on the bottom; dust with salt and pepper; sprinkle with the fat. Break the eggs, one at a time, over the cheese. Add the mustard to the cream and pour over the eggs. Bake in a moderate oven till the whites of the eggs are set (about 15 minutes). Serve hot with potato puffs. Serves 6.

BAKED CHEESE DELIGHT

Temperature: 325°F.   Time: 40-45 minutes

1 cup hot cooked wheat cereal   Dash of pepper and mace
  ½ cup milk   1 tablespoon corn starch
1 cup grated cheese   1 tablespoon cold milk
  1 tablespoon butter   2 eggs, separated
½ teaspoon salt

Heat the wheat cereal and ½ cup of milk in the top of the double boiler; blend until smooth with a dover beater. Add the cheese, butter, seasonings and the corn starch, which has been mixed to a paste with 1 tablespoon of cold milk. Blend well with the dover beater. Remove from the heat; add the unbeaten egg yolks; beat till smooth. Fold in the stiffly beaten egg whites. Pour into an oiled 1½-quart casserole; set in a pan of hot water; oven bake until firm. Test with a silver knife. Serve with sliced tomatoes and cucumbers. Serves 6.

CHEESE AND RICE CASSEROLE

Temperature: 325°F.   Time: 50 minutes

¾ cup rice   3 eggs, separated
  6 cups boiling water   1 cup grated cheese
1 teaspoon salt   ¾ teaspoon salt
  3 tablespoons fat   ¼ teaspoon dry mustard
3 tablespoons flour   Dash of pepper
  ¾ cup milk

Cook the rice in the boiling salted water till tender, about 20 minutes. Drain; rinse with boiling water. Let the rice fluff up in the bowl while the remainder of the dish is being prepared. Melt the fat in a saucepan; blend in the flour; let bubble 3 minutes. Add the milk slowly; cook and stir until smooth and thick. Beat the egg yolks till light; add the cooked rice, the cheese and seasonings. Combine with the milk mixture; fold in the stiffly beaten egg whites. Pour into an oiled 1½-quart casserole; bake in the oven in a pan of warm water till set. Serve hot with escalloped tomatoes and hot brown rolls. Serves 6.

BAKED EGGS IN POTATOES

Temperature: 350°F.   Time: 1 hour

6 large potatoes   6 eggs
  2 tablespoons butter   ½ teaspoon salt
6 thin slices loaf cheese   Dash of pepper and paprika

Scrub the potatoes; brush well with oil and bake in a moderate oven till tender. Cut a slice from the side and scoop out about half the potato. Use this half for potato cakes. Dot the potatoes with butter; lay in the slices of cheese; break in an egg and dust lightly with salt, pepper and paprika. Return to the oven and continue baking till the egg white is set (about 15 minutes). Serve hot with buttered cabbage. Serves 6.

BAKED OMELETTE

Temperature: 350°F.   Time: 30 minutes

2 tablespoons butter   Dash of pepper and paprika
  1½ tablespoons corn starch   1 cup milk
1 tablespoon onion, finely chopped   4 eggs, separated
  1 teaspoon salt   ½ teaspoon dry mustard

Melt the butter in a frying pan; remove from the heat; blend in the corn starch, chopped onion and seasonings. Let bubble over low heat for 3 minutes. Gradually add the milk; stir and cook until the sauce is thick. Remove from the heat; cool slightly. Add the well beaten egg yolks and mustard. Fold in the stiffly beaten egg whites. Pour into a 1½-quart oiled casserole; bake in a moderate oven till a delicate brown. Serves 4.

BAKED CHEESE OMELETTE

Temperature: 350°F.   Time: 30 minutes

3 tablespoons butter   Dash of paprika
  3 tablespoons sifted pastry flour 1 cup milk
1 tablespoon onion, finely chopped   One 4-oz. package cream
  1 teaspoon salt   cheese
Dash of pepper   4 eggs, separated

Melt the butter; blend in the flour, chopped onion and seasonings; let bubble on low heat for 3 minutes. Gradually add the milk; stir and cook until the sauce is thick and smooth. Remove from the heat; add the cream cheese; cool slightly. Add the well beaten egg yolks; fold in the stiffly beaten egg whites. Bake in an oiled 1½-quart casserole in a moderate oven until a delicate brown. This omelette will not fall as quickly as a pan-cooked omelette; it is firmer in texture and moister. Serve with sliced tomatoes and cucumbers. Serves 4.

RICE-EGG OMELETTE

Temperature: 325°F.	Time: 35-40 minutes

4 tablespoons fat	2 cups cooked rice
4 tablespoons flour	¼ teaspoon paprika
1 teaspoon salt	⅛ teaspoon dry mustard
2 cups milk	4 tablespoons cheese, grated
3 eggs, separated	

Melt the fat in a saucepan; blend in the flour and salt; let bubble 3 minutes. Slowly add the milk; cook and stir till smooth and thick. Cook for 5 minutes over low heat, stirring occasionally. Beat the egg yolks; add the rice, seasonings, cheese and the sauce. Fold in the stiffly beaten egg whites. Pour into a 1½-quart oiled baking dish. Bake in a pan of hot water in a moderate oven till firm and golden brown. Serve with escalloped corn and sliced tomatoes. Serves 6.

POTATO OMELETTE

Temperature: 350°F.	Time: 15 minutes

3 eggs, separated	Dash of pepper and paprika
3 tablespoons cereal cream	1 tablespoon onion, grated
1 cup warm, lightly mashed potatoes	1 teaspoon parsley, chopped
1 teaspoon salt	2 tablespoons fat

Separate the eggs; beat the whites till stiff and glossy. Beat the yolks till very light; add the cereal cream, mashed potatoes, seasonings, onion and parsley. Fold in the stiffly beaten egg whites. Heat the fat in a heavy frying pan; turn in the omelette. Cover, reduce the heat and cook until the bottom is crisp and brown. Remove the lid; bake in the oven until crusty. Serve with spiced apple balls. Serves 4-5.

SCOTCH OMELETTE

Temperature: 450°F.	Time: 5 minutes

¾ cup soft white bread crumbs	Dash of pepper and paprika
½ cup hot milk	¾ teaspoon salt
4 eggs, separated	1 tablespoon fat

Cover the crumbs with the hot milk; beat until smooth. Separate the eggs; beat the yolks until thick and lemon colored. Add to the bread; add the salt, pepper and paprika. Fold in the stiffly beaten egg whites. Melt the fat in the frying pan; pour in the egg mixture. Cook over low heat for about 10 minutes, lifting the edges so that the liquid will run out. When nicely browned and firm, place in a hot oven for about 5 minutes to dry. Fold and serve at once. Serves 4.

PUFFY OMELETTE

Temperature: 350°F. Time: 12-15 minutes

6 eggs, separated
  6 tablespoons hot water
¾ teaspoon salt
  Dash of pepper and paprika

½ teaspoon baking powder
  ½ tablespoon onion, grated
    (optional)
1½ tablespoons fat

Separate the eggs; beat the whites until glossy and stiff. Beat the yolks until light and lemon colored; add the hot water, seasonings, baking powder and grated onion. Fold in the stiffly beaten egg whites. Rub a heavy iron or aluminum frying pan with salt; heat the fat until hot but not sizzling. Pour in the omelette mixture; cover and reduce the heat. Cook until puffy and golden brown underneath; bake in a moderate oven until the top is dry. Be sure not to overcook or the omelette is tough. Loosen the edge with a spatula and crease through the centre; with the spatula turn one half over the other. Slide to a hot platter; serve with buttered toast and apple butter. Serves 6.

BAKED HASH OMELETTE

Temperature: 350°F. Time: 35 minutes

2 tablespoons melted fat
  1 onion, finely chopped
1¼ lbs. chuck steak, ground
  2 cups raw potatoes, grated
⅔ cup milk

½ cup tomato juice
  1 teaspoon salt
⅛ teaspoon pepper
  Dash of cayenne
¼ cup chili sauce

Heat the fat in a heavy saucepan; add the onion; cook and stir till golden brown. Mix together the meat, potatoes, milk, tomato juice and seasonings; add to the onion; cook and stir until the meat is tender. Take from the heat and press well down in the pan. Place in the oven; bake until well browned top and bottom. Remove from the oven; spread half the top with the chili sauce; turn over like an omelette and slide to a hot platter. Serve with apple butter and hot biscuits. Serves 6.

CREAMY SCRAMBLED EGGS

Temperature: 350°F. Time: 12-15 minutes

1 tablespoon butter
  4 eggs
¼ teaspoon salt

Dash of pepper and paprika
  ⅓ cup milk
2 tablespoons cooked rice

Melt the butter in a shallow baking dish. Beat the eggs slightly; add the seasonings, milk and cooked rice. Pour this mixture into the baking dish. Bake in a moderate oven till the eggs are creamy, reaching in 3 or 4 times to lift the eggs from the bottom of the dish. Serve over squares of buttered toast. Serves 4.

FRENCH TOAST

1 egg	2 tablespoons fat
½ cup milk	4 slices of bread
⅛ teaspoon salt	

Slightly beat the egg in a deep plate; add the milk and salt. Heat 1 tablespoon of fat in a frying pan. Dip the slices of bread in the egg mixture; pan fry in the hot fat until brown on one side. Lift from the pan. Heat the remaining fat in the frying pan; pan fry the uncooked side. Serve hot with strawberry jam. Serves 4.

NOTE TO THE BRIDE: *For a different flavor, substitute tomato juice for the milk; for a pungent dish, use grapefruit juice instead of the milk.*

BAKED HASH AND EGGS

Temperature: 350°F. Time: 10-12 minutes

1 cup gravy	2 cups mashed potatoes
1½ cups cooked meat, chopped	6 eggs
1 onion, chopped	Salt and pepper
1 teaspoon meat extract	½ cup grated cheese

Combine the gravy, chopped meat, onion and meat extract; heat to boiling. Cover the bottom of an oiled baking dish with the fluffy mashed potatoes; spread with the hash mixture. Make six depressions in the hash mixture; break in the eggs. Sprinkle with salt and pepper; bake in a moderate oven for 5 minutes. Remove from the oven and sprinkle with the grated cheese; continue baking until the eggs are set, from 5 to 8 minutes. Serves 6.

LIMA BEAN SAVOURY

2 cups dried lima beans	2 tablespoons molasses or brown
4 teaspoons salt	sugar
3 tablespoons fat	⅛ teaspoon ginger
1 cup onion, sliced	2½ cups chopped fresh or canned
½ cup celery, chopped	tomatoes
1 tablespoon flour	½ cup loaf cheese, cubed
½ teaspoon dry mustard	

Wash the beans and soak overnight in cold water. In the morning drain, cover with boiling water and add 2 teaspoons of the salt. Cover; simmer slowly till tender (about 1 hour); drain. Heat the fat; add the sliced onions and chopped celery; cook until tender but not brown. Blend in the flour and mustard; add the molasses or brown sugar, the remaining salt, pepper, tomatoes and the beans. Simmer for 5 minutes; add the cheese; cook till the cheese is melted. This is a delicious savoury. Serves 6.

LUNCHEON SPECIAL

1 cup uncooked rice	2 cups milk
2½ quarts boiling water	1 teaspoon salt
1 tablespoon salt	Dash of pepper, mace and paprika
1 tablespoon French mustard	1 cup grated cheese
¼ cup fat	½ cup sweet pickle, diced
4 tablespoons flour	3 hard-cooked eggs, sliced

Cook the rice in the boiling salted water until tender; drain; rinse with boiling water. Stir in the mustard; press into a round baking dish which has been well oiled. Set the rice dish in a shallow pan of hot water; cook over gentle heat for 10 minutes. In the meantime, melt the fat in a saucepan; blend in the flour; let bubble 3 minutes. Slowly add the milk; cook until smooth and thick. Add the seasonings and cheese; stir until the cheese is melted. Remove from the heat; add the sweet pickle and hard cooked eggs. Unmould the rice on a large hot platter; pour the sauce over it and serve at once with chutney and brown bread. Serves 6.

MACARONI AND CHEESE

Temperature: 400°F.   Time: 20 minutes

1 cup broken macaroni	¾ teaspoon salt
2 quarts boiling water	Dash of pepper
1 tablespoon salt	2 cups hot milk
3 tablespoons fat	1 tablespoon chopped onion
3 tablespoons flour	2 cups grated cheese
¼ teaspoon dry mustard	½ cup buttered crumbs

Cook the macaroni in the boiling salted water until tender; drain and rinse. Melt the fat in a saucepan; blend in the flour; let bubble 3 minutes. Add the seasonings, hot milk and onion; add the grated cheese and stir until it is melted. Mix the sauce and the macaroni; turn into a well oiled 1½ quart casserole. Top with the buttered crumbs; bake in a hot oven till brown. Serves 6.

ROLLED NOODLE BROWNIES

1 cup hot mashed potatoes	2 tablespoons fat
1 egg, well beaten	4 eggs, well beaten
½ teaspoon salt	½ cup milk
Dash of pepper and celery salt	½ teaspoon salt
1 cup pastry flour	Dash of pepper

Measure the potatoes into a bowl; add the egg, ½ teaspoon salt, a dash of pepper, a dash of celery salt and the flour; mix well. Flour the hands; take out small pieces of the potato mixture; roll to make pencil-shaped noodles 2″ long. Have ready a pan of boiling salted water; drop in the noddles and let cook for 15 minutes.

Drain well. Heat the fat in the frying pan; pan fry the noodles until golden brown. Combine the well beaten eggs with the milk, salt and pepper; pour over the crisp noodles; stir gently until creamy. Serve at once. Serves 6.

RING OF PLENTY

Temperature: 350°F.   Time: 45 minutes

1½ cups cooked macaroni   1 cup hot milk
   (¼ pound uncooked)   1 egg, well beaten
2 quarts boiling water   1 teaspoon salt
  1½ teaspoons salt   ⅛ teaspoon pepper
1 cup Canadian cheese, grated   1 teaspoon grated lemon rind
  1 cup soft bread crumbs   1 tablespoon lemon juice
1 tablespoon parsley, chopped   2 tablespoons canned pimento,
  3 tablespoons melted fat   chopped
1 medium onion, finely chopped   8 servings cooked green peas

Break the macaroni in short pieces; cook in the boiling salted water until tender. Drain and rinse; there should be 1½ cups. Combine with all the remaining ingredients except the peas. Pour into an oiled 9″ ring mould; bake in a pan of hot water until firm. Remove from the oven and let stand in the warming oven for 10 minutes; unmould on a hot platter; fill the centre with the cooked peas. Serve with brown rolls. Serves 8.

ESCALLOPED POTATOES WITH HAM

Temperature: 350°F.   Time: 1½ hours

1 slice smoked ham, 1½″ thick   ¼ teaspoon dry mustard
  1 tablespoon prepared mustard   Dash of pepper
4 cups raw potatoes, sliced   1 cup cheese, grated
  3 tablespoons fat   ¼ cup green pickle, chopped
3 tablespoons flour   3 tablespoons cornflakes
  1½ cups milk   1 tablespoon melted fat
1 teaspoon salt

Nick the edges of the ham and place on the bottom of an oiled baking dish; spread with the prepared mustard. Peel the potatoes and cut in thin slices; cover with boiling water; let stand till cool; drain well. Melt the fat in a saucepan (bacon fat is delicious); blend in the flour and let bubble 3 minutes. Add the milk slowly; cook and stir till thick and smooth. Remove from the heat; add the seasonings, cheese and chopped green pickle. Cover the ham with alternate layers of sliced potatoes and cream sauce; bake in a moderate oven till the potatoes are cooked. Five minutes before taking from the oven cover with a mixture of the corn flakes and melted fat. Serve with scrambled eggs. Serves 4-5.

MACARONI CASSEROLE

Temperature: 350°F.   Time: 15-20 minutes

2 cups macaroni, broken	4 tablespoons fat
3 quarts boiling water	1 onion, chopped
1 tablespoon salt	¾ cup water
1 pound beef liver	1 can tomatoes (2½ cups)
¼ cup flour	1 teaspoon white sugar
1 teaspoon salt	1 cup grated cheese
Dash of pepper	½ cup dry crumbs
¼ teaspoon dry mustard	

Break the macaroni slowly into the boiling salted water; cook till tender (about 20 minutes); drain. In the meantime, remove the skin and tubes from the liver; to do this, flour the liver, insert a sharp knife under the membrane, then pull and scrape it from the meat. The tubes may be cut out with the scissors. Cut the liver into 1″ cubes; roll the cubes in a mixture of the flour, salt, pepper and mustard. Heat the fat in a large heavy saucepan; sear the liver; add the chopped onion and brown delicately. Add the water, tomatoes, sugar and macaroni. Heat to boiling; pour into an oiled 1½ quart casserole. Top with a mixture of grated cheese and crumbs; bake in a moderate oven till the cheese melts. Serve hot with Melba toast. Serves 6.

DEVILLED EGGS

The first 'must' with devilled eggs is to hard cook them so that there is no discolored dark ring around the yolks. Put boiling water in both bottom and top of the double boiler; put the eggs in top; cook them, covered, for 25 minutes. Hold the eggs under the cold water tap for a moment; tap them gently to crack the shells; chill in cold water. When cold, shell them with the back of a teaspoon; cut in half and remove the yolks; fill with this mixture:

Filling

6 egg yolks	1 tablespoon green pickle, chopped
2 tablespoons softened butter	½ teaspoon salt
2 tablespoons mayonnaise	2 tablespoons green onion,
2 teaspoons prepared mustard	chopped

Mash the egg yolks; add the remaining ingredients. Fill the egg whites with mixture; put together in pairs, wrapping each in a square of waxed paper. There will be a little filling left; use it for sandwiches. Serves 6.

NOTE TO BRIDES: *The filling may be varied by adding cheese, celery, olives, pickles or relish.*

CURRIED RICE

Temperature: 350°F.

Time: 1½ hours

½ cup uncooked rice
2 cups hot water
½ cup tomatoes
¾ teaspoon salt

¼ cup onion, finely sliced
¼ cup green peppers, sliced
2 tablespoons melted butter
¾ teaspoon curry powder

Wash and drain the rice; pour over it the 2 cups of hot water; let it stand where it will be hot but not cook for 45 minutes. Add all the remaining ingredients; blend well. Place the mixture in a baking dish; bake in a moderate oven until the rice is cooked. Stir from time to time so that the rice will spread evenly through the mixture. This is an unusual dish, but really delectable. Serves 5-6.

ENGLISH SAVOURY

Temperature: 350°F.

Time: 40 minutes

8 slices stale bread
½ pound cheese, grated
¼ teaspoon salt
Dash of pepper

3 eggs
2 cups milk
1 tablespoon corn starch

Cut 4 slices of stale bread to fit a long baking dish which has been well oiled; cover with the grated cheese, sprinkle with the seasonings, then add a second layer of bread. Lightly beat the eggs, add the milk and corn starch; beat again. Pour over the bread; let stand 20 minutes. Bake in a moderate oven until puffy and brown. Serve hot; serves 4-5.

SUNDAY SUPPER DISH

Temperature: 350°F.

Time: 45 minutes

½ pound fresh *or* 1 6-ounce
  can of mushrooms
2 green peppers
2 medium onions
3 tablespoons fat
2 eggs, well beaten

1 cup milk
  2 tablespoons grated cheese
¼ teaspoon baking powder
¼ teaspoon salt
Dash of pepper and cayenne
½ teaspoon paprika

Clean and chop the mushrooms; remove the seeds from the peppers and chop. Peel and chop the onions; cook and stir in the hot fat until tender and golden brown. Beat the eggs until light; add the milk, grated cheese, baking powder, salt and condiments; add the chopped mushrooms, peppers and onion. Blend well; bake in an oiled casserole in a moderate oven until firm. Served with a spiced tomato sauce. Serves 6.

CHAPTER 15

Salads and Salad Dressings

BEET-CELERY SALAD

1 tablespoon gelatine
¼ cup cold water
1 cup boiling water
2 tablespoons lemon juice
1 teaspoon lemon rind, grated
¼ teaspoon salt

Dash of pepper and mace
1 tablespoon white sugar
1 cup cooked beets, diced
1 cup celery, diced
1 cup apples, diced

Soak the gelatine in the cold water for 5 minutes. Pour the boiling water over it; stir well till dissolved. Add the lemon juice and rind, the seasonings and sugar; chill until the mixture begins to thicken; add the beets, celery and apple. Pour into an oiled loaf pan; chill until set. Unmould and serve with a plain boiled dressing and hot biscuits. Serves 6.

JELLIED CARROT SALAD WITH HAM

1 tablespoon plain gelatine
¼ cup cold water
1 cup boiling water
¼ cup cider vinegar
½ teaspoon salt
¼ cup white sugar
1½ tablespoons lemon juice

1 teaspoon lemon rind, grated
1½ cups carrots, grated
¼ cup green pickle, finely
 chopped
1 cup cooked ham, ground
1 cup mayonnaise

Soak the gelatine in the cold water for 5 minutes; dissolve in the boiling water. Add the vinegar, salt, sugar, lemon juice and rind; chill until the mixture begins to set. Fold in the vegetables; pour half the mixture into an oiled loaf pan; chill till fairly firm. Cover with the ground ham; pour on the second half of the gelatine mixture. Chill until firm. Unmould on a flat platter and frost with the mayonnaise. Add a frill of parsley at the bottom of the mould. Serve with Cheese Sticks. Serves 6.

JELLIED CHEESE SALAD

1 tablespoon gelatine
¼ cup cold water
½ cup mayonnaise
2 cups cottage cheese or
 cream cheese

¾ teaspoon salt
⅛ teaspoon paprika
¼ cup green pickle, chopped
12 stuffed olives, chopped
¼ cup green onions, chopped

Soak the gelatine in the cold water for 5 minutes; dissolve it by placing it over hot water until it is liquid. Warm the mayonnaise in the top of the double boiler; add the liquid gelatine; blend well. Combine with the cottage or cream cheese; beat till smooth. Add the seasonings, chopped pickled, olives and onion; blend well. Pour into a small oiled ring mould and chill till set. Serve with garden greens and French Dressing. Serves 6.

JELLIED CHICKEN SALAD

1 boiling fowl, approximately 4 pounds	1 cup cold stock
	2 tablespoons cider vinegar
1 onion, chopped	½ teaspoon salt
2 tablespoons celery, chopped	Dash of paprika and celery salt
1 tablespoon salt	
1 tablespoon gelatine	½ teaspoon white sugar

Singe, disjoint and wash a boiling fowl. Place in a saucepan with the onion, celery and salt; cover with cold water; simmer gently till tender. Strain the stock and remove the fat. Take the white meat from the bone and dice; there should be 1½ cups. Soak the gelatine in ¼ cup cold stock for 5 minutes; heat the remaining ¾ cup to boiling and dissolve the gelatine. Add the vinegar, seasonings and sugar. When it begins to set, add the diced chicken. Pour into small moulds or a loaf pan. Chill till set; unmould; serve on lettuce with mayonnaise. Serves 6-8.

BRIDE'S SALAD

2 cucumbers	2 teaspoons onion, grated
2 tablespoons gelatine	1 teaspoon white sugar
½ cup cold water	1½ teaspoons salt
¾ cup boiling water	Dash of paprika
6 tablespoons lemon juice	12 tomato slices
1 teaspoon lemon rind, grated	

Pare the cucumbers and remove the seeds; grate on the coarse side of the grater; there should be 4 cups of pulp and juice. Soak the gelatine in the cold water for 5 minutes; dissolve in the boiling water. Add the lemon juice and rind, grated onion, sugar, salt and paprika; blend in the grated cucumber. Chill until the mixture begins to set. Pour into individual oiled moulds; if you haven't the aluminum moulds, egg cups are just right. When ready to serve, unmould on thick slices of firm tomatoes which have been skinned and chilled. If you prefer one large moulded salad, chill in a bowl; invert the salad on a clear glass plate; garnish with alternating slices of tomato and cucumber. Serves 6.

GINGER ALE SALAD

1 tablespoon gelatine
  ¼ cup cold water
¼ cup orange juice
  ¼ cup white sugar
Dash of salt
  1 cup ginger ale

1½ tablespoons lemon juice
  1 cup sweet grapes, seeded
1 peach
1 apple
1 pear

Soak the gelatine in the cold water for 5 minutes. Heat the orange juice to boiling; add the gelatine; stir till dissolved. Add the sugar, salt, ginger ale and lemon juice. Chill until the mixture begins to set; add the grapes and the various fruits which have been peeled, cored and diced. Turn into a salad mould; let chill until set. Unmould on shredded lettuce; serve with Fruit Dressing. Serves 6.

GOLDEN SALAD

1 tablespoon gelatine
  ¼ cup cold water
½ cup boiling water
  ¼ cup white sugar
¼ cup cider vinegar
  ½ cup orange juice

½ teaspoon salt
  1 tablespoon orange rind, grated
1 teaspoon lemon rind, grated
  3 tablespoons lemon juice
1½ cups carrots, grated
  ½ cup celery, chopped

Soak the gelatine in cold water for 5 minutes; add the boiling water and the sugar; stir till dissolved. Add the vinegar, orange juice, salt, orange and lemon rind and lemon juice. Stir well; add the carrots and celery. Pour into an oiled mould and chill until set. Unmould on lettuce; serve with a plain boiled dressing. Serves 6.

GREEN SALAD

1 tablespoon gelatine
  ¼ cup cold water
1½ cups boiling water
  Green vegetable coloring
½ teaspoon salt
  1 tablespoon lemon juice

1 teaspoon lemon rind, grated
  ½ cup mayonnaise
¼ cup green pickle, chopped
  ¼ cup horse-radish
2 grapefruits

Soak the gelatine in the cold water for 5 minutes; dissolve in the boiling water. Add enough vegetable coloring to tint a delicate green; add the salt, lemon juice and rind. Let chill till the mixture begins to set; add the mayonnaise, pickle and horseradish. Beat till fluffy; pour into an oiled ring mould. Chill till firm. Unmould; serve with sections of grapefruit and French Tomato Dressing. Serves 6.

FRUIT SALAD

2 tablespoons gelatine	One 4 oz. package plain
½ cup cold water	cream cheese
1½ cups orange juice	¼ cup mayonnaise
1 tablespoon red cherries,	1 orange, sectioned
chopped	1 grapefruit, sectioned
1 tablespoon sweet green pickle	1 red apple, diced
1 tablespoon parsley, chopped	

Soak the gelatine in cold water for 5 minutes. Heat the orange juice; stir in the gelatine till dissolved; let chill until the mixture begins to set. Add the chopped cherries, pickle and parsley. Combine the cream cheese and mayonnaise; beat till light; add to the chilled gelatine mixture. Peel the orange and grapefruit; separate into sections. Dice the apple with the skin on. Pour half the salad mixture into a ring mould or loaf pan. Add a filling of the fruit; pour over it the remaining half of the gelatine mixture. Chill until firm; unmould in a bed of lettuce; serve with Fruit Dressing. Serves 6.

JELLIED GREEN SALAD

1 tablespoon gelatine	1 teaspoon lemon rind, grated
¼ cup cold water	½ cup celery, finely chopped
1 cup boiling water	¼ cup cucumber, finely diced
2 tablespoons white sugar	¼ cup raw spinach, finely chopped
½ teaspoon salt	¼ cup green pickle, finely chopped
¼ cup cider vinegar	6 maraschino cherries
2 tablespoons lemon juice	

Soak the gelatine in cold water for 5 minutes; dissolve in the boiling water; add the sugar and stir till dissolved. Add the salt, vinegar, lemon juice and rind. Chill until the mixture begins to set; fold in the chopped vegetables and pickle. Drain the cherries and cut petalwise; arrange in the bottom of an oiled loaf pan. Pour in the jellied salad; let chill until set. Unmould on a clear glass platter and garnish with parsley. Serve with mayonnaise mixed with a little chili sauce. Serves 6.

MUSTARD RELISH

1½ teaspoons gelatine	⅓ cup boiling water
2 tablespoons cold water	1 cup mayonnaise
1 teaspoon dry mustard	

Soak the gelatine in the cold water for 5 minutes. Sprinkle with the mustard; add the boiling water. Stir until dissolved; chill until it begins to thicken. Fold in the mayonnaise. Spoon in small oiled muffin pans and chill until firm. Unmould; serve with cold meat plates. Yield: 8 moulds.

FRESH PINEAPPLE SALAD

2 tablespoons gelatine
½ cup cold water
3½ cups fresh pineapple, finely diced
¾ cup white sugar

1 tablespoon orange rind, grated
¾ cup orange juice
5 tablespoons lemon juice
2 egg whites

Soak the gelatine in the cold water for 5 minutes. Finely dice the pineapple; sprinkle with the sugar and let stand for half an hour; simmer gently until the pineapple is tender. There should be 3½ cups pineapple and syrup; if necessary, add sufficient hot water to make this amount. Add the soaked gelatine; stir till dissolved. Cool the mixture; add the orange rind and fruit juices. Chill until the mixture begins to set; fold in the stiffly beaten egg whites. Pour into an oiled 9″ ring mould, chill until firm. Unmould and serve with Fruit Dressing. Serves 6.

JELLIED SALAD SQUARES

1 tablespoon gelatine
¼ cup cold water
1 cup hot orange juice
4 tablespoons white sugar
1 tablespoon lemon juice
1 tablespoon orange rind, grated

1 teaspoon lemon rind, grated
8 maraschino cherries, chopped
Liquid from cherries
12 sections tangerines or oranges

Soak the gelatine in the cold water for 5 minutes; add the hot orange juice and sugar; stir till dissolved. Add the lemon juice, orange and lemon rind, chopped cherries and liquid. Pour half the mixture into an oiled pan 8″ x 8″; chill until slightly set. Press tangerine sections into the jelly in an even pattern; you want 12 squares. Cover with the remaining jelly and chill till firm. When ready to serve, unmould on an oiled cookie sheet. Cut in squares; use as a garnish for cold meat plates. Yield: 12 squares.

SALMON AND EGG MOULD

1 tablespoon gelatine
2 tablespoons cold water
3 tablespoons butter
3 tablespoons pastry flour
½ teaspoon salt

Dash of mace, pepper and paprika
2 cups hot milk
2 cups canned or cooked salmon, flaked
1 tablespoon lemon juice
4 hard cooked eggs

Soak the gelatine in cold water for 5 minutes. Melt the butter in a saucepan; mix in the flour and seasonings; stir gently over low heat for 3 minutes. Add the hot milk; stir and cook till smooth and thick. Add the soaked gelatine; stir till dissolved. Add the salmon and lemon juice. Shell the eggs; remove the whites from the yolks. Save the yolks for sieving; add the finely chopped whites to the salmon mixture. Pour into an oiled loaf pan 9″x 5″x 3″; chill until firm. Unmould on a bed of lettuce and frost with mayonnaise. Press the yolks through a sieve over the dressing; decorate with long narrow leaves cut from green pepper or sweet pickle. Serve with whole wheat bread and a salad bowl. Serves 6.

TOMATO-CHEESE SALAD

1 tablespoon gelatine	1 cup mayonnaise
½ cup cold water	¼ cup green onion, chopped
One 10 oz. can condensed	¼ cup young radishes,
tomato soup	chopped
One 4 oz. package plain cream	2 hard cooked eggs
cheese	1 tablespoon parsley, chopped

Soak the gelatine in the cold water for 5 minutes. Heat the soup to boiling; remove from the heat. Add the cheese; beat with a dover beater till smooth and well blended. Add the soaked gelatine; stir till dissolved. Chill until the mixture begins to thicken; add the mayonnaise, onions and radishes. Pour into an oiled pan 8″ x 8″; chill until firm. Cut into circles with a 2½″ cookie cutter. Shell the eggs; finely chop the yolks and whites. Brush the edge of the circles with mayonnaise; roll them in the chopped eggs, then the parsley. Serve the pin-wheels on lettuce. Serves 6.

BEET AND EGG SALAD

1 quart small beets	4 whole cloves
¾ cup cider vinegar	½ teaspoon salt
¼ cup water	4 hard cooked eggs
½ cup white sugar	½ cup cucumber, diced
¼ teaspoon allspice	½ cup celery, diced
1 stick whole cinnamon	Mayonnaise to moisten

Top and scrub the beets; cook in boiling water till tender; slip off the skins and chill. Score down the outside with a fork and hollow out the inside; the scooped-out centre may be served as a plain vegetable. Heat together the vinegar, water, sugar, spices and seasoning; boil 5 minutes; strain to remove the spices. While still warm, add the beets and the whole hard cooked eggs; let stand overnight. Drain; fill the cooked beets with a mixture of diced cucumbers and celery, moistened with mayonnaise. Serve on lettuce with the hard cooked eggs, cut in half. Use the pickling liquid as a sauce for hot beets. Serves 6.

TOMATO JELLY

1 tablespoon gelatine
4 tablespoons cold water
2 cups tomato juice
1 tablespoon lemon juice
1 teaspoon lemon rind, grated

1 teaspoon onion, finely chopped
1 teaspoon white sugar
½ teaspoon salt
Dash of pepper, cayenne and celery salt
½ teaspoon Tabasco (optional)

Soak the gelatine in the cold water for 5 minutes. Heat the tomato juice to boiling; remove from the heat. Add the soaked gelatine; stir till dissolved. Add all the remaining ingredients; pour into an oiled 9″ ring mould or into individual moulds. Let chill; unmould on lettuce; serve with Boiled Dressing and Cole Slaw. Serves 6.

MARY'S COLE SLAW

¼ cup cider vinegar
1 teaspoon salt
¼ teaspoon pepper
½ teaspoon dry mustard
1 tablespoon white sugar

1 tablespoon salad oil
1 egg
2 tablespoons cereal cream
3 cups cabbage, chilled and shredded

Measure the vinegar, salt, pepper, mustard, sugar and salad oil into a saucepan; heat to the boiling point. Slightly beat the egg; pour the hot mixture over it. Blend well and cook until thickened; use low heat—never let the mixture actually boil. Remove from the heat; beat in the cream. Pour hot over the cabbage. Chill; serve very cold. Serves 6.

NOTE TO BRIDES: *For Cheese Cole Slaw, add ½ cup grated cheese just before serving.*

HOT POTATO SALAD

4 potatoes, medium size
6 slices breakfast bacon
1 onion, diced
2 tablespoons white sugar
¼ cup cider vinegar

¼ cup water
1 teaspoon salt
Dash of pepper and cayenne
2 hard cooked eggs, chopped
1 tablespoon parsley, chopped

Scrub the potatoes; cook until tender in their jackets; while still warm, peel and dice. Dice the bacon and pan fry till crisp; drain; add the crisp bits of bacon to the potatoes. Strain and pour ¼ cup bacon fat back into pan; pan fry the onion very gently, stirring and cooking till it is golden brown; add the sugar, vinegar, water and seasonings. Heat to boiling; pour over the diced potatoes; add the chopped eggs. Reheat in the top of the double boiler; add the chopped parsley just before serving. Serve hot. Serves 6.

POTATO SALAD

4 cups cooked potatoes, diced
4 tablespoons hot fat
1 tablespoon lemon juice
½ cup green onions, chopped
2 hard cooked eggs
¼ cup green pickle, chopped
¼ cup young radishes, sliced
1 teaspoon salt
⅛ teaspoon pepper
Mayonnaise to moisten
Green pickle, sliced, or raw
carrots, sliced

Cook the potatoes in their jackets till tender. Cool and skin them; dice in fairly small pieces. Heat the fat to boiling; pour over the potatoes and shake so that each piece is coated with the fat. Add the lemon juice and onions; mix well; let stand 2 hours. Shell the eggs and dice the whites; reserve the yolks for garnish. Combine the potato mixture with the chopped egg whites, pickles, radishes and seasonings; add enough mayonnaise to moisten. Spoon into a loaf pan and press until firm; unmould on a flat platter. Ice with mayonnaise; press the yolks through a sieve over the mayonnaise coating. Garnish with sliced green pickles or raw carrots; the carrots should be scraped, scored with a fork, thinly sliced and chilled. Add the garnish just before serving. Serves 8.

TOSSED GREEN SALAD

6 lettuce leaves, pulled in pieces
½ cup radishes, sliced
1 cup raw spinach, chopped
1 tart apple, pared and diced
¼ cup cider vinegar
2 hard cooked eggs, sliced
1 teaspoon white sugar
½ teaspoon salt
¼ teaspoon celery seed
Dash of paprika and cayenne
6 tablespoons mayonnaise
¼ cup chili sauce

Prepare and combine the lettuce, radishes, spinach and apples; add the vinegar and toss. Chill till ready to serve. Shell and dice the eggs; add all the remaining ingredients and chill. Combine with the vegetables just before serving. Serve with cold roast bacon. Serves 6.

SALAD BOWL

1 cup raw spinach, chopped
1 cup celery, chopped
1 cup green cabbage, shredded
1 onion, diced
½ cup radishes, sliced
¼ cup cider vinegar
½ cup mayonnaise
2 tablespoons chili sauce
2 tablespoons green pickle, chopped
1 tablespoon onion, diced
1 hard cooked egg

Wash the spinach in hot water; shake well and chop. Add the chopped celery, shredded cabbage, onions and radishes. Add the cider vinegar; chill in the refrigerator. Combine the mayonnaise, chili sauce, pickles and diced onion. Chop the egg whites and add to the dressing; press the yolks through a sieve into the dressing. Chill; toss with the salad greens just before serving. Serves 6.

OLD FASHIONED POTATO SALAD

8 medium potatoes
  4 slices breakfast bacon, diced
1 medium onion, diced
  2 tablespoons pastry flour
½ cup cider vinegar
  ½ cup water
2 teaspoons salt

½ teaspoon dry mustard
  ⅛ teaspoon pepper
2 tablespoons sugar
  ½ cup celery, diced
4 hard cooked eggs, shelled
  and diced
½ cup boiled salad dressing

Cook the potatoes in their jackets in boiling salted water till tender. Drain and cool; peel and dice—there should be 5 cups. Cook the diced bacon and onion in a frying pan till the bacon is crisp and the onion golden brown. Blend in the flour; add the vinegar, salt, water, mustard, pepper and sugar; cook over low heat till the mixture thickens, stirring continually. Combine the diced potatoes, celery and chopped eggs; pour the hot dressing over the mixture and toss lightly with a fork. This salad is delicious hot or cold. If served hot, omit the salad dressing; if served cold, chill and add the salad dressing just before serving. Serves 6-8.

SPRING SALAD

2 cups cabbage, shredded
  1 cup raw carrots, shredded
1 cup unpeeled red apple,
  diced
3 tablespoons lemon juice
  2 tablespoons green pickle,
    parsley or green pepper,
    chopped

1 tablespoon onion, chopped
  1 teaspoon salt
Dash of pepper and paprika
  ⅓ cup cream
1 teaspoon dry mustard
  1 tablespoon chili sauce
1 tablespoon cider vinegar

Combine the cabbage, carrots, apple and lemon juice; toss lightly with a fork. Add the chopped greens and the onion. Combine all the remaining ingredients; mix well with the cabbage mixture. Chill before serving. Serve with boiled salad dressing. Serves 6.

WALDORF SALAD

1½ cups tart apples, diced
  1 tablespoon lemon juice
1 teaspoon lemon rind, grated
  1 cup celery, diced

¼ cup nuts, chopped
  ½ cup seedless raisins
Boiled dressing to moisten

Peel, core and dice the apples; sprinkle with the lemon juice and rind. Add all the remaining ingredients; toss well and chill; serve in lettuce cups with thinly sliced Cheese Bread. Serves 6.

TOSSED SUMMER SALAD

1 cup cucumbers, sliced
  1 cup tomatoes, cut in eighths
1 cup onions, sliced
  1 cup cooked green beans,
    sliced

3 tablespoons vinegar
  1 tablespoon white sugar
1 teaspoon salt
  Dash of pepper and nutmeg
1 cup thick sour cream

Peel the cucumbers; remove the seeds and slice. Scald and skin the tomatoes; cut in eighths and drain. Peel and thinly slice the onions. Sliver the beans lengthwise; cook in boiling salted water and drain. Combine all the vegetables in a bowl.. Measure the vinegar, sugar, seasonings and cream into a jar. Shake well; pour over the vegetables. Blend and chill before serving. Serves 6.

Salad Dressings

COOKED SALAD DRESSING

3 tablespoons white sugar
  2 teaspoons salt
1 teaspoon dry mustard
  3 tablespoons flour
Dash of paprika

2 eggs, unbeaten
  1½ cups milk
½ cup cider vinegar or lemon
  juice
2 tablespoons butter

Measure the sugar, salt, mustard, flour and paprika into the top of a double boiler. Add the unbeaten eggs; beat till smooth. Add the milk and vinegar; beat with the dover beater. Cook over boiling water till the mixture is smooth and thick (about 20 minutes), stirring occasionally. Remove from the heat; add the butter; beat until light. Yield: 2½ cups.

CREAMY SALAD DRESSING

1 tablespoon white sugar
  1 teaspoon dry mustard
1 teaspoon salt
  Dash of cayenne
1 cup 18% cream

1 egg, unbeaten
  1 tablespoon sifted flour
1 tablespoon butter
  ⅓ cup cider vinegar

Combine all the ingredients except the vinegar in the top of a double boiler; beat until smooth; cook over boiling water until smooth and thick. Add the vinegar; continue cooking for 5 minutes. Remove from the heat; beat until smooth. Pour into a sterile jar; do not cover until cold. This recipe may be doubled and lemon juice may be substituted for the vinegar. Yield: 1½ cups.

RICH COOKED SALAD DRESSING

2 eggs	1 teaspoon salt
4 tablespoons white sugar	Dash of pepper and paprika
2 tablespoons corn starch	1½ cups thick sour cream
1 tablespoon dry mustard	½ cup cider vinegar

Break the eggs into the top of a double boiler; add the sugar, corn starch, mustard, salt, pepper and paprika; beat till smooth. Add the sour cream; blend with the dover beater. Cook over boiling water until the mixture begins to thicken; add the vinegar slowly; continue cooking for 10 minutes. Strain; pour into a sterile jar. Do not cover till cold. Yield: 2½ cups.

PLAIN FRENCH DRESSING WITH VARIATIONS

½ cup salad oil	Dash of pepper
¼ teaspoon onion, scraped	1 teaspoon sugar
¼ teaspoon dry mustard	2 tablespoons cider vinegar or
½ teaspoon paprika	tarragon vinegar or lemon
½ teaspoon salt	juice

Measure all the ingredients into a quart jar and shake vigorously. Store in the refrigerator; shake well before using. Vary the recipe by adding:

1. Grapefruit juice instead of vinegar.
2. Half lemon juice, half vinegar and ¼ cup chili sauce.
3. Finely chopped parsley and green peppers.
4. 1 teaspoon strained tomato juice and a few drops onion juice.

Yield: ¾ cup dressing.

NEW FRENCH DRESSING

1 tablespoon gelatine	¾ teaspoon dry mustard
1 tablespoon cold water	1½ teaspoons salt
2 tablespoons boiling water	Dash of pepper and paprika
1 tablespoon brown sugar	⅓ cup cider vinegar
Dash of cayenne	1 cup salad oil

Soak the gelatine in the cold water for 5 minutes; dissolve in the boiling water; chill until the mixture begins to set. Measure all the dry ingredients into the vinegar; add the salad oil; beat vigorously with dover beater until well blended. Add the chilled gelatine; again blend well. Let stand 15 minutes; beat vigorously; chill well before serving. Yield: 1½ cups.

QUICK FRENCH DRESSING

¾ cup salad oil
¼ cup lemon juice or vinegar
¾ teaspoon salt

Dash of pepper and paprika
¼ cup brown sugar

Combine all the ingredients; beat with a dover beater till well blended. Use for salad greens. Yield: 1¼ cups.

FRENCH TOMATO DRESSING

One 10 oz. can condensed
  tomato soup
¾ cup cider vinegar
1 teaspoon salt
½ teaspoon pepper
1 teaspoon dry mustard

Dash of cayenne
5 tablespoons brown sugar
1 teaspoon onion, finely
  chopped
1½ cups salad oil

Combine all the ingredients in a quart jar; shake vigorously; chill. Shake again just before serving. Yield: 3½ cups.

FRUIT DRESSING

1 teaspoon corn starch
¼ teaspoon salt
¼ cup white sugar
4 tablespoons lemon juice

1 egg, well beaten
One 4 ounce package plain
  cream cheese
1 cup 18% cream

Mix together the corn starch, salt and sugar; add the lemon juice and the egg. Blend well; cook over boiling water till smooth and clear, about 10 minutes. Chill the cheese and cream in the refrigerator; combine; beat with the dover beater until like whipped cream. It may be necessary to chill the mixture again during the beating. When light and fluffy fold into the chilled lemon mixture. Yield: 2 cups.

NOTE TO BRIDES: *This is a salad dressing you'll make over and over again and use for everything from salads to ice cream.*

CLEAR FRUIT DRESSING

2 eggs, separated
⅛ teaspoon salt
3 tablespoons white sugar

¾ cup orange juice
1 tablespoon lemon juice
1 teaspoon lemon rind, grated

Separate the eggs; beat the yolks till light; add the salt and white sugar. Add the fruit juices and rind. Cook over boiling water until thickened, stirring constantly. Cool slightly; fold in the stiffly beaten egg whites. Chill before serving. Yield: 1½ cups.

COOKED FRUIT DRESSING

2 tablespoons white sugar
1½ teaspoons salt
2 teaspoons dry mustard
2 tablespoons sifted flour
3 egg yolks

Dash of cayenne
1¼ cups rich milk
6 tablespoons lemon juice
1 teaspoon lemon rind, grated
1 tablespoon butter

Measure the sugar, salt, mustard, flour, egg yolks, cayenne and milk into the top of a double boiler, beating well after each ingredient goes in; cook over boiling water until the mixture thickens, about 10 minutes. Add the lemon juice and rind; continue cooking for 5 minutes. Strain; add the butter and beat with the dover beater. Pour into a sterile jar and store in the refrigerator. This is a delicious dressing for fruit salads. Yield: 2 cups.

FRESH FRUIT DRESSING

½ cup lemon juice
½ cup salad oil
1 teaspoon salt
½ teaspoon paprika

Dash of cayenne
3 tablespoons white sugar
1 tablespoon maraschino
cherries, chopped

Measure the lemon juice and salad oil into a quart jar, add the salt, paprika and cayenne; add the white sugar. Shake well and chill; just before serving, add the maraschino cherries. Use as a dressing for raw fruit salads. Yield: 1¼ cups.

TOSSED SALAD DRESSING

1 tablespoon hard cooked egg,
chopped
1 tablespoon chutney or chili
sauce
¼ teaspoon curry powder

1 tablespoon lemon juice
9 tablespoons salad oil
3 tablespoons cider vinegar
¼ teaspoon salt
1 teaspoon sugar

Measure all the ingredients into a quart jar; shake well and chill. Shake vigorously before using. Yield: 1 cup.

PIQUANT SALAD DRESSING

1 egg
1 teaspoon salt
1 teaspoon dry mustard
1 tablespoon corn starch

⅛ teaspoon curry powder
½ cup sour milk
½ cup cider vinegar

Slightly beat the egg in the top of a double boiler. Add the remaining ingredients in order given; mix with a dover beater. Cook over boiling water till smooth and thick. Remove from the heat; beat again till creamy. Serve with jellied salads. Yield: 1¼ cups.

PIQUANT MAYONNAISE

1 cup mayonnaise
2 tablespoons chili sauce
2 hard cooked eggs, chopped

2 tablespoons dill pickle, chopped
¼ cup whipping cream

Combine all the ingredients except the cream 3 hours before using. Just before serving, stiffly whip the cream and fold into the dressing. Yield: 2 cups.

JIFFY MAYONNAISE

¼ cup corn starch
  ¼ cup cold water
¾ cup boiling water
  1 egg
2 tablespoons white sugar

1½ teaspoons salt
  2 teaspoons dry mustard
⅛ teaspoon paprika
  ¼ cup cider vinegar
¾ cup salad oil

Measure the corn starch and cold water into the top of a double boiler; mix to a paste; add the boiling water. Stir and cook over direct heat until smooth and thick; continue cooking over boiling water for 7 minutes. Place all the remaining ingredients in a mixing bowl; pour on the hot starch; beat with a dover beater until the mixture thickens and turns light yellow in color. Pour into a sterile jar; do not cover till cold. Yield: 3 cups.

GREEN SALAD DRESSING

1 small potato
2 teaspoons white sugar
¼ teaspoon salt
  ¼ teaspoon paprika

¼ teaspoon dry mustard
6 tablespoons salad oil
2 tablespoons cider vinegar

Cook the potato until tender; drain and mash with a fork till very fine; there should be ¼ cup. Measure into a bowl the sugar, salt, paprika, mustard, 1 tablespoon salad oil and 1 tablespoon vinegar. Beat till smooth; add the potato and beat again. Add the remainder of the oil and the vinegar; beat till light and smooth. Chill; serve with vegetable salads. Yield: 1 cup.

30-MINUTE SALAD DRESSING

¼ cup lemon juice
  ¼ cup cider vinegar
⅔ cup salad oil
  1½ teaspoons salt
Dash of cayenne

1 teaspoon white sugar
Dash of paprika
1 tablespoon parsley, chopped
1 tablespoon green pickle, chopped

Combine all the ingredients in a quart jar. Shake well; chill thirty minutes before pouring over salad. Yield: 1¼ cups.

CHAPTER 16

Sandwiches

CHEESE SANDWICH FILLINGS

Toast rounds of bread; spread with a sauce made by heating together condensed tomato soup and grated cheese. Serve hot.

Roll tea biscuit batter thinly; spread half of it with grated cheese; fold over, cut in squares and bake in a hot oven. Serve warm.

Cream ½ cup plain cream cheese; add 1 tablespoon finely chopped onion, 2 tablespoons grated raw carrots and ¼ teaspoon salt. Blend well.

Grate ¼ pound nippy Canadian cheese, add 2 finely chopped hard cooked eggs, 1½ teaspoons chopped onion and chopped sweet green pickle; add salt and pepper to taste and enough mayonnaise to make it spread easily. Use whole wheat or rye bread. This is a grand mixture for a toasted open face sandwich. Toast the bread on one side, spread the untoasted side with the filling and toast in a hot oven till the cheese runs. It teams up well with cole slaw.

CHEESE SPREAD

⅓ cup butter
2 tablespoons flour
¾ cup white sugar
3 teaspoons dry mustard
1 teaspoon salt
Dash of pepper and paprika
2 eggs, lightly beaten

¾ cup cider vinegar
Two 4 ounce packages plain cream cheese
¼ cup cereal cream
2 tablespoons pimento, chopped
2 tablespoons green pickle, chopped

Melt the butter in the top of the double boiler; blend in the flour and let bubble gently over direct heat for 3 minutes. Add the sugar, mustard, salt, pepper, paprika and eggs; blend well; cook and stir over boiling water till thickened. Add the vinegar, cheese and cream; cook again over boiling water till well blended. Remove from the heat; beat in the pimento and pickle. Pour in sterile jars; chill well before using. You will have 3 cups of delicious sandwich filling.

TOMATO-CHEESE SPREAD

1 can tomatoes (28 oz.)	1 sweet green pepper, chopped *or*
2 tablespoons salt	½ cup sweet green pickle, chopped
½ cup white sugar	1 tablespoon dry mustard
¾ cup cider vinegar	½ cup corn starch
1 medium onion, chopped	½ cup grated cheese

Combine in a saucepan the tomatoes, salt, sugar and ½ cup vinegar; heat to boiling; strain through a sieve. Put the onion and green pepper or pickle through the food chopper; combine with the tomato mixture in the top of a double boiler; heat thoroughly. Mix the mustard and corn starch to a paste with the remaining ¼ cup vinegar; stir into the hot mixture; cook over direct heat till smooth and thick. Cover; cook over boiling water for 20 minutes, stirring occasionally. Remove from the heat; add the grated cheese; stir till melted. Seal in sterile jars. Yield: 2½ pints. This filling will keep indefinitely if well chilled; it makes a tasty addition to a sliced meat sandwich.

CHICKEN SALAD SANDWICHES

2½ cups diced, cooked chicken	1½ cups tart apple, finely
¾ cup salad dressing	chopped
2½ cups celery, finely diced	Lemon butter
4 hard cooked eggs, diced	Lettuce
1½ teaspoons salt	White Bread
Dash of pepper and paprika	

Cook a boiling fowl till tender; cool; dice the meat with a pair of scissors. Use 2½ cups of this chicken meat; if chicken is scarce, cooked ham may be substituted. To the chicken or ham add the salad dressing; marinate for 1 hour; add the chopped celery. Shell the eggs and dice them; add to the chicken mixture; add the seasonings and apple. Add 1 tablespoon lemon juice and 1 teaspoon grated lemon rind to the butter; mix till creamy; spread the bread with it. Lay a lettuce leaf on one slice; spread the other with the chicken salad filling; pair and cut in quarters. Yield: 12 sandwiches.

EGG SANDWICH FILLINGS

Chop 4 hard cooked eggs; moisten with ¼ cup mayonnaise; add ¼ cup finely chopped celery and a dash of salt and pepper. Spread whole wheat bread with plain cream cheese; fill with the egg mixture.

———————

Chop 3 hard cooked eggs; add ¼ cup butter, 1 tablespoon finely chopped onion, ½ teaspoon dry mustard and a dash of salt and pepper. The bread need not be buttered.

SPRING SANDWICH LOAF

A spring sandwich loaf is one of the prettiest dishes for a supper party or a sewing group luncheon. It isn't any harder to make than ordinary sandwiches and looks as decorative as a rose-bud in the hair. Made up 2 fillings:

Meat Filling

Put ½ pound cooked ham or jellied tongue through the chopper; add 2 tablespoons chopped sweet pickle, 2 tablespoons boiled salad dressing and 1 tablespoon lemon juice. Mix well.

Egg Filling

Chop 4 hard cooked eggs; add 2 tablespoons salad dressing, 1 tablespoon chopped onion, 2 tablespoons chopped greens (celery tops, green cabbage, onion tops), ½ teaspoon salt and a dash of pepper.

Cut the crusts from a loaf of bread; slice lengthwise in slices about ½" thick. Butter each slice lightly on 1 side. Spread the bottom slice with the ham mixture; cover with bread; spread the next slice with the egg mixture; continue until the loaf is complete.

Frosting

Cream three 4-ounce packages cream cheese with 1 tablespoon lemon juice and enough salad dressing to make it spread evenly. Frost the top and sides of the sandwich loaf and chill well before serving.

Here is a pretty top garnish: cut slices of red tomatoes, moisten the edges with a bit of salad dressing and then roll in chopped parsley. Place the pin wheels on top of the loaf just before serving. This sandwich loaf will cut into 8 large or 10 medium servings.

MEAT SANDWICH FILLINGS

Ham and Peanut Butter Spread

1 cup boiled ham, ground	1 tablespoon prepared mustard
¼ cup peanut butter	¾ teaspoon Worcester Sauce
3 tablespoons mayonnaise	

Blend all the ingredients; spread between thin slices of buttered rye bread.

Liver and Egg Spread

½ cup cooked liver, chopped	¼ teaspoon salt
1 hard cooked egg, chopped	Dash of pepper and celery salt
1 teaspoon onion, chopped	2 tablespoons mayonnaise

Finely chop left-over cooked liver; add all the remaining ingredients. This quantity will make 6 sandwiches.

Liver Paste

2 pounds pork liver	½ teaspoon salt
1 cup milk	¼ teaspoon onion salt
1 tablespoon cider vinegar	Dash of pepper and paprika
3 tablespoons fat	1 teaspoon lemon juice
½ pound fresh or canned mushrooms	2 tablespoons rolled oats

Cut up the liver; soak in the milk and vinegar all night. Drain (save the liquid); pan fry the liver in the hot fat till tender; for the last 10 minutes add the sliced mushrooms. When tender, finely chop both the mushrooms and liver; run them through the food chopper if you want them nicely done. Add the seasonings, lemon juice, rolled oats and the reserved liquid to the paste; heat to boiling; continue cooking over boiling water 10 minutes. Turn into a loaf pan; chill until set. Slice for sandwiches or mix to a paste with butter and spread on whole wheat bread.

Liverwurst

You can buy the prepared liverwurst mixture; it comes in a casing about 2½″ wide and is jam-full of energy. We find it rather rich when used straight; it's nicer mixed in this proportion: ½ pound liverwurst, 1 teaspoon horse-radish, 1 teaspoon chili sauce, 2 tablespoons mayonnaise, a dash of salt and pepper. Try this filling with rye bread; it's good!

Chopped Meat Spread

3 pounds cooked meat (veal and chicken, mixed)	¼ cup canned tomatoes
	½ teaspoon salt
3 medium heads celery, finely chopped	Dash of pepper
	Mayonnaise to moisten
¼ cup green pickle, chopped	

Put the meat through the coarse knife of the food chopper; add all the remaining ingredients. This is a tasty sandwich filling and one that doesn't get tiresome or monotonous.

Another tangy meat combination is this: 1 cup chopped cooked meat, 2 tablespoons chopped mustard pickle, a taste of onion juice and a dash of salt and pepper.

SWEET SANDWICH FILLINGS

Cream one 4-ounce package plain cream cheese with 1 tablespoon jam or marmalade; for extra flavor add 2 tablespoons chopped celery and ¼ teaspoon salt. That's a delicious spread.

Spread stale bread with raspberry jam; dip in egg and milk; pan fry in a little hot fat until golden brown. Cut in squares and serve hot.

Cream one 4-ounce package plain cream cheese with ¼ cup butter; add 1 tablespoon grated orange rind and 1 tablespoon orange juice; mix well.

Blend ¼ cup butter with ½ cup orange marmalade; use to fill brown and white sandwiches.

Measure equal quantities of Spiced Apple Butter and plain cream cheese into a bowl; blend well; spread between slices of buttered whole wheat bread. To vary the appearance of the sandwiches, cut bread slices into rounds; cut the top slices in the centre with a thimble. Fill with plenty of the spread; it will come up through the circle in the tops.

SANDWICHES—LARGE AMOUNTS

1 large (3 pound) sandwich loaf cuts to 70 slices.

1 small (24 ounce) sandwich loaf cuts to 20 slices.

One 3-pound loaf requires ½ pound of butter for spreading and 1 pound of meat or cheese filling.

Sandwich Filling

3 pounds cooked meat, chopped (veal, chicken or ham)	¼ cup sweet pickle or green pepper, chopped
3 medium heads celery, chopped	1½ teaspoons salt
¼ cup pimento, diced	¼ teaspoon pepper
	2 cups mayonnaise

Combine all the ingredients; blend well. This amount of filling is sufficient for 150-180 large sandwiches, or 300-360 small sandwiches.

CHAPTER 17

Soups

CREAM OF ASPARAGUS SOUP

1½ pounds fresh asparagus	3 tablespoons butter
¼ cup onion, chopped	3 tablespoons flour
¼ cup celery, chopped	½ cup cereal cream
2 cups water	2 cups rich milk
½ teaspoon salt	Dash of pepper and paprika

Brush the asparagus; cut in 1″ lengths. Place in a saucepan with the onion, celery, water and salt. Simmer until tender; press through a sieve. Melt the butter in a saucepan; blend in the flour; let bubble for 3 minutes. Slowly add the cream, milk, seasonings and asparagus puree. Heat to boiling; serve with crisp crackers; serves 6.

POT BARLEY SOUP

4 pounds shin bone or shank	2 cups potatoes, diced
3 quarts cold water	¼ cup carrots, diced
3 teaspoons salt	¼ cup celery, diced
¼ teaspoon pepper	½ cup onion, chopped
3 whole cloves	¼ cup turnip, diced
1 bay leaf	1 cup barley
1 teaspoon white sugar	

Have the butcher crack the shin bone so that the marrow will cook out. Cover with the cold water; add the seasonings and sugar. Cook slowly for 3 hours or until the meat falls from the bones. Add the vegetables and barley; simmer another hour. Serve hot. Serves 6.

SPLIT PEA SOUP

2 cups split peas	½ teaspoon salt
1 smoked ham bone	⅛ teaspoon pepper
8 cups water	Butter
1 medium onion, chopped	

Soak the peas overnight. Put the ham bone in a saucepan with 8 cups water; let simmer for one hour. Add the peas, chopped onion, salt and pepper; cook slowly for another hour, adding water as needed. (Water from carrots, cabbage, etc. is ideal for this purpose.) Just before serving, add enough boiling water to double your soup; dot with butter. Serves 6.

BEAN SOUP

2 cups black or lima beans
2 quarts cold water
4 stalks celery, chopped
½ cup cabbage, finely chopped
1 onion, finely chopped
1 teaspoon salt
¼ teaspoon pepper

¼ teaspoon dry mustard
4 tablespoons butter
2 tablespoons flour
1 tablespoon vinegar
10 thin slices lemon
2 hard cooked eggs

Wash the beans; soak overnight in cold water. In the morning drain; cover with fresh water; add the celery, cabbage, onion, salt, pepper and mustard. Cover and cook gently until the beans are tender, about 3 hours. Press through a sieve; there should be about 8 cups. Melt the butter in a saucepan; blend in the flour; let bubble 3 minutes. Add to the bean puree; add the vinegar. Bring the mixture to a boil; serve hot with one slice of lemon and one slice of hard cooked egg in each serving. Serves 10.

ONION SOUP

2 cups onion, sliced
½ cup water
3 tablespoons fat
1 tablespoon flour
1 teaspoon salt
Dash of pepper and paprika

4 cups soup stock *or*
2 condensed meat cubes dissolved in
4 cups hot water
Rounds of thin toast
Grated cheese

Slice the onions thinly; simmer in the water till tender. Drain; save what water there is for the stock. Heat the fat in a saucepan; add the onions; sauté till they are tender and golden brown. Add the flour and seasonings; stir and cook gently for 3 minutes. Add the soup stock or the dissolved meat cubes; let simmer for half an hour. Pour into an oven-proof bowl; add the toast rounds; sprinkle with grated cheese. Place in a hot oven (450°F.) till the cheese melts and runs. Serve hot. Serves 6.

CREAM OF POTATO SOUP

5 cups raw potato, thinly sliced
1 onion, sliced
¼ cup celery, chopped
1 cup cold water
2 teaspoons salt

3 tablespoons butter
2½ cups milk
1 tablespoon parsley, chopped

Peel and thinly slice the potatoes; put in a heavy saucepan. Add the onion, very thinly sliced; this soup is not sieved and the onion slices when cooked should be almost transparent. Add the chopped celery, water and salt; cook until all the vegetables are tender; mash in the liquid. Add the butter, milk and chopped parsley. Heat to the boiling point; serve at once. Serves 6.

CLEAR TOMATO SOUP

2 tablespoons fat	Dash of pepper and paprika
1 onion, chopped	Bay leaf
1 tablespoon celery, diced	1 tablespoon corn starch
6 cups fresh tomatoes	1 tablespoon cold water
1 tablespoon white sugar	1 tablespoon butter
1½ teaspoons salt	

Heat the fat in a heavy saucepan; add the onions and celery; cook and stir till the vegetables are tender but not brown. Add the tomatoes, the sugar, salt, paprika, pepper and bay leaf. Simmer till the tomatoes are tender; press through a sieve. Heat the mixture to boiling; stir in a paste made by mixing the corn starch and the water. Cook and stir over low heat for 5 minutes. Remove from the heat; beat in the butter. Serves 6.

CREAM OF TOMATO SOUP

PART I

4 tablespoons fat	1 teaspoon whole pickling spice
1 cup onions, sliced	2 teaspoons sugar
1 apple, diced	¾ teaspoon salt
1 can tomatoes (2½ cups)	Dash of pepper and paprika

PART II

2 tablespoons fat	Dash of pepper and paprika
2 tablespoons flour	2 cups milk
1 teaspoon salt	

Heat 4 tablespoons fat in a heavy saucepan; add the sliced onion and apple; cook and stir till tender. Add the tomatoes, spice, sugar and seasonings. Bring to the boil; let simmer for 5 minutes. Rub through a sieve; there should be 2 cups of puree.

Melt 2 tablespoons fat in a saucepan; blend in the flour and seasonings; let bubble for 3 minutes. Slowly add the milk; cook and stir till smooth and thick. Remove from the heat; combine with the tomato puree. Beat with a dover beater; serve with small salted crackers. 6 servings.

VEGETABLE SOUP

8 cups cold water	1 tablespoon white sugar
One 2 pound beef bone, cracked	1 stalk celery with leaves,
2 pounds beef brisket	chopped
1 large onion, chopped	6 carrots, diced
2 cups canned tomatoes	1 onion, diced
1 tablespoon salt	

Measure the water in a large kettle; add the beef bone and the brisket. Add the chopped onions, the tomatoes, salt, sugar and celery. Simmer gently for 3 hours. Strain; add the diced carrots and onion; simmer again till the vegetables are tender. Serve hot with salted crackers. Serves 6.

CHAPTER 18

Vegetables and Vegetable Sauces

ASPARAGUS

Buy fresh asparagus with close tips; one large bunch will give you 3 servings. Break off each stalk as far down as it snaps off easily; save the tougher ends for soup. If you want the asparagus whole, tie it in bundles again and stand, tips up, in the bottom of a double boiler which has been almost filled with boiling salted water. Invert the top of the double boiler over the asparagus so that the tips will steam tender. Cook about 25 minutes; lift to a hot platter; serve with melted butter.

BUTTERED ASPARAGUS

Temperature: 350°F.   Time: 15-20 minutes

2 pounds asparagus	Dash of pepper and paprika
2 tablespoons butter	2 cups milk
2 tablespoons flour	½ cup cheese, grated
½ teaspoon salt	½ cup buttered crumbs

Wipe the asparagus; cut in 1″ lengths; cook in a small quantity of boiling salted water till tender, about 20 minutes. Drain and reserve the liquid; there should not be more than ½ cup. Melt the butter; blend in the flour and seasonings; let bubble 3 minutes. Slowly add the reserved asparagus liquid and the milk, cook and stir till smooth and thick; add the cheese. Remove from the heat; stir till melted. Place alternate layers of cooked asparagus and sauce in an oiled baking dish; cover with the buttered crumbs. Bake in a moderate oven till golden brown. Serve with bacon sandwiches. Serves 6.

ASPARAGUS CASSEROLE

Temperature: 325°F.   Time: 45 minutes

2 bunches asparagus	Dash of pepper and paprika
¼ cup hot milk	1½ tablespoons melted butter
1 cup soft bread crumbs	1 tablespoon onion, finely chopped
2 eggs, lightly beaten	1 tablespoon parsley, finely
¼ teaspoon salt	chopped

Scrub the asparagus; cut the tender parts into 1″ lengths; cook in boiling salted water till tender; drain. Pour the hot milk over the bread crumbs; beat till smooth. Add the lightly beaten eggs, seasonings, butter and onion; add the asparagus. Oil a 1½-quart casserole; sprinkle the bottom with the chopped parsley. Pour in the asparagus mixture. Set the casserole in a shallow dish partially filled with hot water. Bake in a moderate oven till firm. Unmould; serve with scrambled eggs. Serves 6.

BEETS WITH BACON

12 beets, with tops
  3 slices breakfast bacon,
    diced
1 teaspoon salt

¼ teaspoon pepper
  1 teaspoon sugar
½ cup cider vinegar

Cut off the beet tops; wash and cook in boiling salted water; chop coarsely. Cook the beets till tender; rub off the skins and chop. Combine the cooked tops and beets. Cook the bacon till crisp; add the seasonings and vinegar; heat to boiling. Pour over the beets and greens; serve immediately. Serves 6.

HARVARD BEETS

1 tablespoon fat
  1 tablespoon flour
2 tablespoons boiling water
  3 tablespoons brown sugar
2 tablespoons cider vinegar

¼ teaspoon salt
  Dash of pepper
Dash of mace and powdered
  cloves
1¼ cups cooked beets, diced

Melt the fat in the top of a double boiler over direct heat; blend in the flour; let bubble 3 minutes. Add the boiling water slowly; cook and stir until smooth and thick. Add the brown sugar, vinegar, seasonings and spices; blend well. Add the diced beets; let stand over boiling water till piping hot. Serves 4.

WESTERN BEETS

Temperature: 400°F.
24 small new beets
  1 teaspoon orange rind, grated
1 cup orange juice

Time: 55 minutes
1 tablespoon brown sugar
  1 teaspoon salt
2 tablespoons fat

Top the beets and save the greens. Scrub and peel the beets; they will lose very little color. Place them in an oiled casserole. Combine the orange rind and juice, brown sugar, salt and fat; heat and pour over the beets. Cover and bake till tender, (about 45 minutes). Baste with the liquid; bake, uncovered, for an additional 10 minutes. Serve hot. Serves 6.

GREEN BEANS-MUSTARD SAUCE

1 quart pencil beans, slivered lengthwise	Dash of pepper
	1 tablespoon flour
¼ cup green onions, chopped	1 egg, well beaten
¾ cup milk, scalded	1 tablespoon cider vinegar
1 teaspoon dry mustard	2 tablespoons butter
1 teaspoon salt	

Cook the beans and onions in a tightly covered saucepan with a small quantity of boiling salted water; drain. In the meantime, scald the milk. Mix the mustard, salt, pepper, flour, egg and vinegar to a paste; stir into the hot milk; cook and stir till smooth and thick. Remove from the heat; add the butter; pour over the hot beans. This quantity will serve 6.

BAKED BEANS

Temperature: 300°F.   Time: 6 hours

1½ cups dried lima beans	¼ cup sweet green pepper, chopped
¼ pound salt pork, diced	
2 cups cooked tomatoes, sieved	½ teaspoon salt
	⅛ teaspoon pepper
2 tablespoons onions, chopped	2 tablespoons molasses or corn syrup
½ cup celery, chopped	

Cover the beans with cold water; bring slowly to the boil. Drain; cover again with water; let simmer until the skins burst. Pour off the liquid; add all the remaining ingredients. Pour into the bean pot or casserole; oven bake in a slow oven for 6 hours. Serves 5-6.

SAVOURY BAKED BEANS

Temperature: 325°F.   Time: 3 hours

½ pound lima beans	¾ cup molasses
⅛ teaspoon baking soda	½ teaspoon salt
¼ cup salt pork, diced	½ teaspoon pepper
1 large onion, diced	½ teaspoon dry mustard
1 cup canned tomatoes	

Cover the beans with water; add the soda; let stand overnight. In the morning, drain and rinse. Cover with boiling water; cook slowly until tender; drain. Dice the salt pork; fry till crisp. Add the onion; cook and stir until golden brown. Add the remaining ingredients; simmer gently for 10 minutes. Put half the beans in a bean pot; cover with half the tomato mixture. Add remainder of the beans and the remainder of the tomato mixture. Cover and cook in moderate oven for 3 hours. These beans are delicious. Serves 5.

BUTTERED BROCCOLI

Remove the tough leaves and lower stems; split each stalk lengthwise in halves or quarters. Wash well; soak in salt water (2 teaspoons salt to 4 cups water) for 1 hour. Drain; tie in a bunch. Cook in boiling salted water till tender. Serve buttered or with Hollandaise Sauce.

BRUSSELS SPROUTS

Clean, wash and soak the sprouts in salted water (as broccoli) for 30 minutes. Cook in boiling salted water till tender (about 20 minutes). Serve buttered and seasoned to taste.

CABBAGE BAKED IN CREAM

Temperature: 315°F. Time: 45 minutes

4 cups cabbage, finely chopped	¼ teaspoon salt
2 eggs, lightly beaten	Dash of paprika and cayenne
1 tablespoon melted butter	1 cup cheese, grated
½ cup cereal cream	½ cup buttered crumbs

Cook the cabbage in very little boiling salted water for 7 minutes. Drain and press dry; place in an oiled casserole. Lightly beat the eggs; add the melted butter, cream, seasonings and cheese. Pour over the cabbage; bake in a slow oven for 35 minutes. Sprinkle with the buttered crumbs; return to the oven till lightly browned. Serves 6.

NEW CABBAGE WITH BUTTER-SWEET DRESSING

6 cups cabbage, finely chopped	½ teaspoon salt
4 tablespoons fat	Dash of pepper and paprika
1 tablespoon brown sugar	¼ cup cider vinegar
¼ teaspoon dry mustard	

Chop the cabbage finely; cook till tender in boiling salted water. Drain well; keep hot. Heat the fat in a saucepan; blend in the brown sugar, mustard and seasonings. Add the cider vinegar and the cabbage; cook and stir till piping hot. Pour into a heated dish; serve with fish or meat dishes. Serves 6.

GLAZED CARROTS

8 medium carrots	¼ cup water
1 teaspoon lemon juice	½ teaspoon salt
3 tablespoons white sugar	1 tablespoon fat

Scrape the carrots; cut lengthwise in quarters. Add all the remaining ingredients; cover tightly; cook over low heat till the carrots are glazed and tender. Serves 4.

GOLDEN CARROT BALLS

Temperature: 375°F.   Time: 20 minutes

8 carrots
  ¼ cup 18% cream
½ cup buttered crumbs

½ teaspoon salt
  Dash of pepper and mace

Scrape the carrots and cook whole; drain; when cool enough to handle, scoop out with a ball cutter. Roll the carrot balls in the cream, then in the buttered crumbs. Dust lightly with the seasonings; place on an oiled cookie sheet. Bake in a 375°F. oven till hot and crisp on the outside. Serves 4.

DEVONSHIRE CARROTS

Temperature: 350°F.   Time: 25 minutes

3 tablespoons fat
  1 onion, finely chopped
2 cups raw carrots, scraped
  and shredded
1 teaspoon salt

1 teaspoon sugar
1 teaspoon lemon juice
1 teaspoon lemon rind, grated
1½ cups water

Heat the fat; add the onions; cook till tender. Add to the carrots; place the mixture in an oiled baking dish. Combine all the remaining ingredients; pour over the carrot-onion mixture. Cover and bake till tender. Serves 4.

FILLED CARROT ROLLS

Temperature: 375°F.   Time: 30 minutes

6 large whole carrots
  3 tablespoons cream
2 tablespoons onion, chopped
  2 tablespoons cracker crumbs
½ cup weiners, chopped

½ teaspoon salt
  Dash of pepper and poultry
    dressing
¼ cup top milk
½ cup dry bread crumbs

Cook the carrots whole; scoop out the centres. Chop the scoop-outs; mix with the cream, onion, cracker crumbs, weiners and seasonings. Pack back in the carrots. Roll each in the top milk and bread crumbs. Bake in a moderate oven till golden brown. Interesting and amusing. Serves 6.

CARROT MOULD

Temperature: 350°F.   Time: 45-50 minutes

3 tablespoons fat
  1 onion, finely chopped
4 tablespoons flour
  1 egg, lightly beaten

1 teaspoon salt
  3 cups cooked carrots, mashed
Dash of pepper and paprika
  1 teaspoon brown sugar

Heat the fat in a heavy pan; add the diced onion; cook and stir till tender but not brown. Add the flour and blend well; let bubble for 3 minutes. Remove from the heat; add the remaining ingredients and mix well. Pour into an oiled 9″ ring mould; bake in a moderate oven in a pan of hot water till firm. Unmould and serve with green peas. Serves 6.

CARROT SOUFFLE

Temperature: 350°F.   Time: 1 hour

2 cups cooked carrots, mashed   ½ cup carrot liquid
   4 tablespoons fat   ⅔ cup top milk
   4 tablespoons flour   2 eggs, separated
   ½ teaspoon salt   1 tablespoon corn starch
Dash of pepper and paprika

Cook diced carrots till tender in a small quantity of boiling salted water. Drain; reserve ½ cup carrot liquid. Mash the carrots; there should be 2 cups. Melt the fat in a saucepan; blend in the flour and seasonings; cook and stir over low heat for 3 minutes. Add the carrot liquid and milk; cook and stir till smooth and thick. Add the carrots and blend well; remove from the heat. Beat the egg yolks till light; blend in the corn starch. Add to the carrot mixture and blend; cool slightly; fold in the stiffly beaten egg whites. Pour into an oiled 1½-quart mould; bake in a pan of hot water in a moderate oven till firm. Unmould and serve with broiled ham. Serves 6.

USES FOR YOUNG CARROTS

Pack grated carrots into muffin tins; turn out on lettuce leaves; serve with a spoonful of cottage cheese and a boiled dressing.

Combine grated carrots with chopped early apples and celery for a new version of Waldorf Salad.

Roll balls of cottage cheese in mayonnaise, then in grated carrots; it's a bonus with a vegetable salad.

Scrape the carrots and cut in thin slices. Nick the edges like a Maltese cross; crisp in cold water till ready to serve. The thin slices spread in the water are very decorative.

CAULIFLOWER

Cook a large head of snow white cauliflower in boiling salted water until tender (about 20 minutes). Drain upside down; cut the stem flat and close to the flowerlets so that the cauliflower will sit squarely on the serving platter. Cut green peppers in small fan-shaped scallops and insert between the flowerlets at the outer edge; just before serving, sprinkle with grated cheese and glaze in the oven. Serves 6.

MAIN DISH CAULIFLOWER

Temperature: 325°F.

Time: 1¼ hours

1 head cauliflower
  4 tablespoons butter
1 tablespoon onion, chopped
  4 tablespoons flour
1¼ cups milk

1 teaspoon salt
  Dash of pepper and paprika
1 cup loaf cheese, cubed
  3 eggs, separated

Break the cauliflower in pieces; cook in boiling salted water till tender. Drain and chop coarsely; there should be 3 cups. Melt the butter in a saucepan; add the onion; cook until tender. Blend in the flour; simmer for 3 minutes. Add the milk slowly; cook and stir till smooth and thick. Add the seasonings and cheese; pour over the lightly beaten egg yolks, stirring constantly. Add the cauliflower; fold in the stiffly beaten egg whites. Pour into an oiled 2-quart casserole; bake in a moderate oven in a shallow pan of hot water until set. This will take the place of a meat dish; serve with Escalloped Tomatoes, with Applesauce and hot Gingerbread for dessert. Serves 5-6.

CELERY-CHEESE CUSTARD

Temperature: 325°F.

Time: 40 minutes

2 cups celery, coarsely
  chopped
2 tablespoons butter
  2 tablespoons flour
2 cups rich milk

⅓ cup cheese, grated
  ½ teaspoon salt
Dash of pepper, mace and paprika
  2 eggs, separated

Cook the celery in boiling salted water; drain well. Melt the butter in a saucepan; stir in the flour; bubble 3 minutes. Add the milk slowly; cook and stir till smooth and thick. Add the cheese and seasonings; stir till the cheese is melted. Beat the egg yolks till light; mix with a little of the hot liquid; add to the sauce. Simmer over low heat for 3 minutes; fold in the stiffly beaten egg whites. Pour into an oiled 1½-quart casserole; bake in a pan of warm water in the oven till firm. Serve hot. Serves 4.

NOTE TO BRIDES: *If you fold a piece of newspaper, place it on the bottom of the baking dish and place the moulds on top the custard will not separate or water.*

CORN ON THE COB

Remove the husks and silk from the corn. Cook in half skim milk and half water till tender, (about 7 minutes). Butter; serve hot.

SWISS CHARD

Wash the greens thoroughly; shake; cook in the moisture that clings to the leaves. Season with salt, pepper and butter.

CUCUMBERS IN CREAM SAUCE

6 medium cucumbers
  1½ tablespoons butter
1½ tablespoons flour
  1½ cups rich milk and
    cucumber water, mixed

½ teaspoon salt
  Dash of pepper, paprika and
  mace
1 tablespoon parsley, chopped

Peel the cucumbers; quarter and remove the seeds; if the cucumbers are large, cut in eighths. Cook in boiling salted water until tender; drain, saving the liquid. Melt the butter in a saucepan; blend in the flour; bubble gently for 3 minutes. Slowly add the mixture of milk and cucumber water (we use ¾ cup of each). Cook and stir till smooth and thick; add the seasonings; beat with the dover beater until light. Pour over the cucumbers; sprinkle with the chopped parsley. Serves 6.

SAUTEED EGG PLANT

Cut a large egg plant in ¼" slices crosswise; sprinkle the slices with salt, pepper and a little flour. Sauté in hot fat till golden brown.

ONION CASSEROLE

Temperature: 375°F.

Time: 25 minutes

12 medium onions
  1 cup celery, cooked and diced
1 cup canned peas, drained
  2 hard cooked eggs, shelled
    and sliced
1 tablespoon butter

1 tablespoon flour
  ½ teaspoon salt
Dash of pepper and paprika
  1 cup milk
  ½ cup cheese, grated
  ½ cup buttered crumbs

Boil the onions gently until tender; drain. Arrange all the vegetables in an oiled 2-quart casserole with the sliced eggs on top. Melt the butter in a saucepan; add the flour and blend; let bubble 3 minutes. Add the seasonings and milk; cook and stir till smooth and thick. Remove from the heat; add the cheese; stir till dissolved. Pour over the vegetables and eggs; sprinkle with the buttered crumbs. Bake in a moderate oven for 25 minutes. Serve with mustard pickles and rye bread; a Baked Lemon Pudding is just right to end the meal. Serves 6.

BAKED ONIONS WITH MUSHROOMS

Temperature: 400°F.

Time: 12-15 minutes

6 medium sized, firm onions
  2 tablespoons fat
1½ cups fresh or canned
  mushrooms
1 tablespoon flour
  ⅓ cup rich milk
  ½ teaspoon salt
  Dash of pepper and paprika

1½ tablespoons butter
  1½ tablespoons flour
  ¾ cup milk
  ¼ teaspoon salt
Dash of cayenne
  ½ cup buttered crumbs
6 rounds toast

Peel the onions; cook in boiling salted water till tender. Drain; hollow out the centre with a pair of scissors; dice and save the centres for the mushroom sauce. Heat 2 tablespoons fat in a heavy saucepan; add the mushrooms; cook and stir till tender. Blend in 1 tablespoon flour; let bubble 3 minutes; slowly add ⅓ cup rich milk and the seasonings. Cook and stir till smooth. Add the diced onion centres. Fill the onions with this mixture; place in a baking dish. Melt 1½ tablespoons butter and blend in 1½ tablespoons flour; add the milk; cook and stir till smooth. Add the seasonings; pour over the stuffed onions. Sprinkle with the buttered crumbs; bake till golden brown. Serve on rounds of buttered toast. Serves 6.

GLAZED ONIONS

12 medium onions
  ¼ cup white sugar
1 teaspoon dry mustard

¾ teaspoon salt
  Dash of pepper and paprika
  ¼ cup melted butter

Peel and cook the onions till tender; drain and place in shallow baking dish. Mix the sugar, mustard, seasonings and butter; pour over the onions. Bake, uncovered, in a moderate oven for 20 minutes. Serves 6.

STUFFED PEPPERS WITH CORN

Temperature: 350°F.

Time: 25 minutes

6 peppers
  2 cups cooked corn

2 slices breakfast bacon
  2 tablespoons cream

Wipe the peppers; remove the seeds and veins; parboil for 7 minutes; drain. Slice the corn off the cobs. Dice and pan fry the bacon; add the corn and the cream. Stuff the peppers with this mixture. Bake in a moderate oven; serve with tomato slices. Serves 6.

PARSNIPS

6 small parsnips
¼ cup milk
¼ cup fine bread crumbs

½ teaspoon salt
Dash of pepper and dry mustard
2 tablespoons fat

Peel the parsnips; cook them whole; when tender, drain and cool slightly. Dip in the milk; roll in a mixture of crumbs, salt, pepper and a little dry mustard. Heat the fat; pan fry till crisp and brown on the outside. Serves 4.

PEAS AND CUCUMBERS

2 cups peas, shelled
2 cups cucumbers, pared and diced
2 teaspoons salt

1 tablespoon brown sugar
1 teaspoon vinegar
2 tablespoons butter

Combine the peas and cucumbers; cook together till tender in a small amount of salted boiling water. Drain; add the sugar, vinegar and butter. Shake and serve. Serves 6.

POTATOES

Here is a simple source of Vitamin C, particularly if they are cooked in their jackets. Scrub the potatoes; cook in boiling, salted water till tender. Drain and shake dry.

BAKED POTATOES

Select 6 potatoes of medium size; scrub well. Prick with a fork; brush over with salad oil. Bake in a moderate oven (375°F.) for one hour and 15 minutes or until tender.

SAUSAGE STUFFED BAKED POTATO

Scrub large potatoes; core lengthwise and stuff with uncooked sausage. Brush with salad oil; bake in a fairly hot oven till tender.

POTATO DUMPLINGS

2 cups cooked potatoes, riced
2 tablespoons flour
1 teaspoon melted shortening

1 egg, slightly beaten
½ teaspoon salt
Dash of pepper and nutmeg

Mix all the ingredients and blend thoroughly; chill for 2 hours. Lift out by spoonfuls and roll between the palms of your hands; there should be twelve small dumplings. Drop into the stew, cover tightly and steam 15 minutes; serve at once. The dumplings are certainly good—they add the last touch to that long, slow-cooked stew. Serves 6.

BAKED POTATOES WITH CHEESE

Scrub the potatoes and core them right through the centre. Fill the core with the grated cheese. Rub with oil; bake in a 400°F. oven till the potatoes are tender.

COMPANY POTATOES

Temperature: 350°F.   Time: 1 hour, 15 minutes

8 cups raw potatoes, thinly sliced
2 tablespoons dried bread crumbs, rolled

½ cup soft butter
3 teaspoons salt
½ teaspoon pepper
½ cup onion, thinly sliced

Pare and thinly slice the potatoes; let them stand in cold water for 20 minutes. Drain and dry well (use a clean bath towel). Oil a 2-quart casserole; sprinkle the inside with the crumbs. Arrange the first layer of potatoes on the bottom of the dish with the edges overlapping; dot with butter, sprinkle with pepper and salt; cover with a thin layer of onion. Continue in this way till the entire dish is filled; there should be about 5 layers in all. Cover tightly; bake until the potatoes are tender. Place a large hot plate over the casserole and invert; the whole golden brown round will come out like a cake. Garnish with slices of jellied meat loaf and pickled peaches. This is a honey! Serves 8.

NEW POTATOES WITH CHEESE

Temperature: 325°F.   Time: 20-25 minutes

12 small new potatoes
½ teaspoon salt
Dash of pepper and mace

1 cup loaf cheese, grated
4 tablespoons cereal cream

Scrub the potatoes; cook in boiling salted water till tender but firm; drain and shake over heat to remove all moisture. Place in a shallow oiled baking dish; sprinkle with the seasonings and grated cheese. Pour the cream over the potatoes; bake in a moderate oven till the cheese is melted and the potatoes browned. Turn them once during the baking so that they will brown evenly. Serve hot with slices of spiced beef and a tossed salad. Serves 6.

PANCAKE POTATOES

4 medium sized potatoes
1 medium sized onion
½ teaspoon salt

Dash of pepper
Dash of celery salt
2 tablespoons fat

Wash and grate the potatoes on the medium grater; press dry. Grate the onion and add to the potatoes; add the seasonings. Heat the fat in a heavy iron frying pan; spread the potato mixture over it; press down well in the pan, then shake to loosen from the bottom. Cover and cook over low heat; invert the cake on a flat dish. Add a little more fat to the pan; heat and slide in the potato cake with the uncooked side down. Cover and cook again till tender and well browned. Serve on a flat platter and cut in wedges like pie. Serves 6.

ESCALLOPED POTATOES

Temperature: 350°F.   Time: 1 hour, 15 minutes

4 cups raw potatoes, sliced   Dash of pepper
  3 tablespoons fat   1 cup cheese, grated
3 tablespoons flour   ¼ cup green pickle, chopped
  1½ cups milk   3 tablespoons cornflakes
1 tablespoon salt   1 tablespoon melted fat
  ¼ teaspoon dry mustard

Peel the potatoes and cut in thin slices; cover with boiling water and cover tightly; let stand till cool; drain well. Melt the fat in a saucepan (bacon fat is delicious); blend in the flour; let bubble for 3 minutes. Add the milk slowly; cook and stir till thick and smooth. Remove from the heat; add the seasonings, cheese and chopped green pickle. Oil a 2-quart baking dish; fill it with alternate layers of sliced potatoes and cream sauce. Bake in a moderate oven till the potatoes are cooked. Five minutes before taking from the oven cover with a mixture of the cornflakes and melted fat. It makes a delicious topping. Serves 6.

HASHED BROWN POTATOES

3 tablespoons bacon fat or butter   ¼ cup milk
  3 cups cooked potatoes, diced   1 teaspoon salt
3 tablespoons sifted pastry flour   Dash of pepper and cayenne
  2 tablespoons onion, chopped

Measure 2 tablespoons of fat into a heavy 9″ iron or aluminum frying pan. While it heats, mix the potatoes, flour, onion, milk and seasonings in a bowl. Turn the potato mixture into the fat and pat it down solidly, shaking the pan vigorously from side to side so that the potatoes will not stick. Cook over medium heat until the bottom is golden brown and crusty (about 15 minutes); turn out the potato cake on a flat dish. Wipe the frying pan, heat the remaining tablespoon of fat and slide the potato cake back again, crusty side up; continue cooking, shaping the cake with a spatula and shaking the pan again to keep the cake from sticking and thus losing its even shape. Cook until brown; turn out on a hot platter. Cut in pie-shaped wedges and serve with creamy scrambled eggs. Serves 6.

SLICED POTATO PIE

6 medium sized potatoes	1 teaspoon salt
4 tablespoons bacon fat or butter	Dash of pepper and paprika

Peel the potatoes; cut in very thin slices. Soak in cold water for 2 hours; drain and dry between towels. Heat half the fat in a heavy frying pan; add half the potatoes. Dot with the remaining fat; add the remainder of the potatoes and the seasonings. Heat over a hot burner until the potatoes are brown on the bottom; cover and reduce the heat. Do not stir at any time; keep the heat low enough to cook but not high enough to burn. When the potatoes are tender (about 40 minutes) remove the cover, dot with butter and brown in a hot oven. Cut in wedges like pie and serve hot. Serves 6.

CASSEROLE OF SWEET POTATOES

Temperature: 350°F.   Time: 15 minutes

6 hot cooked medium sized sweet potatoes	1½ teaspoons salt
6 tablespoons cream	2 teaspoons lemon rind, grated
4 tablespoons brown sugar	1 cup hot milk

Peel and cook the sweet potatoes till tender; mash. Beat in the cream, brown sugar and salt; add the lemon rind and the hot milk; beat till smooth. Place in a buttered casserole and bake in a moderate oven for 15 minutes. Serves 6.

BAKED SQUASH

Temperature: 400°F.   Time: 50 minutes

½ medium squash	1 teaspoon salt
¼ cup butter	2 tablespoons lemon juice
¼ cup brown sugar	1 teaspoon lemon rind, grated

Pre-heat the oven to 400°F. Peel the squash and cut in 1" pieces; place in a shallow oiled pan. Melt the butter in a small saucepan; add the brown sugar, the salt, lemon juice and rind; pour over the squares of squash. Cover and bake in a hot oven for 50 minutes; remove the cover after 30 minutes baking. Baste with the liquid in the pan. This squash is very lovely to look at and quite as good to eat. Serves 6.

SQUASH WITH SAUSAGE

Peel the squash; cut in squares and cook till tender; drain well and mash. Beat up with a little butter or cream, some salt and pepper; put in an oiled casserole. Cover with little pork sausages which have been steamed. Bake in a hot oven (400°F.) until the sausages are golden brown.

CREAMED SPINACH

2 pounds spinach	1 tablespoon flour
2 tablespoons hot cream	½ teaspoon salt
1 tablespoon butter	Dash of pepper
1 tablespoon onion, finely chopped	1 cup rich milk

Wash the spinach and cook without water; there will be enough moisture clinging to the leaves; use a flat-bottomed saucepan and a tight-fitting lid. Drain the spinach and chop; add the hot cream; press into an oiled ring mould. Keep the mould in the warming oven till ready to serve. Unmould on a hot platter; serve with the following sauce: Melt the butter; add the chopped onion; cook till golden brown. Add the flour; blend; let bubble for 3 minutes. Add the seasonings and rich milk; cook and simmer till smooth and thick. Pour over the spinach mould. Serves 6.

NOTE TO BRIDES: *To complete the picture, fill the centre of the spinach ring mould with buttered carrots. Cook the carrots, drain and chop. Toss lightly with 2 tablespoons of melted butter to which you have added a dash of salt, pepper and mace.*

SPINACH FONDUE

Temperature: 350°F.	Time: 1 hour
1⅓ cups milk	3 egg yolks, beaten
1⅓ cups soft bread crumbs	1 cup cooked spinach
½ teaspoon salt	1 cup cheese, cubed
4 tablespoons melted fat	3 egg whites

Heat the milk in the top of the double boiler; add the soft bread crumbs. Beat till smooth; add the salt and melted fat. Beat the egg yolks; add to the milk mixture. Cook over hot water until the mixture thickens; add the spinach and the cubed cheese. Fold in the stiffly beaten egg whites; pour into an oiled 1½-quart baking dish. Bake in a pan of hot water in a moderate oven until firm, about 1 hour. Serves 6

BROILED TOMATOES

4 firm tomatoes	1 tablespoon brown sugar
1 teaspoon salt	1 teaspoon dry mustard
⅛ teaspoon pepper	

Scald and skin the tomatoes; cut in 1″ slices. Sprinkle with salt; let chill 1 hour; drain. Place on an oiled sheet; sprinkle with a mixture of the pepper, sugar and mustard. Broil or bake in a moderate oven till tender. Serves 6.

BAKED TOMATOES

Temperature: 375°F.   Time: 15-18 minutes

2 tablespoons fat   ¾ teaspoon salt
  1 onion, chopped   3½ tablespoons brown sugar
4 cups canned tomatoes   1½ cups buttered bread crumbs

Heat the fat in a saucepan; add the chopped onions; cook and stir till tender but not brown. Add the tomatoes, salt and 2 tablespoons brown sugar; heat till the sugar is dissolved. Turn the mixture into a 1½-quart oiled baking dish; cover with a mixture of 1½ tablespoons brown sugar and the crumbs. Bake in a moderate oven till brown. Serve with stuffed pork chops. Serves 6.

ESCALLOPED TOMATOES

Temperature: 375°F.   Time: 15 minutes

1 tablespoon fat   Dash of pepper
  1 onion, chopped   1 teaspoon white sugar
2½ cups canned tomatoes   1½ cups soft bread crumbs
  1 teaspoon salt   ¼ cup loaf cheese, grated

Heat the fat in a saucepan; pan fry the onion till tender; add the tomatoes, salt, pepper, sugar and 1 cup of the crumbs. Pour into an oiled 1½-quart baking dish. Top with a mixture of the remaining ½ cup of crumbs and the grated cheese; bake in a moderate oven till the cheese is melted (about 15 minutes). Serves 6.

TOMATOES WITH MINT

They're delicious, these tomatoes; you'll want them again and again. Scald and skin large firm tomatoes; slice them in thick slices. Heat ½ cup cider vinegar with 2 tablespoons white sugar and ¼ teaspoon salt. Pour over 1 tablespoon chopped mint. Chill; pour over the sliced tomatoes. Let stand in the refrigerator for 1 hour before serving.

TURNIP WITH APPLES

3 tart apples   Dash of pepper and mace
  1 medium turnip   1 teaspoon white sugar
1 teaspoon salt   2 tablespoons butter

Core and cut the apples in eighths; do not peel. Cook in very little water till soft; press through a sieve; there should be about 1 cup of pulp. Cook the turnip in boiling salted water till tender; drain and mash; there should be about 3 cups. Combine with the apple pulp and beat well; add the seasonings, sugar and butter. Serve hot; it's delicious. Serves 6.

TURNIP DELIGHT

Temperature: 350°F.   Time: 12-15 minutes

3 cups hot mashed turnips   ⅛ teaspoon pepper
2 tablespoons butter   ⅛ teaspoon mace
2 egg yolks   ¼ cup hot cream
½ teaspoon salt

Mash the turnips and mix with the butter; add the well beaten egg yolks and seasonings. Beat in the hot cream until the mixture is light and fluffy. Pile into an oiled 2-quart casserole; cover with the following meringue:

Meringue

2 egg whites   ¼ teaspoon salt
½ cup cheese, grated   ¼ teaspoon baking powder

Stiffly beat the egg whites; fold in grated cheese which has been mixed with the salt and baking powder. Spread over the turnip mixture. Brown in moderate oven (350°F.). Serves 6.

VEGETABLE PLATTER

Temperature: 350°F.   Time: 25 minutes

1 whole cauliflower   Green peppers
1 tablespoon lemon juice   Tomato slices
Meat stuffing

Cook the cauliflower whole, adding the lemon juice to the boiling water to keep it white. Cut the stem ends off the peppers, take out the seeds and veins; parboil for 8 minutes, then drain. Mix ½ pound seasoned hamburger with ¼ cup thinly sliced onion; pan-fry for 2 minutes. Fill the pepper cases with the mixture; bake in a moderate oven for 25 minutes. Serve around the cauliflower alternately with thick slices of Broiled Tomatoes. Serves 6.

Vegetable Sauces

BITTERSWEET SAUCE

1 teaspoon salt   1 teaspoon white sugar
⅛ teaspoon pepper   ¼ cup cider vinegar
1 teaspoon paprika   ⅓ cup salad oil
1½ teaspoons dry   1 teaspoon onion, finely chopped
mustard

Blend all the dry ingredients in a saucepan; add the vinegar; mix till smooth. Add the salad oil and onion; heat to boiling. Pour over the cooked vegetable just before serving. Serves 6.

EGG SAUCE

1 egg, well beaten   1 tablespoon lemon juice
   ¼ cup cereal cream   ½ teaspoon lemon rind, grated
⅛ teaspoon salt   1 tablespoon butter
   ⅛ teaspoon nutmeg

Beat the egg until light; add the cream, salt and nutmeg. Cook and stir over boiling water till thick. Remove from the heat; add the lemon juice, rind and butter. Beat well and pour over cooked cauliflower or asparagus. Serves 6.

HOLLANDAISE SAUCE

2 egg yolks   Dash of cayenne
   ½ teaspoon salt   ½ cup melted butter
Dash of paprika   1 tablespoon lemon juice

Beat the egg yolks till thick and lemon colored; add the salt, paprika and cayenne. Add 3 tablespoons melted butter, beating in one teaspoon at a time. Add the remainder of the butter alternately with the lemon juice. Serve with hot asparagus, beans, broccoli or kale. Serves 5.

LEMON BUTTER FOR VEGETABLES

¼ cup butter   1 teaspoon grated lemon rind
   1 tablespoon lemon juice   1/16 teaspoon paprika

Cream the butter till soft but not oily; add the lemon juice, rind and paprika. Blend and shape into small balls. Chill; serve on asparagus tips, young carrots or green beans. As the butter melts, you get all the butter flavor plus the pungency of the lemon. Serves 6.

VEGETABLE SAUCE

1 tablespoon butter   Dash of pepper and mace
   1 tablespoon sifted flour   1 egg yolk, lightly beaten
1 cup potato water   1 teaspoon lemon juice
   ¼ teaspoon salt   ¼ cup cheese, grated

Blend the butter and flour together in a heavy saucepan over low heat; let bubble 3 minutes. Add the potato water; cook and stir till smooth and thick. Add the seasonings; keep hot until just before serving. Add the beaten egg yolk; let cook without boiling for 3 minutes longer. Add the lemon juice and cheese; stir till melted. Pour at once over cooked, drained broccoli, cauliflower or cabbage. Serves 6.

CHEESE SAUCE

2 tablespoons fat	1 cup milk
2 tablespoons sifted flour	Dash of pepper and paprika
½ teaspoon salt	¼ cup cheese, grated

Melt the fat in a saucepan; blend in the flour and seasonings; let bubble 3 minutes. Add the milk slowly; cook and stir till smooth and thick, about 3 minutes. Remove from the heat; add the grated cheese; stir till the cheese is melted. Pour a little hot sauce over each serving of vegetable. Serves 6.

NOTE TO BRIDES: *A little chopped onion may be added to the fat, cooked and stirred till tender before the flour is blended in.*

BASIC RECIPE FOR WHITE SAUCE

Thin White Sauce: This sauce is used for making creamed soups—pea, bean, onion, corn, potato—any kind of cream soup.

1 tablespoon butter	1 cup liquid
1 tablespoon flour	Dash of salt

Medium White Sauce: This sauce is used for creamed dishes—creamed fish, chipped beef or chicken.

2 tablespoons butter	1 cup liquid
2 tablespoons flour	Dash of salt

Thick White Sauce: We use this sauce for souffles and croquettes.

3 tablespoons butter	1 cup liquid
3 tablespoons flour	Dash of salt

Measure the butter into a heavy pan and melt. The butter should never get so hot as to brown or s-s-s; if it does, you lose the delicate butter flavor which makes the sauce. Lift the pan from the heat to blend in the flour; stir till it is smooth. Place again on low heat; stir and cook for about 3 minutes. Add the liquid slowly; add the salt; cook and stir till smooth and thick. Before serving, beat the sauce with the dover beater until it's like velvet. Serves 6.

CHAPTER 19

Eat and Keep Slim

This diet is for the woman who really wants to reduce, who feels that she will look better—and feel better—if she takes off the surplus pounds round her waist, her hips and her thighs.

Food Makes Fat: First of all, face the fact that food and food only makes fat. Don't fool yourself with that airy nonsense about not eating enough to keep a sparrow alive. If you don't eat at the table you probably eat between times and would be horrified if you knew how often you nibble.

Must I Starve Myself? No, indeed. You can pick satisfying, slimming diets that make you comfortable and give you your ideal figure as quickly or as gradually as you choose.

What About Tea and Coffee? Neither tea nor coffee will add one ounce to your weight—but that means clear tea and black coffee. Add cream and sugar and you have all the makings of a spare tire. Lemon in the tea is an excellent substitute for sugar; it gives a pungent tang and a bit of Vitamin C.

What About Soft Drinks? From the standpoint of health, there is nothing against soft drinks. They are pure, satisfying, and palatable. But the average 6-ounce bottle of soft drink contains the equivalent of three teaspoons of sugar.

What About Milk? If milk were all cream it *could* add to your weight, but the fat content of milk is not excessive and you should drink at least a glass a day. It gives you calcium, without which you couldn't move a muscle, and for lack of which your heart would stop beating. If your diet calls for skim milk, comfort yourself with the fact that it's almost as valuable as whole milk.

How Quickly Can I Lose Ten Pounds? In ten days if you really work at it. But first, check up with your doctor, see that you are in good condition, then start eating your way to slenderness and beauty.

BREAKFASTS

MONDAY: 3 stewed prunes; 1 cup black coffee.

TUESDAY: 1 boiled egg; 1 slice whole wheat toast (dry); 1 cup black coffee.

WEDNESDAY: Tomato juice; 1 cup black coffee.

THURSDAY:　1 poached egg; 1 slice whole wheat toast (dry); 1 cup black coffee.

FRIDAY:　1 boiled egg; 1 slice whole wheat toast (dry); 1 cup black coffee.

SATURDAY:　1 sliced orange: 1 cup black coffee.

SUNDAY:　Grapefruit juice; 1 poached egg; 1 cup coffee.

MONDAY:　1 boiled egg; 1 slice whole wheat toast (dry); 1 cup black coffee.

TUESDAY:　1 grapefruit; 1 cup black coffee.

WEDNESDAY: 1 boiled egg; 1 slice whole wheat toast (dry); 1 cup black coffee.

LUNCHES

MONDAY:　2 patties broiled hamburger (all lean meat); lettuce, tomato, cabbage or apple salad (no dressing); ½ glass whole milk; tea or coffee.

TUESDAY:　1 egg, boiled or poached; 1 serving cooked carrots; ½ glass skim milk; tea or coffee.

WEDNESDAY: Lean, small steak (broiled); ½ cup string beans or turnip; cole slaw; ½ glass whole milk; tea or coffee.

THURSDAY:　1 poached or boiled egg; ½ cup cooked spinach, broccoli or kale; 4 sticks celery; ½ glass skim milk.

FRIDAY:　1 poached egg with spinach; 1 serving cauliflower; ½ glass skim milk; tea or coffee.

SATURDAY:　Lean steak, broiled; cole slaw; 1 serving green vegetable; ½ glass whole milk; tea or coffee.

SUNDAY
DINNER:　1 cup consomme; 1 serving lean roast beef (no fat, no gravy); 1 serving carrots or turnip; tomato and lettuce; tea or coffee.

MONDAY:　1 poached egg, 1 serving stewed tomatoes; 1 cup shredded cabbage with parsley or green pepper; ½ glass skim milk; tea or coffee.

TUESDAY:　2 patties broiled hamburger (all lean meat); 1 cup cooked cabbage; ½ glass whole milk.

WEDNESDAY: 2 boiled eggs; cole slaw; ½ cup stewed tomatoes; ½ glass skim milk; tea or coffee.

DINNERS

MONDAY: Grapefruit juice; lean steak, broiled; ½ cup cooked beans, peas or spinach; 4 stalks raw celery; tea or coffee.

TUESDAY: 1 cup clear consomme; 1 serving pan-broiled liver (no fat in the pan); ½ cup cooked cauliflower; 1 serving green salad; tea or coffee.

WEDNESDAY: 1 cup consomme; 2 pork chops, broiled (no fat); ½ cup cooked celery; green salad; tea or coffee.

THURSDAY: 1 cup bouillon; chicken (breast meat); tossed green salad; 1 orange, sliced; tea or coffee.

FRIDAY: 1 cup clear consomme; 1 serving fish with lemon (haddock, sole, halibut, cod, etc.); raw salad (shredded cabbage, grated carrot, diced apple); tea or coffee.

SATURDAY: Tomato juice; 2 lamb chops or pork chops, broiled (no fat); 1 serving turnip; tea or coffee.

SUNDAY
SUPPER: 2 slices lean roast beef (cold); 1 serving tossed salad; ½ glass whole milk; 2 halves canned peaches; tea or coffee.

MONDAY: Orange juice; 2 broiled veal chops (no fat); ½ cup cooked celery; ½ grapefruit (no sugar) tea or coffee.

TUESDAY: Tomato juce; 1 serving pan-broiled liver; 1 serving green vegetable (spinach, beet greens, kale, broccoli); 2 stalks raw celery; tea or coffee.

WEDNESDAY: 1 cup clear consomme; 2 slices roast beef (no fat); green salad; tea or coffee.

NOW GET WEIGHED!

Drink as much water, clear tea and black coffee as you wish.

Use saccharine to sweeten tea and coffee.

Use vinegar, salt and pepper to dress green salads.

Take a teaspoonful of baking soda daily.

The milk allowance may go into your beverage.

Don't fry the eggs or meat—broil them.

AND DON'T GO BACK TO NIBBLING, OR YOU'LL GAIN ALL YOU HAVE LOST.

CHAPTER 20

Measurements and Substitutions

The essential tools of a good cook are a good sifter, a standard measuring cup and standard measuring spoons. Here are four simple rules for success in baking:

1. Sift all flour before measuring.
2. When filling cups with liquids, place the cup on the table so that the measure is accurate.
3. Have shortening room temperature so that it may be accurately and easily packed in the cup.
4. All measurements are level.

TABLE OF MEASUREMENTS

Dash	Less than ⅛ teaspoon
3 teaspoons	1 tablespoon
4 tablespoons	¼ cup
5 tablespoons plus 1 teaspoon	⅓ cup
8 tablespoons	½ cup
10 tablespoons plus 2 teaspoons	⅔ cup
12 tablespoons	¾ cup
16 tablespoons	1 cup
4 cups or 2 pints	1 quart
16 cups or 4 quarts	1 gallon
8 quarts	1 peck
16 pecks	1 bushel
16 ounces (dry measure)	1 pound

TABLE OF EQUIVALENTS

	Unit	*Equivalent*
Baking Powder	1 teaspoon	¼ teaspoon baking soda plus ½ teaspoon cream of tartar
Butter	1 pound	2 cups
Cheese	1 pound, grated	4 cups
Currants	1 pound	3 cups
Dates	1 pound, pitted	2 cups

TABLE OF EQUIVALENTS (*Continued*)

	Unit	*Equivalent*
Eggs	5 Grade A Large	1 cup
Egg Yolks	16 Grade A Large	about 1 cup
Egg Whites	8-10 Grade A Large	about 1 cup
Flour (all-purpose)	1 pound	4 cups
Flour (pastry)	1 pound	4½ cups
Lemons, medium size		
Juice	1 lemon	2 to 3 tablespoons
Rind, grated	1 lemon	1½ teaspoons
Nuts	1 pound	4 cups
Oranges, medium size		
Juice	1 orange	½ cup
Rind, grated	1 orange	1 tablespoon
Raisins	1 pound	3 cups
Rice	1 pound	2 cups
Sugar (white)	1 pound	2 cups
Sugar (brown)	1 pound	2½ cups, firmly packed

SUBSTITUTIONS

1 ounce (1 square) unsweetened chocolate	=	¼ cup cocoa (in cakes and cookies increase shortening by 1½ teaspoons)
1 tablespoon corn starch (for thickening)	=	2 tablespoons flour (approximate)
1 cup cake flour	=	⅞ cup all-purpose flour (i.e. 2 tablespoons less)
1 cup milk	=	½ cup evaporated milk plus ½ cup water
OR		4 tablespoons dried milk plus 1 cup water
1 cup honey	=	¾ cup sugar plus ¼ cup liquid
1 cup brown sugar (firmly packed)	=	1 cup granulated sugar

SUGAR SUBSTITUTES

HONEY: For sweetness, ¾ cup honey equals 1 cup sugar. If honey is used in place of sugar, reduce the liquid 1/5 cup for each cup of honey used. In baking, use a slightly cooler oven.

CORN SYRUP: For sweetness, 2 cups corn syrup equal 1 cup sugar. If corn syrup is used in place of sugar, reduce the liquid ¼ cup for every cup of corn syrup used.

MOLASSES OR
   MAPLE SYRUP: For sweetness, 1½ cups of molasses or maple syrup equal 1 cup of sugar. If molasses or maple syrup are used in place of sugar, reduce the liquid by ¼ cup for every cup of molasses or maple syrup used.

Leavening: Use ½ teaspoon baking soda for each cup of molasses or ¼ teaspoon baking soda for each cup of maple syrup in addition to the regular leavening. Have the oven slightly cooler than for sugar.

SACCHARIN: Fortified Sugar with Saccharin: Roll 30-½ grain Saccharin tablets fine with the rolling pin; add to 1 cup white sugar. The fortified sugar is twice as sweet as ordinary sugar. In baking, it may be substituted for ordinary sugar, using half the amount called for in the recipe. The most successful dishes are cakes, pies, muffins, applesauce and desserts.

TABLE OF FRUIT YIELDS

	Unit as Purchased	*Approximate Yield*
Apples	1 pound	2½-3 cups, diced
		1½ cups applesauce
Apricots	1 pound	3 cups cooked
Bananas	1 pound	2 cups sliced
Berries	1 quart	3½ cups
Cherries	1 pound or	
	1 quart	2¾ cups stemmed and pitted
Figs, dried	1 pound	2⅔ cups, chopped
Grapefruit	One	⅔ to ¾ cup juice
		1¼ cups diced pulp
Peaches	1 pound	2-2½ cups, sliced
Pears	1 pound	2½ cups, cooked
Pineapple	One	2½-3 cups, diced
Plums	1 pound	2 cups, cooked
Prunes	1 pound	4 cups, cooked
		2 cups, cooked and pitted
Rhubarb	1 pound	2 cups, cooked

CHAPTER 21

Oven Guide

Slow Oven:	275°F. – 325°F.	Custards, sponge cakes, fruit loaves, meats.
Moderate Oven:	325°F. – 375°F.	Cakes, some muffins, cake desserts.
Fairly Hot Oven:	375°F. – 425°F.	Muffins, yeast breads, most cookies.
Hot Oven:	425°F. – 500°F.	Tea biscuits, pastries.

KATE AITKEN

. . . is well known to thousands of Canadian women for her practical approach to the everyday problem of food.

She is perhaps best known as the food editor of *The Standard*. However, this position is the culmination of a long career in inventing and writing about new dishes.

Mrs. Aitken has conducted a daily radio program for many years . . . previous to the war, she was Director of Women's Activities at the Canadian National Exhibition and Director of the Exhibition Cooking School . . . she has conducted cooking schools in many cities and towns throughout Canada, and also at the Chicago Exposition and in Southern United States . . . in addition, she has owned and operated a fruit and vegetable farm and canning plant and has lectured for both the Ontario and Dominion Departments of Agriculture.

At present, Mrs. Aitken, as food editor, writes and conducts the food pages of *The Standard*, a national Canadian weekend newspaper. At her test kitchen, all her recipes are tested and tasted before publication. One indication how practical her recipes are, is the high readership her food pages in *The Standard* enjoy.

Two out of every three of *The Standard*'s 225,000 women readers, read Kate Aitken's recipes in *The Standard* every week.

RECIPE INDEX

RECIPE CLIPPINGS